Destiny of Choice

Destiny of Choice

Part 1 & 2

By Mary Jordan

Mary Jordan is an active sponsor to organisations supporting victims of human trafficking.

Dolphin Marketing Press Ltd
Southampton

Dolphin Marketing Press Ltd Southampton
www.dolphinmarketingpress.com
www.maryjordannovels.co.uk
ISBN 13: 978-0-9932452-7-5
eBook ISBN 13: 978-0-9932452-0-6
eBook ISBN 13: 978-0-9932452-1-3

Disclaimer

I have tried to recreate events, locales and conversations from my memories of them. In order to maintain their anonymity in some instances I have changed the names of individuals and places. I may have changed some identifying characteristics and details such as physical properties, occupations and places of residence. Any resemblance to real persons, living or dead, events and places are purely coincidental. The views expressed in this book are the author's.

Acknowledgments

I would like to express my most sincere gratitude to everyone involved in the publication of Destiny of Choice.

Contents

Disclaimer v

Acknowledgments vi

Part 1 1

  1. The Nightmare Of My Childhood.............................. 2

  2. Goodbye Forever to My Home 12

  3. Love Excitements.. 41

  4. Accident or The Finger of Fate 49

  5. Hospital Woes 51

  6. The Disruption 55

  7. Excruciating Breakup 58

  8. Again With Krasi's Gang 65

  9. The Smell Of The Seaside And Money.................... 69

 10. Criminal Business 71

 11. Nostalgia 79

 12. Assassination And Breakup 82

 13. Guests From The Afterlife. Shock And Reality........ 97

 14. In The Clutches Of Trafficking Or Welcome To Hell....116

 15. The Daily Life Of A Prostitute 129

 16. Fraudulent Hopes 133

 17. Indecent Proposal With The Taste Of Olives 145

 18. Sex, Money, And Diamonds 154

 19. Hell's Door Is Opening Slightly 156

 20. The Glow Of My Lucky Star 173

Part 2 is not chaptered intentionally 186

Part 1

My star,
Glinting with ethereal
Beauty!
I can't understand
What you are saying
To me!
But one thing I do know,
You walk with me
On my journey through life.
At my crossroads, please,
Don't leave me!
Don't betray me!

By Mary Jordan

CHAPTER 1

The Nightmare Of My Childhood

"Ioana, come here immediately!" The rasping voice of my father aroused me from my daydreaming as I stared at the poster of Michael Jackson. All my friends were mad about him. So was I.

"Ioana!"

He was clearly not going to leave me in peace.

"Yes, daddy!"

"Ioana! Run down to the shop and buy me a bottle of vodka and five beers!"

I looked into the sitting room. There were two strangers playing backgammon and my father was talking to a third visitor.

My father used to be a sportsman. He was once a wrestler. He liked to show his guests all his medals and prizes. I found that a bit immodest but I wouldn't have dared tell him. He was a severe man and imposed his own will on everyone.

With a sigh I went to the front door where my father's voice caught up with me again.

"And make sure you don't get Tsarevets vodka like last time!"

God! How I was fed up with it all! Going to shop every day was killing me! One bottle of vodka and five beers. And make sure it isn't Tsarevets! The same thing every day! I wanted to revolt and shout out, "I'm not going! Everyone knows who I am, always carrying that shopping bag filled with bottles. Go and get it yourself!" But I didn't say anything. To get my own back I deliberately bought him Tsarevets.

He would kill me. Who cares! I was used to it by now. I was twelve years old and I cared about what I looked like and what the boys thought of me. I knew that I couldn't impress them with anything in particular since I had been wearing the same clothes for two months – my school dress. It was summer and all the other girls were vying with each other to wear tee shirts and jeans while I felt severely punished. For the whole summer I was allowed to wear only a grey tracksuit and my school dress. My punishment was for the daring "fringe" I had cut myself.

My father was particularly inventive in his punishments and in his beatings, he had no equal. I had been beaten with a belt, cable and with his fists. Anything that occurred to him. I was only five years old when he punished me by making me kneel on stones with my arms raised high holding a five litre bottle. The punishment was for breaking my doll by accident.

My mother didn't have enough courage or strength to stop him. Before they got married, she had been a beautiful and vivacious young girl. At least that's what she looked like in the photographs. The change in her was eloquent enough. Now my mother was a quiet, silent, gloomy woman.

I no longer cried when my father beat me. I just clenched my teeth and told myself that sooner or later I would run away from this hell.

I walked back towards the house with these unhappy thoughts in my head, carrying that hateful shopping bag. It was a hot summer's day. The sun was mercilessly beating down and everything was hiding in the shade. The two skinny boys standing like sentinels before the entrance to our block of flats, tried unsuccessfully to bring a bit of life into the prefabricated environment.

I could hear a drunken argument between one of the guests and my father. I knew what was going to happen to me when I presented them with the bottle of Tsarevets I had deliberately bought.

I was right. The bottle struck my head, and in a hail of curses and threats I was locked in my room.

It was the 18th of August, the day of the Ilienden Preobrazhenski uprising. I remembered that very well because I had been tested on that very lesson at school.

It was time for my own uprising.

I gathered some underwear, my jacket and a book of photographs of my girlfriends in a small bag. I took the money out of my savings box. It wasn't very much – eight levs. But that didn't alter my decision. I would be better off without a home and with no money than the tyranny of that animal. I started planning my escape. Actually I didn't need a plan. I just had to wait for my father to fall asleep and jump off the balcony in my room. It wasn't dangerous since we lived on the ground floor.

Later that evening I put my plan into action. And there I was, free and independent. So free that I didn't even know where to go. I went to the Central Station. It was always full of people and I wouldn't be alone. I sat down on a bench next to a family with a child.

"Where are you going, little girl?" a woman with a baby asked me.

She spoke with a pleasant, throaty voice and looked at me curiously.

I reacted immediately.

"To Bourgas. I'm going to stay with my aunt."

"Goodness me, why are you travelling alone?" she asked in amazement.

"Mummy and daddy are divorced and I live with my grandmother. But she's in the hospital and can't look after me. So I'm going to my auntie's."

I was lying with a soft, mellifluous voice, staring her straight in the eyes. I didn't even blush. I was enjoying watching the woman with the baby telling the story to her husband.

"Some people are completely irresponsible!" the poor woman said angrily. "How can they abandon a child like that? And leave her to her grandmother. And her sick as well!"

Then the entire family began to collect their bags hastily and left me quickly.

Well done, Ioona! I congratulated myself. *You did well.* I couldn't wait to see what the next day would bring me. I fought against sleep for a long time but eventually fell asleep clutching my bag of treasures.

I woke up early in the morning aching all over but in an excellent mood. I was dying of hunger and went to look for something to eat.

There were cafes down in the Rotunda, but I realized that their sandwiches were very expensive and so I went for a walk in the town.

I had a wonderful breakfast of hot buns and milk in a milk bar and then went into the first cinema I came across.

I wandered around the town for a long time and the day imperceptibly disappeared along with my capital. What were eight levs in a town like Sofia? And then there was the matter of where I would sleep. It was already dark and I was back at the station. I sat in the ladies' toilet and waited until the voice of the woman at the cash desk abruptly startled me.

"Hey, little girl, will you help me for a moment?"

I looked at her without blinking and without answering. The lady spoke to me reassuringly with a soft voice.

"I hope you don't mind, when you've done what you're doing in the toilet, will you hold my wool for me, because it's got all tangled up."

"I can wind it all up for you, auntie, I'm in no hurry."

"Oh, thank you! May you be healthy and happy!"

A couple of minutes later I was in her little room. It had a clothes hanger for her clothes and a small sofa covered with a faded sheet. *I could sleep on that,* I thought, and said out loud, "Let me see if I can get those tangles out!"

"You'll see for yourself, but the wool's no good anyway. I'm fed up with it! It keeps on snapping and then tangling. If it wasn't my sister's, I would have chucked it away by now. My name's Auntie Penka," she introduced herself. She was short, plump and kind.

"I'm Lily and I'm from Bourgas."

"What are you doing here, child?" Auntie Penka asked in her kind and curious voice. "What are you doing hanging around the station? This place is full of murderers and thieves. They haven't done anything to you because they haven't seen you yet. Just one look at how well-developed and pretty you are, and someone will be licking their lips when they see you."

I gulped, took the wool with both hands and began a heart-rending story.

"Auntie Penka, I'm an orphan. Mummy died two years ago. She had cancer and when she died my daddy started drinking out of his grief. He lost his job at the factory where he worked. And he's been drinking ever since. He started hitting me." This last statement was absolutely true. "But Auntie Penka, I put up with it and waited for him to come to his senses. But he didn't come to his senses, but completely lost his mind. A couple of evenings ago he brought a friend home. They were both drunk. Daddy's friend offered him money to sleep with me. He agreed and took the money without thinking."

The poor woman sitting opposite me stared in astonishment and the ball of wool fell onto the floor. She sat there for a couple of moments, speechless, before speaking hesitantly.

"Why didn't you cry out to get the neighbours, little one? Why did you go along with them?"

"Wait a moment, Auntie Penka, I didn't go along with them. I pretended that I had to go down into the cellar. Then I locked them in and ran away. I had a little bit of money, so I got on the train and came to Sofia. The worst thing of all is that I don't have anywhere to sleep and I've run out of money."

The kind-hearted woman was moved to tears and offered me just what I wanted – the little sofa to sleep on.

So that's how I got to know the people at the station. I gradually got to know them all. I had enough money. Until then I hadn't known that people could be so kind and sympathetic, qualities which sleep deeply within each one of us just waiting to be awakened. I was like an alarm clock for their emotions and lived quite well. I met another girl with a story like mine. She bought me a lovely red and black tracksuit. It felt like silk, and I was on top of the world.

A month had passed by since I had run away from home. There were only a couple of days left until the beginning of the school year. My entire heart was singing. I wouldn't have to wear a school pinafore, or go to any stupid lessons, nor get beaten or punished for running away from school. I was free, independent and happy.

That day Eli, that was my friend's name, had planned to go around the shops. The shopping trip began with a purple tracksuit bottom and a black elastic skirt for me. I looked so happy and I thought to myself that it was just too good to be true. That was what my grandma used to say. I wondered what would happen to me, and I didn't find any answer. I suppressed the little worm of doubt in my mind and gave myself up to enjoyment. And life with Eli was full of fun. At about lunch time we met up with her old friend, Raggy Veso.

"Hi, my little kittens!" He was a tall man with a deep voice which seemed to come from beneath the earth itself. His jeans were ragged and it was a miracle they hadn't fallen apart. They were full of holes and tears. His blue eyes looked upon the whole world with anger, with the exception of the tender and youngest part of the population.

"What are you up to? Why don't you come with Uncle Veso? We're having a party at a friend's house and they want a few girls there. It'll be fun!"

I looked at Eli without saying anything. She was in charge here.

"Why not, Raggy?" she quickly agreed. "Where's the party?"

"In Boyana. My friend's old man built a shack there and we're going to celebrate it. It's all clean fun."

Raggy Veso shuffled us into a taxi and we drove off.

It was a hot, sunny, muggy day. The cloud of smog hung over the town, but in Boyana it was quiet, cool and green. The "shack" was a luxury villa on two floors with discreet shutters on all the windows and a big lawn. A fine gravel path led up to the front door.

The moment we crossed the threshold, an inner voice spoke to me. Something was going to happen, but what? It was a mystery to me. Otherwise everything seemed fine. It was a great place. Spacious and well decorated. The owner had to be a rich man. He looked at us arrogantly and judgementally, then a condescending and casual smile appeared on his face.

"Gin, whisky, vodka?" the host began to play his role. "I'm Dimo," he introduced himself.

I mumbled my name and cast a quick glance at the others. The company consisted of four young men of uncertain age. They could have been eighteen years old, but their punk hairstyles, blue and coloured tattoos, the earrings in the ears and noses made them unrecognisable. They were very colourful, but very unpleasant looking.

Dimo was the exception. Designer jeans, blue sports shirt and training shoes, like I had never seen before.

"What would you like to drink?" The question was directed at me.

"Coca Cola," I said nervously.

They all laughed and looked at me with the eyes of hungry cats.

"We've only got tonic, little one." A hairy hand reached over to the table and poured some tonic into a beautiful crystal glass.

"Sit down and make yourself at home!" Dimo politely and somewhat ambivalently sat me down on a comfortable, leather couch.

My drink was immediately served to me. Eli was happily clinking glasses with everyone, and I gulped down my glass of tonic with ice and lemon. I was very hungry. I was very surprised when I started feeling hot instead of cooler. Someone had poured a good quantity of gin into my glass. Whether I was scared or whether it was the result of the alcohol, my head began to spin and I closed my eyes for a moment. I had never drunk alcohol before and I began to feel ill. When I opened my eyes, I realized that they were planning something for me and that I had to get away from there. No one seemed to be paying me any attention. The stereo system was playing very loudly and Eli was dancing, something between an erotic dance and striptease. They were watching her intently, drinking quietly. *It's calm for the moment,* I thought to myself. I gradually relaxed and drank another glass of tonic. This time I poured it for myself to be sure. But it had already gotten ahold of me. *It's time I got out of here,* I said to myself. But as I tried to get up (my legs were strangely wobbly), the man with the hairy hands came over to me.

"Little one, come on, get up, I want to show you something."

His punk hair looked really funny and I laughed out loud.

"Get out of here, cocky! I know what you want to show me. I just want to tell you that I haven't been unsealed yet, and I'm not in the mood at the moment."

I was trembling inside. Not that I had decided to die a virgin, but I didn't like the look of this idiot.

"Johnnie, did you hear what you said?" my budding lover said as he grabbed hold of me.

The Johnnie in question laughed and poured fat onto the fire.

"Come on Rimmer, you're not going to tell us that that little slut's going to stop you? You've got your reputation to think of!"

The situation was getting hot. I looked for Dimo but he had disappeared. I clearly couldn't rely on anyone else's help or protection.

The voice of Auntie Penka was echoing through my head. "Why didn't you cry out and get the neighbours?" I had to shout for help. Except there weren't any neighbours around and the music was too loud for anyone to hear. It would have deafened any shouts. The window was right opposite me, but it was tightly closed. Eli had whispered that the house had air conditioning. I had no time to lose. I grabbed the heavy crystal ashtray full of cigarette butts, and threw it with all my strength at the window.

The glass smashed with a crash onto the floor and at the same time the siren of the alarm system began to wail insistently. *Great!* I thought. Everything happened in the space of a second. By the time they had realized what was happening I had jumped out of the window. That was my patented trick. I ran along the path as fast as I could. I reached the street and turned around. No one was chasing me, but I continued running. I had overcome my fear and was already thinking how I was going to get back to the town. I decided to take a taxi. I didn't stop running because I wanted to get a safe distance from the house. There was a car driving after me. I turned around and froze. It was a police car. I tried to look as calm as possible and walked on trying to restrain my panting. But they came closer to me and stopped. I wished I wasn't feeling so dizzy.

"What are you up to, little girl?" a young, nice-looking policeman asked me.

"Nothing, just running."

"Keeping fit?" He looked at me questioningly.

"Something like that," I mumbled, and bent over and vomited.

I was so ashamed of myself.

"You don't look very fit to me." The nice looking policeman took my hand carefully. "Where do you live?"

Oh, no, not that. I prayed silently, although I had never been to a church.

"At home, of course," I answered and thought about my father. "I was just on my way home."

"All right. We'll take you."

What now? I tried one last time to get away from them.

"I live really close by. Thank you, but there's no need. It'll be easier if I walk."

"Get in!" the policeman insisted.

This is the end, I thought, and got into the car.

"Tell me your address, please." The policeman turned around.

There was nothing left to do. I looked at him and mumbled, "I don't have a home."

The driver and his colleague looked at me in astonishment.

"What do you mean, you haven't got a home?"

"Very simple. I ran away from home."

"Vasilev, drive to the police station," the young lieutenant ordered.

I said nothing during the journey. They took me into a room where there was a man dressed in civilian clothes sitting behind a huge desk. When I went in, he frowned at me, and when the other officers made their report, they left us alone.

I sat on the uncomfortable chair in silence. The man opposite me was in no hurry to speak either. He was arranging some papers in files, signing other documents and crossing things out. He didn't even seem to notice I was there. I felt terrible. My head was aching, I had a bitter taste in my mouth and I really wanted a drink of Coca Cola.

"Excuse me, can I have a glass of water?"

The man behind the desk smiled at me and asked politely, "Wouldn't you prefer a glass of Coca Cola?"

"Thank you."

Five minutes later there were two glasses of my favourite drink on his desk.

"Now tell me your story, slowly, we're in no hurry. All right?"

I hesitated, took a deep breath and told him the story of my life. Two hours later I was standing in front of my father.

I waited obediently for the beating to begin, but to my amazement it didn't happen. My father was sitting with his head on his chest in silence. My mother looked anxiously at me and then at him, and didn't know what to do with her hands. The total silence hung heavy in the room and made me feel nervous. Suddenly, my father asked me in a depressed voice, "Ioana, tell me why you did it?"

I turned my head to look through the window. Children were skipping on a rope outside the window, and a boy and girl were kissing a little further away. I continued to say nothing.

"I want you to tell me!" My father raised his voice and my mother jumped up in fright. "I have to know why my daughter doesn't want to live in my home!"

I felt a storm rising inside me. The anger was making my heart race. Did I have to explain to him? Me? Had he forgotten how he had punished me to kneel on stones in the corner? Had he forgotten about the scars on my body which wouldn't heal? Had he forgotten about the endless humiliation he had forced upon me? Or the litres of tears I had shed? Did I have to explain about the terrible family quarrels which drove me crazy and made me ashamed in front of my neighbours? No. He wouldn't have understood me. He wasn't going to hear a word from me. My heart boomed in my ears and I heard my father's muffled voice as though I had cotton wool in my ears.

"I understand that you are ashamed of what you have done and that is why you are saying nothing, but I want to come to an agreement with you. You will promise me that it will not happen again, and I won't beat you or punish you for what you have done. Do you agree?"

How noble he thought he was! *All right, if that's what you want. We'll play the game, but I would score the winning goal!*

"All right!" I rasped.

"Go and sort your clothes out and get ready for school. You start on Monday, don't you?"

"I think so," I replied with a sigh.

The school year started on Monday.

CHAPTER 2

Goodbye Forever to My Home

Life went on in the way I had known it for years – school, homework, shopping. I was pleased to notice that my father was trying to be kind with me. The ban on my clothes was lifted. He didn't shout at me or humiliate me. Visitors continued to come to our house, they continued to drink, but my little sister did the shopping for them, so I could breathe more easily.

My friends at school were green with jealousy when I told them of my adventures. My mother tried to find out what I had been doing when I was away from home, but I was as silent as the grave. I assumed that my father had told her to find out as much as possible, but he never raised the subject. So the months passed relatively peacefully. There was one problem, however, which concerned me. I didn't want to go to school. I liked to study, but only things I was interested in. Everything else seemed a waste of time and I got bored. I started skipping school. This started happening more and more frequently until the end of the first term. My results were atrocious. I had nine F's. The situation was made even more complicated by the fact that my father wanted to see my report card. I got hold of another report card with excellent grades, faked a stamp and signatures.

"Well done, my girl!" My father was over the moon with my grades.

I even got a present, but I was worried inside. My intuition had never let me down and now it was warning me that I wasn't going to get away with it. It was Friday, and as always we had visitors. My poor mother was pacing between the kitchen and the living room with glasses and plates.

I sat in the kitchen, and I tried to help her as far as I could. I heard my father calling for me. I went to see the visitors who were passionately arguing about something. My father, of course, was the most passionate of them all.

"Just look how pretty she is! A bit crazy like me, but she's a good looker, isn't she?" He was very drunk and very proud of me. They all smiled and one of the lady guests said,

"You'll be very pretty when you grow up! Green eyes, black hair and those thighs! The child's got everything!"

The visitors laughed and my father laughed with them. He was very happy and vociferous.

At that very moment the doorbell rang.

"Ioana, go and see who it is!"

I ran and opened the door and stood frozen to the spot. My class teacher was standing in the doorway.

"Hello, Ioana. Can I come in?"

"Not now, Miss!" I whispered in fright. But my father was right behind me.

"Good evening. I'm Ioana's class teacher."

"Come in. I'm very pleased to meet you!"

My father shook her hand, and I stood aside for her to come in.

"No, thank you. I shall call some other time. It's clearly not very convenient at the moment."

She clearly saw the situation but she didn't know my father.

"On the contrary, please come in! It's very convenient."

"I shan't come in, thank you. I just wanted to check that you got Ioana's report card. Because of that injury to her leg she couldn't come and resit her tests to improve her F grades...."

"What injury? What F's?" My father looked at her in astonishment.

"What do you mean, what leg?" the class teacher asked him in annoyance. "Ioana hasn't been to school for a month and a half. I was told that you had had a car accident and that her leg had been broken in two places. I can see that she's much better now and I hope you make much more effort next term to avoid having to repeat the year!"

I would have been happy if the ground had opened to swallow me up, or if I had fainted at least. But no! I stood there staring at them unable even to blink.

My father went bright red, right down to the roots of his hair. He shouted at me,

"Is that true?"

At the same time, he struck me with all his strength across my face. I flew to one side and fell to the floor.

"Don't do that, please!" my class teacher cried out.

"Valeria!" My mother went pale and begged with my father to stop.

"Keep out of this!" he shouted out and dragged me into my room. He pushed me to the ground. I don't remember anything after that. I woke up with my mother holding a compress to my head. She was crying and trying to arrange the room. I felt sorry for her but I didn't have the strength to cry. My father came back into the room like an enraged bull. He pushed my mother out of the way and shouted,

"Filthy slut! You deserve to be thrown out onto the street. That's where you belong. But I'm a very tolerant man and I'm going to give you your last chance. You're going to leave school and I'll find you a job washing dishes. You're going to pay to live here, for your food and your bed. Is that clear?"

Fuck off! I thought, but I closed my eyes and didn't move until he left. Somewhere from the flat I heard my father's thunderous voice. He was calling for my mother.

Tortured by beating, tears and grief, I fell into a deep sleep.

The next day I got out of bed at about lunch time. It would be going too far to say I stood up. I slowly raised my body, with a lot of effort and pain. I had pains in my kidneys, my back and my head, most of all. I felt as though I had fallen off the top floor onto the roof tiles. God, my face! It was completely bruised and swollen, purple and blue, and one of my eyes was completely closed. The other was still bleeding. I went back to bed. My head was throbbing. I just lay there and groaned quietly. My mother applied all sorts of creams and compresses to my face. Nothing helped.

"Mummy, has daddy changed his mind?"

"What are you talking about? You know what he's like!"

"I don't want to mummy, please!"

"What can I do about it, darling? You know that he'll beat me if I stand up for you."

My father's stubbornness was very well known to me, but I still lived in hope. I hoped that after the beating he had given me, his conscience would guide him. However, I couldn't have been more wrong. But I had no intention of washing dishes in some fourth-rate restaurant, or paying for my food and bed in my own home. A couple of days passed in relative calm. I almost didn't leave my room. Only when my father wasn't at home would I leave my room and walk through the flat. The rest of the time I just lay on my bed. I tried to read but nothing went into my head. My eyes ran over the lines, but I didn't understand anything of what I was reading. I was tormented by the thought that I had to do something. I began to treat my bruises and the swelling on my face. I made compresses and bindings, until at the end of the second week you couldn't tell that my face had been beaten at all.

It was Sunday. I made the most of the fact that I was alone at home. I collected some clothes in a little bag, took my jacket – the one which had been a present for the "excellent" grades – and slammed the front door behind me.

I took my fate in my own hands again.

Naturally, I went to the Central Station again. Nothing seemed to have changed there. The barefoot, snotty gypsy children with their noses stuck in bags of glue occasionally looked up at the passers-by with a dull faraway stare. The thieves and crooks were standing in the usual places. They were looking for naïve travellers. Behind the kiosks in the Rotunda there were the usual people playing dice and other gambling games. Further on down, the queers and underage gypsy prostitutes were standing outside the toilets. They charged next to nothing, but still couldn't get any clients.

I looked over the familiar faces and felt at home. I stopped next to a group of boys. I knew one of them. Krasi was the king of the dice players and no one could beat him. He was playing with a stranger at that moment. The multi-coloured dice rattled over the top of the box. Full house! The spectators sighed in admiration. Krasi took the money, picked up the dice and stood up.

"That's how you do it, brother! Congratulations!" He smiled and turned around. It was then that he saw me.

"Oh, baby! Where have you been?"

"Around the world!" I said importantly.

"You brought me luck! Let me buy you coffee. We'll have a chat!"

"I'd love you to buy me a coffee!" I shouted out happily, and Krasi grinned radiantly.

"You've haven't changed, baby! I'm really pleased to see you."

I took him by the arm and we went to the café opposite. It was smoky and noisy, but nice all the same. The bartender saw us from afar and waved at us. Krasi sat me down at a little table to the side of the bar and went to talk to the bartender. They spoke quietly and I couldn't hear anything, but I wasn't really interested. I could tell, however, that they were talking about something serious, because Krasi's face had become serious, even severe.

He brought over some sandwiches, Coca Cola and peanuts. He sat opposite me, smiled cheerfully and asked,

"Tell me then, little one, where have you been hiding all this time?"

I told him everything very quickly. I trusted him completely. When I had first run away from home, he had helped me out with money and other little favours from time to time. If it hadn't been for him, I would have been raped at least three times. He protected me and everything had been all right until that unforgettable day when Eli had taken me to that party in Boyana. He listened to me very carefully and coughed.

"Yes, yes… Let me think how I can help you."

While Krasi was thinking seriously, I looked at him closely. He was all right! Tall, darkish fair hair, with a narrow straight face, ironically squinting bright blue eyes. He always wore jeans and a denim jacket. He had a heavy gold pendant around his neck, which glinted softly. His eyes captured everything and everyone. Nothing escaped him. He made me feel safe and protected. Quite simply I felt calm with him.

"Let's go to the seaside, baby!" Krasi slapped the table cheerfully.

I looked at him in surprise and decided that he was having a laugh. Who goes to the seaside in February?

"I've forgotten my swimming costume and my boots. I can't go."

Krasi laughed for a long time at my stunned face and then repeated his invitation.

"Baby, we're not going to the seaside to sunbathe, don't get upset! We really are going to the seaside, but we're going to work."

I looked at him with unconcealed curiosity.

"Don't look at me as though you're going to swallow me up! Haven't I ever told you how pretty you are with those eyes of yours?"

"Don't flatter me! When are we going then?"

"Hold your horses! What's the hurry? I've got something I need to do today. If it works out, we'll go tomorrow evening. Have you got anywhere to sleep tonight? Oh, I forgot, you've just run away from home. Well, we'll have to find somewhere for you to sleep for one night, perhaps two."

Krasi furrowed his eyebrows tensely for a moment and lit a cigarette. I felt guilty that I had created problems for him, which were difficult to sort out.

"Krasi, I can look for somewhere at the station..."

He looked at me and said,

"Those times have passed, little one. The place is full of prostitutes and gypsies now. Your place isn't here! We'll go to Itso's."

"I don't know him. Is he OK?"

"He's not bad. I needed to see him anyway. We'll sleep there tonight, and tomorrow morning I'll give you a nice little job to do, while Uncle Krasi's away working."

"I'm very curious to find out what that is."

"All in good time, baby! It's time to go now!"

It was beginning to get dark. The thin snow falling on the Sofia streets was turning into a wet sludge. Krasi and I walked together happily and boldly, despite the gloomy and cold winter evening. We joked and laughed until we choked, and the few passers-by whom we met looked disapproving.

The Itso in question lived in a snobbish district called Lozenets. His block of flats was on a quiet and discreet street. There wasn't a single broken street lamp, unlike our district, where there wasn't a single working one. There wasn't a single overflowing rubbish bin either. Everything was as tidy and clean as a chemist's shop. All the houses and blocks of flats had their own garages. It was like an image from a picture book. The outside door was locked. We rang the front door bell and after about a minute waiting the door opened automatically. There were no name plates on the heavy oak doors. The door handles were in all sorts of strange shapes. I had never seen anything like them. Finally, we reached the door of young Itso. I don't know why, but I already hated him. Perhaps it was because of the differences between us in our so-called classless socialist society.

Itso was waiting at the door, but by the way he invited us to come in, I realized that he was OK. He was a small, thin little boy, dressed in an ordinary pullover and jeans.

"Krasi! Where have you been all day? I've been expecting you since this afternoon."

"Hi, Itso! This little sweetie held me up. Can I introduce you?"

"Nice to meet you, my name's Itso!"

"Ioana," I muttered and slipped into the hallway.

"I'm alone, there's no one else here," Itso declared. "So come into the living room."

His living room was so big, that ours could have fit into it twice over. There was a fireplace burning. It was the first time I had seen a real, burning fireplace, and I stood staring at it as though enchanted. God, how could I have ended up in a place like this on my first night away from home? Was this a sign? I looked at Krasi with gratitude. He seemed to read my thoughts and burst into laughter. Itso stared strangely, not knowing what we were laughing about.

"Baby's never seen anywhere as posh as this before, Itso."

"What? This? This is all so stupid and I'm so bored with it all..." He smiled in embarrassment, as though apologetically.

Because you've got it, idiot! I thought, and stuck my tongue out at Krasi for shaming me.

I continued looking around with curiosity. The house was amazing. Your feet just sank into the soft carpet and I felt as though I was walking on clouds. There were paintings hanging on the walls, and above the fireplace there was a huge mirror in a golden frame. On either side of the fireplace there were golden candlesticks. It would take a while but I eventually began to tell the difference between gold and brass. The furniture was mainly made out of solid wood and carved like it was from the last century. I settled down into one of the armchairs to the side of the fireplace and looked into the flames. The flames flickered to and fro, and from time to time sparked like little diamonds jumping out of the fire. I found it hard to take my eyes off the captivating fiery dance, but looked at Krasi and Itso. They were doing some serious calculations and nothing else seemed to interest them. *What could be of so much interest to them? I* thought. I didn't really care. It was so nice here, so warm and cosy, that I would have wanted to stay here for a long, long time! What a load of nonsense! Who cared what a little, lonely, twelve-year old girl wanted? A girl who didn't even have a home? A little human being who dared to stand up to her cruel, tyrannical father. My heart was wrenched with grief. *Why is fate so kind to some and so cruel to others? What made that unprepossessing boy with glasses who didn't appreciate what he had, any better than me? It wasn't just. At school we were forever being told that in our socialist society all children lived happily, and that everyone had to work, in order to reach our goal of a prosperous future. Whoever lived here didn't seem to live in that society.* I wondered what his parents did for a living. Not work in a factory like mine, that was for sure. Who cared? Why was I feeling so sorry for myself? So what – he had a home with carpets, crystals and a fireplace! I didn't care that there was someone to make his breakfast and give him pocket money. I was free! I was going to have everything! *I will!*

These thoughts whirled around inside my head and, looking boldly into the future, I fell asleep without realizing.

I woke with the unpleasant feeling of someone looking at me. It was light and the winter sun was peering in through the window. I rubbed my eyes and the first thing I saw was Krasi smiling at me playfully. He was standing over my bed staring at me with his hands behind his back.

"Baby, be so kind as to get your pretty little backside out of the sheets and trot along to the bathroom and get washed. We're late as it is!"

I stretched out lazily and looked at myself. I had fallen asleep with my clothes on. Someone had carried me from the armchair in front of the fire into this cosy bedroom, all in white and gold.

"You're worse than my father! I don't want to get up!" My words were accompanied with a heart-rending yawn.

"And you're more sleepy than a bear in winter!" He grinned and his eyes sparkled cheerfully.

There was no way out of it. I got up unwillingly and lazily left my sleepy heaven.

The huge bathroom glistened with cleanliness. I looked longingly at the bath but I had had strict instructions not to hang around. I washed my face quickly and straightened my hair.

"Baby, you're not drowning are you? Come on out, or I'm coming in!" his cheerful, impatient voice asked.

I laughed joyfully, without knowing exactly why, and muttered, "Thank you God for sending him to me!"

The aroma of fresh toast showed me the way to the kitchen. Like all the other rooms in the flat, it was Olympian, but I was no longer surprised. Itso, our host, was right, you can get used to anything.

There was everything you could ask for on the table. Ham, butter, strawberry jam, cheese, and of course, toast.

"I'm as hungry as a wolf!"

"Bon appétit, then!" Itso smiled politely and I noticed that in daylight, he looked even nicer.

I ate as though there was no tomorrow, and neither of the boys could believe how much I had eaten.

"Baby, you're on great form, but I'm just worried that you don't get sick."

Krasi looked at me anxiously.

"Don't worry, I can eat more!" I replied jokingly and peeled a banana. At home we only had bananas at Christmas, and that was one of the things that we traditionally placed on the Christmas table.

After the filling breakfast, my life seemed as beautiful as a song, and I even forgave It so the opportunity of having been born and grown up in a PRIVILEGED family. I waved to him cheerfully at the door and skipped down the stairs.

It had snowed during the night and the street, trees and houses glistened in their new white clothes. The sun shone welcomingly and the people deceived by the good weather were in no hurry to go home. I trustingly put my arm under Krasi's and asked him innocently,

"What are we going to do now, Krasi?"

"What do you want to do?" He looked at me craftily and those beautiful blue eyes of his completely confused me. They were ironical, and slightly sarcastic, but at the same time piercing and kind. In one word: beautiful.

"Well, I don't know!" I stuttered.

Krasi coughed to sound more authoritative, said nothing for a moment or two, then,

"Baby, we'll have to go our separate ways."

I felt as though a gun had been held to my head. I started to tremble and a lump came to my throat. I looked at him downfallen and asked quietly,

"Why?" I suddenly felt so sad, that I almost burst into tears.

"Because I hate shopping, especially with a girl."

I didn't know what he was getting at and looked at him with a confused expression. I must have been very funny, because he burst into laughter as he looked at me.

"You silly little girl! You fell for my little joke. I didn't think you were so naïve. It's just that today you're going to have the pleasure of shopping, and I've got business to attend to, because we're leaving tonight..."

"You stupid idiot! You nearly gave me a heart attack! You should be ashamed of yourself!" I started beating his chest with my little fists, while he laughed until his sides nearly burst. The people waiting at the tram stopped and looked at us curiously, but I didn't care. I only stopped when I didn't have the energy to hit him anymore. At that moment I realized how comical the situation must have looked and burst into laughter myself. We weren't interesting anymore and our audience was looking in the other direction, waiting for the tram to come. When I had calmed down, Krasi looked at me seriously and said,

"That's enough fun now! Time to get down to work!"

"What work do you want me to do?" I asked calmly and filled with curiosity.

"Believe me, it's much more pleasant than mine. By the way, have you looked at your feet recently?"

This last comment made me laugh again. My old boots leaked from everywhere. Not to mention the fact that the heels were completely worn down.

"You're very demanding! My father's not a millionaire!"

"He might not be a millionaire, but he could at least have bought you some decent winter boots! It doesn't matter, Krasi's a generous lad and has even more generous fingers! Take this." He put a thick wad of notes into my hand. "Buy yourself a few things. But don't come back without boots!"

My heart jumped. What a wonderful day lay ahead of me! I flung my arms around his neck and kissed him gratefully on his prickly chin.

"Jesus, you're true dynamite! And you weigh a ton as well! I'm putting you on a diet from today!"

"I'll only stop eating when I'm dead." I grinned back at him and kissed him once again. Then I let go of his aching neck and Krasi began to rub it, rather exaggeratedly.

"Baby, I want you at eight o'clock in the café at the station. Bye for now."

"I'll be there. Bye for now!"

As happy as a free bird, I ran to the shops. It was an indescribable experience. God, what a day it was! I didn't have any strength left by the end of it. Or any money either. But I got a pair of beautiful knee boots, two pairs of trousers, two sweaters, three silk blouses, a dozen pairs of luxury tights, underwear, a huge sport's bag, and handbag and most important of all – I manage to fill it with all sorts of make-up and lipstick. That was my weak point. Deep down inside I harboured the consequences of a particularly terrible punishment and even more terrible beating because I had dared to put some lipstick on. I enthusiastically filled my new bag with all manner of eye pencils, eye shadow and lipstick. I imagined myself returning home and standing in front of my father, showing him my new acquisitions. I imagined his face and smiled, "Is that enough now? Yes? Well I have to be going now!" Dressed and made-up I couldn't recognize myself in the mirror of a shop. I was dying with impatience to show myself to Krasi. I used the last of my money to get a taxi. The station café was full, but Krasi wasn't there. I went over to the bartender and he let me sit at his table. I sat down exhausted on the chair and put my treasure-filled bag next to me on the ground. I watched it constantly out of a fear that it might be stolen. I was already getting very impatient when he arrived. He went straight over to the bartender who pointed at me. Krasi looked at the table, but looked straight past me. Then he looked around the entire café and back towards me. I felt a wave of surprise overcome him, then admiration and finally laughter, and an ironical expression appeared on his face. I was proud of myself and couldn't sit still with joy.

"Baby, has anyone ever told you how beautiful you are?"

"Quite frequently!"

"Baby, you're not just beautiful! You're unique! Tell me why you hide your age? I think you told me you were twelve years old. But I reckon you're at least five or six years older. I can't see the point. I know that women do that sort of thing when they're past twenty-five."

"You know, Krasi, you're not paying me a compliment saying that I look seventeen. But I'll forgive you. I'm happy but don't forget that I am really only twelve!"

"OK, let's not argue about it! But you still look fantastic. I'm really pleased that you've gone to all that trouble."

"Are we going?" I wasn't listening to him.

"Calm down, just wait here for a moment."

He went back to the bar and he went with the bartender into the kitchen behind the bar. Krasi appeared a moment later with a travelling bag. He grabbed my new bag and said commandingly,

"Let's go!"

The train to Bourgas left in an hour's time.

"I'm hungry," I said, smiling like a little devil.

I hadn't forgotten his threat of putting me on a diet.

"I didn't hear what you just said." He smiled craftily.

"If you think you're going to torture me with hunger, I'm going back to Daddy. He might beat me but he lets me eat." I stood in front of him provocatively and gave him a belligerent look.

"I give up!" Krasi raised his hands theatrically and looked at me from head to toe. "I'm just sorry that your wonderful curves will be lost in the jungle of your greed."

"Fool!"

I gave him a friendly slap and we went to have dinner together.

The train was relatively empty and we got a compartment to ourselves. I stretched out on the seat, imagining the wheels of the train rattling along and me falling sweetly asleep.

"Baby, I'll get out for a moment. A friend's come to see me off."

I opened my eyes in surprise, but Krasi was gone. I rolled down the window and looked outside. It was dark and I couldn't see them clearly, but could make out that Krasi's friend was short and stout. I saw him give Krasi a package. That was all. Then they parted. The train was just pulling out when Krasi appeared with a bright and mysterious smile. He was holding something in his hands, which made me think. This secret package fired my curiosity but I pretended not to notice. I could see that he was hiding something from me. I decided to observe him carefully. Krasi sat in front of me, lit a cigarette and blissfully blew out smoke towards the ceiling.

"Baby, what are we going to do all night?"

"We're going to sleep!" I said harshly. "I'm still little and I have to sleep and eat regularly, to grow up big and strong." I wagged a finger in front of his face. He assumed an expression of comic, religious reconciliation and crossed himself.

"Dear Lord, help her to grow vertically and not horizontally!"

"And I hope you live to see me fat, fool!" I hissed and we both burst into laughter.

I really was beginning to feel sleepy and soon travelled into the world of dreams. I was woken by a fatherly tap on the shoulder.

"Wake up, sleepy head! You sleep like a log! You've fallen onto the ground twice, and I've had to pick you up. I was worried you would get a concussion."

"Don't take the mickey! You're the one with a concussion!" I kicked him amicably and sat up.

I was still sleepy but noticed the dark shadows beneath his eyes.

"I haven't slept a wink. I can't stand these trains!"

I laughed and looked through the window. We had already arrived in Bourgas. It was a damp, misty morning. There wasn't a soul at the station with the exception of a few taxi drivers who were looking carefully and cheerfully around for clients.

"I'm hungry."

"Be patient, baby! We'll have breakfast in Sozopol."

"I'll be dead by then!"

"No comment! We have to get out of here quickly!"

Krasi shoved me into the first taxi, sat next to the driver and said curtly,

"Sozopol!"

The driver was happy to get such a good fare, and screeched off like a rally driver. We were soon out of the city. I tried to follow the countryside, but I gave up and fell asleep again. I was woken by an impatient tugging on my sleeve.

"Baby, wake up, you've slept your life away again! You've got such a talent for sleeping!"

"If you don't sleep, you won't grow up!" I muttered and dragged myself out of the case. "Where are we?"

"On the Earth."

"To be more precise?"

"Sozopol."

"I'm hungry. You said that we'd eat when we got to Sozopol."

"I don't remember saying that. I said other things as well that I don't remember. We've got to go to find an address first of all, get a little job done and then I'm all yours."

I wanted to argue with him, but said nothing. We walked in silence down a quiet and pretty street. Even the cold, unwelcoming morning couldn't take away from the charm of the romantic sea-side town. I had been here with my parents and my sister on holiday, and now, without inviting them, a flood of memories came back to me. My sister and I used to come here every evening to play on the enormous swings. We'd spend hours at the shooting range where the top prize was a fantastic doll. We never did manage to win it, but just dreaming of it was enough. We liked playing on the dodgems and bumping into each other, which made us feel dizzy... Now that was all irreversibly lost and would never happen again. A lump came into my throat, making it hard to breathe and my mouth dry and bitter. Overtaken by memories, I didn't notice that we were standing in front of a two-storied house with wide verandas all around it. Krasi left our bags on a pretty little bench and rang the bell. A moment later, the door of the house opened and a tousled little boy stood there in his pyjamas.

"Is Miroslav at home, my friend?"

"My brother's not back from work yet. Do you want to leave him a message?"

"Tell him that Krasi was looking for him. He knows why. I'll be back at lunch time."

"All right."

The boy shut the door and we walked up the street.

"Can we eat now?" I asked hopefully.

"Yes, we're going to have breakfast now!" Krasi replied with my same tone of voice.

A few minutes later we were sitting in a café. I was delighted with the freshly baked cheese pastries, chocolate rolls, vanilla doughnuts. Everything you could possibly wish for! I ate until I thought I would burst. All washed down with Coca Cola. When I could no longer eat any more, I asked Krasi,

"What are we going to do until lunch time?"

"We'll take your new boots for a walk along the beach."

"I don't want to, it's too cold. Why don't we sit here in the warm and wait? I really like the music they're playing."

"Whatever you say, baby." He smiled kindly at me and lazily dragged on his cigarette. His face was stubbly, and he had shadows beneath his eyes, but the expression on his face was one of strength and supremacy.

We sat and listened to the music in the half-empty café. The speakers were playing a slow melody which brought tears to my eyes. Without realizing it, the tears started rolling down my cheeks.

"Baby, what's up?" Krasi looked at me in astonishment. "Is everything all right?"

I felt embarrassed.

"No, everything's OK, Krasi. I just want to say thank you. For everything. You're great. I know, but I want you to tell me why you're doing all this for me? You're not even trying to get it on with me!"

He looked at me for a long time with his expressive, penetrating blue eyes.

"Because you're alone, baby. And because little girls like you need protection. Your heart is wounded like a little bird, and it needs to get better. I'm your good old doctor for broken hearts."

"You're never serious with me. And you're doing it again."

"Take a piece of advice from me, baby! Never take life too seriously. Smile and try to see the funny side of things. It's more fun and you'll live longer. So no more tears! Wipe your nose and put a smile on yourself! Otherwise Miro will think that everyone from Sofia is miserable!"

I drank another Coca Cola, sorted myself out and we left the café.

This time Miro was at home. He met us topless and barefoot in his garden. He was wearing just a pair of jeans. He was chopping wood and you couldn't tell he had just come from work.

"Hi, come in!"

He invited us into his room which was full of sports gear.

"Come on in, I'll just have a shower and I'll be with you." Our host disappeared through the door and we remained alone. Krasi sat down in a chair and thought to himself. I put a pair of boxing gloves on and stood in front of the mirror. I looked very funny and turned to Krasi so he could see me. At that moment, I saw the mysterious package in his hands.

"What's that?" I asked innocently.

"People who ask questions grow old very quickly," Krasi replied very quickly.

"Tell me what it is!" I threw down the gloves and tried to grab the package.

"Ioana! Please!" He grabbed me in his arms and put me down on the bed. "Just sit still. There are some things the less you know about the better."

We sat there in silence. I realized that it wasn't the time to play around and just sat there patiently. The host soon returned, showered, shaved and dressed.

"Have you got the goods?" The question was directed at Krasi.

"Yes, but before I give it to you, I want to say that I only want green for it."

"No problem, as long as it's good."

Miro took the mysterious package, which looked heavy for its size, and disappeared. I stared at the ceiling and pretended that I didn't care, although I was thinking feverishly. It was clear that Krasi was selling something. But what was he selling? Was it drugs? I shook at the thought. I looked at him furtively. He was serious and slightly nervous, drumming his fingers on the desk. Miro came in carrying another package. It was much smaller in comparison with the other. He gave it to Krasi.

"Everything's OK, Dandy!"

I stared in amazement. What was that all about? Was that his nickname? The aforementioned Dandy opened the package and took a huge wad of dollars out of it. He flicked his fingers through them, one by one.

"Don't worry. It's been checked."

Krasi put the money in his inside pocket and stood up. The deal was over.

"Miro, I'll see you tonight in the Greek tavern about six. We'll have more time to talk. We're tired now and we want to find somewhere to sleep."

"You can stay here, if you like…"

"No, we want to find somewhere with a sea view." My friend from Sofia laughed and led me outside.

He stopped at the door, turned around and asked,

"Have you seen Bobby?"

"Yes, he's just out of the army and he's being spoilt by his parents… I might just bring him along."

"I'll be pleased to see him."

"Bye then, see you tonight!"

When we got out into the street, I couldn't hold back any longer and asked him,

"Krasi, what was in that packet? Please tell me, I promise not to tell anyone!"

"People who ask too many questions…"

"I know, grow old quickly… Don't you trust me? It wasn't drugs, was it?"

He looked at me in a mixture of amusement and anger.

"You've got a very vivid fantasy, baby. All right, I can see I'd better tell you rather than let your imagination run wild. It was gold and other things."

"What other things?"

"God, won't you let it go! If you give in to a woman, there's no end to it!" he complained sarcastically. "Valuable things. Things which he sells to filthy rich collectors. Happy now?" Krasi sighed with feigned emotion.

"And I've got another question," I muttered with embarrassment. "Why did he call you Dandy?"

He laughed out loud and dropped our bags to the ground. I looked at him in shame and hurt. He hugged me and said cheerfully,

"A long time ago, even though I was poor, I liked to wear suits. I had an entire collection of suits and ties and everyone made fun of me. That's when they gave me the nickname and they still use it today."

"So Dandy means someone who likes to dress like a snob?"

"You could say that. Is that all you want to know, miss know-it-all?"

"For now, yes."

This was followed by an eloquent silence. I walked next to him, deep in thought, but suddenly stopped again.

"Isn't it dangerous?"

"I thought you weren't going to ask any more questions? No, it's not dangerous. Now we can enjoy ourselves! I'm so tired my head's spinning. Let's go and find somewhere to sleep."

We found some lodgings in a wonderful old house full of locked rooms waiting for the beginning of the season. The owner was a reasonable man and didn't ask us for any ID documents. Not that Krasi would have had a problem, but I would. He immediately went into the bathroom. Curiosity immediately got the better of me and I quickly went through his pockets. I found his ID card, wallet filled with levs and, of course, the wad of dollars. I counted them at lightning speed – four thousand dollars. Jesus, what a lot of money! I put everything back and went to bed. I pretended to be asleep when Krasi came in.

"I trust you, baby, and I don't want to lose my trust."

I opened my eyes and looked at him.

"What are you talking about?"

"About this..." He lifted up his jacket with one finger and said, "I know how I left my clothes."

"I'm sorry, my bloody curiosity! I won't do it anymore. I didn't take anything."

"I know, just don't do it again."

We fell asleep and woke up at about 7.30.

"Come on, we're late. Put on something pretty."

I got dressed quickly and we rushed along to the restaurant.

Contrary to our expectations, Miro was there waiting for us. He was sitting at the table with another person.

When we got closer I looked at the stranger. I don't know what happened to me, but I couldn't take my eyes off him. He was about 20, with thick chestnut hair and big green, slightly elongated eyes. He was dark-skinned, almost African looking. He was very slim and dressed in elegant sports clothes.

We were introduced. His name was Boiko. I sat next to him speechless. I wasn't following the conversation at all. The only thing I knew about him was that he came from Bourgas.

The evening was fun. I wasn't interested in anything else apart from my new friend. I noticed that his attention was directed at me as well. That made me happy.

"Do you want to dance?" The question was directed at me, of course, by Boiko.

"Yes, with pleasure."

His touch was sensational. God, was this love? If it was, I was all for it! I couldn't eat or drink.

We decided to go to a bar nearby. Krasi and Miro didn't stop talking. I could understand them. Business was the most important thing for them. They seemed to have forgotten about us. At one time I could feel Krasi's penetrating eyes staring at me. I didn't care. I was in love. As they say, "love at first glance". For the first time – I hadn't believed that such a thing could exist. But the fact struck me on the head.

At about 3.00 we decided to leave. We chatted for a few minutes in front of the bar and then we parted. As we left, Boiko whispered into my ear,

"Can I see you tomorrow before you leave?"

"Yes," I replied briefly.

"I'll be waiting for you here at 10.00."

"I'll be here," I agreed excitedly and left.

We didn't speak on the way back to the lodgings. It was freezing cold and a harsh wind was blowing in our faces. It was as warm as toast in the house. Krasi left the room while I got ready for bed. When he came back in I was already in bed.

His quiet voice made me jump.

"Baby, aren't you a bit young for love?"

"I don't understand! What do you mean?" I mumbled.

"You know exactly what I mean, darling. You just like being told. You're too stubborn to want my advice. But I will tell you all the same; your heart is still too small for a big love. And let me tell you something

– things will get very serious. Boiko is a good guy, but I know him very well and he'll want a lot more than a dance. Believe me, baby, leave the child in you a little longer..."

"It's too late, Krasi. I'm madly in love with him."

"That's not true! It's only your imagination. You're only twelve years old for goodness sake. Even though you look seventeen. I love you baby and want to save you for myself. I just want to wait for you to grow up!"

This was like a bolt of lightning. Krasi was in love with me. I almost fell out of my bed.

"Is that true, Krasi? Or are you making fun of me again?"

"It's absolutely true. I just thought it was too early to tell you."

"I'm sorry, I love you too. But like a father, like an older brother, if you like. But I can't stop my feelings now."

I suddenly burst into uncontrollable tears. Krasi sighed deeply and smiled eloquently.

"OK, baby! Let's not get upset about it. I won't stop loving you. Always, remember that. You can always rely on me. I'm leaving tomorrow. I assume I'm not going to enjoy your company on the way back. If you need me, you can find me though the bartender in our café. All right?"

"Thanks, Krasi." I continued crying inconsolably.

He moved closer to me, hugged me and held me for a long time, stroking my hair. I finally fell asleep exhausted in his arms.

The morning came very soon. I hadn't slept very well and I was upset. At the same time, I was excited about my meeting with Boiko. But I could no longer look at Krasi calmly. As always he was cheerful and smiling. He joked as he packed the bags.

We paid for the room, and we went to the bar where I was due to meet Boiko. As we got closer, Krasi stopped. He took out a wad of money, about the same amount as he had given to me previously. He said as he gave it to me,

"This is for emergencies. Hold on to it! And now hold your head up, baby! I want you to be happy! This is far as I go. Come on, give me a kiss and smile! Wish me luck! You know...!"

I stood up on my tiptoes, hugged him and kissed him on the cheek. There was a huge lump in my throat and I couldn't swallow. I wanted to say something to him.

Krasi smiled happily, but his eyes, oh God, his eyes. They spoke to me, those incredible eyes. They looked at me with such pain that I couldn't bear it. I turned around and ran down the street. I arrived first at the arranged place. I was happy because I didn't want him to see me upset. I forced myself to calm down and not think about Krasi.

A moment or two later, a car stopped in front of me. Boiko was inside. My heart leapt when I saw him. He looked even more handsome than yesterday.

"Hello, Ioana!" He smiled cheerfully. "How much time do we have?"

He thought I was leaving when he saw me with my bags.

"All the time in the world." I laughed and my legs felt weak.

"What does that mean? You mean you're not leaving today?"

"It took a while for you to catch on."

"Ioana, I don't know if you realize how happy that makes me to hear that! I didn't even dream that you would stay. You're a beautiful little magician!"

He leant over, raised my chin and kissed me long and passionately. This was my first real kiss, my first real love.

"Let's go, Ioana!"

"Where?"

"On the happiest journey of my life! To my home!"

I got in the car, like in a dream.

He turned on the radio, smiled and we drove off. He drove fast and madly, but I didn't feel afraid for a single moment.

I watched him as he drove. He had an elegant, and at the same time masculine, profile.

Bourgas. In some strange coincidence of circumstances all my dreams of living in this city were about to become reality. I had started on this unknown journey into the future without thinking, without fear. I had no one behind me, no "emergency exit" with the exception of Krasi. He also remained somewhere behind me in my life, but I hadn't drawn the line on him. I knew that if I needed him, I could look for him, and if I found him, he would help me, whatever the problem.

The car stopped suddenly and I looked around anxiously. We were in a small, quiet side street. There was a line of houses, all different styles, with different façades and sizes. The car had stopped in front of a carefully trimmed hedge covered with snow. Beyond the hedge there was a large garden with lots of trees in it. Everything was white and beautiful. At the end of the garden there was a house.

"Have you had a good look?"

Boiko was looking at me, smiling kindly.

"More or less. Is that your house?"

"Mine. Or rather my parents. Do you like it?"

"I don't know."

"Well in that case, please come in."

Boiko led me to the front door.

When we entered, he took my jacket and hung it up. He turned around and pulled me towards him. Then he kissed me, the most amazing kiss which made my head spin.

"I love you, Ioana! You drive me crazy! But I don't want to be inhospitable. Let me show you the room, and then you can take a shower and we can have some breakfast. OK?"

"All right. But won't your parents mind me being here?"

Boiko looked at me from head to toe, and smiled mysteriously.

"Don't worry, darling!"

We went up to the second floor. There were a few rooms and a bathroom. We went into one of the rooms. It was luxuriously furnished. Where was I? I would find out the answer to this question and many others for myself.

I loved to lie in the bath with thousands of bubbles caressing my body. I loved to make waves and then calm them. I loved playing with huge clouds of foam. I lay in the bath for a long time, and then dressed quickly, dried my hair and sat on the bed. It was covered with a thick silk sheet decorated with tender roses. The curtains were made of the same material. There was a small dressing table, with a miniature stool upholstered in the same silk. Part of the wall was covered by a low, white chest of drawers. Upon it there were a number of small statuettes and an old clock made of black polished wood.

I thought, *what am I doing here?* Only because I had been caught up in my "first love," I was trying to live with someone whom I didn't know at all. Was this normal? Thousands of girls in the world fell in love, but they didn't do what I was doing. Yes, but I wasn't like the others. I didn't have a home or parents. Or rather I did, but I didn't want them. I didn't want them as they were. My soul longed for other relationships, for a calm life, without screaming, without beatings and without arguments. I didn't want broken furniture, thrown around during drunken orgies. I didn't want to witness the endless scenes of jealousy, after which my mother hid the scars on her body and face. I couldn't take any more of it. That's why I had taken my destiny in my own hands. I would shape my own future from now on. I had to admit that so far luck had not abandoned me. We would see what fate held in store for me. But I was prepared to fight and to defend my right to be happy in this life. But at what price? The quiet knocking on the door woke me from my thoughts.

"Come in, please!" I had to be as polite as possible. I felt that I had come to a place where politeness and good manners were very important.

"Are you ready, darling? Shall we have breakfast?" Boiko smiled at me.

"I'm very hungry. As hungry as a wolf. What can you cook?"

"You'll see! Just follow me!"

We went down to the first floor. The kitchen and the dining room were linked by a sliding door. At first glance they seemed as richly appointed as everywhere else. I hadn't seen such a tiny oven before, and Boiko put a sandwich into it and it started rotating. In a couple of minutes, it was piping hot.

"What sort of oven is that?"

"It's a microwave. It cooks in minutes."

"You owe me an explanation. What do your parents do?"

Boiko laughed out loud.

"They're quite normal and sometimes even banal. My father's 46. He's a ship's captain on long distance voyages. My mother's an ordinary accountant at Neftohim. My father's name is Ivan, and my mother is Svetla. She's 43. I'm 20. I got out of the army in the autumn and I'm taking a rest now. In the summer I'm going to apply to the University of International Relations. That's my short autobiography. Happy now?"

"More or less."

"Now it's your turn to tell me something about you."

"Tonight. I want to have something to eat now."

"You're very mysterious. But I don't mind. Enjoy your breakfast."

I've always had a good appetite, but now I was worried. Should I tell him the whole truth? Or should I lie to him? The sandwiches were wonderful, but I found it hard to swallow. Would he be angry, if I told him everything? Or did he guess? What normal girl would go to live with the first boy she met, after just one meeting? I decided to leave these questions for later. Why should I spoil such a wonderful day?

After breakfast we went into the town. We visited a few cafés and we went to the harbour as well.

His father's ship was at sea somewhere, in the ocean. But there were many other ships in the harbour. We stood on the quay for a long time. I looked into the blue endless sea, the thick waves crashing against the breakers, and it filled with me with fear and impatience at the same time. I loved him with all the power of which I was capable, and I thought that I should tell him the entire truth. If he understood me properly, then he might understand everything. Because I didn't feel guilty. But he had lived in a completely different environment, in luxury and polite relations. Even the words he used had nothing in common with the way my other friends from the station used to speak.

"Ioana, you're not thinking of throwing yourself into the sea, are you?" Boiko took me by the arms and looked into my eyes. "Why are you so gloomy? Have I offended you in some way? I'm sorry about the sea, I was joking."

"It's all right, Boiko! In the winter the sea is very sad and frightening, do you think so?"

"Oh, my little magician has a poetic soul! Did you write poems when you were little?"

"Do you think I'm grown up?" I muttered and hugged close to him. "Let's go."

We got into his car. Before driving off, Boiko asked me hesitantly, "Where would you like to have dinner? At home or in a restaurant?"

"Your mother will make me nervous."

"My mother's a modern woman, but if you like we'll leave introductions for tomorrow! Do you like grilled fish?"

"Yes, I love it."

We went to a small restaurant which had only four tables. But it was wonderful, clean and cosy. We ordered all sorts of sea foods. After dinner Boiko asked me,

"Isn't it time you told me something about yourself?"

"Not yet," I whispered, "I want to go now and I'm tired."

We said nothing on the way home. I noticed happily that when the car stopped in front of the house, all the rooms were dark.

We entered quietly and went upstairs. The first thing I did was to go to bathroom. I was about to do something which I had only heard about. Boiko had not even suggested that he wanted anything more than a kiss from me. He was so tactful and polite. But I had made my mind up. Now or never! I went out from the bathroom and tiptoed to his door. I knocked softly and the door opened immediately. He was standing there looking at me in expectation. He drew me towards him, and I closed the door. He kissed me with such passion that I thought, *God, I'll die from love!*

At that moment, I let the bathrobe fall from me and I stood completely naked in front of him. His face bore an expression of astonishment, and for a few moments we stood in silence.

"Ioana, you're beautiful! I must be dreaming!"

He lifted me up and carried me over to the bed. He undressed with trembling hands. I had never seen a naked man before and he possessed all the qualities of his sex.

With all the tenderness of which I was capable, I hugged him and whispered,

"I love you! I want to be with you!"

His hands caressed my body and burnt me. His lips touched me in such a way that I quivered with love and desire. His body was smooth and hard.

"Oh, Ioana! You're driving me crazy! How can you be so beautiful!"

Everything disappeared from my mind. Darkness, infinity, sun, stars, sky and sea – everything merged into one and whirled around in a wild wind. I felt as though I was travelling into oblivion or perhaps returning from there. I understood nothing, but felt only one thing – love. Enormous and boundless love for this man-boy, who was making love to me so tenderly. I felt a sharp pain and then realized that I was no longer what I was a moment ago. Boiko stopped in surprise. He turned my head towards him and asked me in a whispering voice,

"Ioana, you... I'm your first, is that true?"

I sighed softly and asked,

"You're not disappointed, are you?"

"How can you joke at a moment like this? This is a special occasion! So momentous! Oh, my darling, my little magician!"

He covered me in quiet kisses of gratitude like a soft hail storm.

My first night, my night as a woman – something I will always remember as long as I live! The happiest night of my life.

The morning came imperceptibly. Exhausted, we slept tightly in each other's arms. We woke up about lunchtime. In the daylight I felt slightly ashamed, but Boiko was wonderful. He treated me like a queen. And I had nothing against it.

We lay in bed together in silence. Suddenly, I began to speak. In a quiet voice, slowly and methodically, trying not to omit any detail I told him all about my life. I didn't hide anything. When I finished, I lay trembling, waiting for my judgement. My heart was pounding and I could hardly breathe. Several minutes passed during which the atmosphere in the room lay heavy. I stole a glance at Boiko. *It's all over,* I thought. *He'll throw me out now.*

"Ioana, darling, I'm shocked!"

The sound of his voice made me jump. There was so much pain and sympathy in it.

"I love you so much and I will never let anyone hurt you again. Even by looking at you. Please, marry me! I want you to be my wife. Right away!"

He wrapped his strong arms around me as though he wanted to hide me from the entire world. His lips caressed my face and closed my eyes. It was too good to be true.

"I can't, Bo! I'm only 12 years old." I had omitted to tell him this, naturally.

A bomb dropped! Boiko stared at me. He went as white as snow. When he spoke, I couldn't recognize his voice.

"You're mad! You must be joking? Tell me you're joking, please!"

"No, it's the truth!" I looked at him pitifully.

"But you, you look so much older. This is not real. You can't be only 12! God, you're only a child! This is a right mess!"

"Oh, please don't get angry and scream!" I cried. "Don't worry. I'll go and you won't have anything to be scared of!"

"No, darling. You don't understand! I love you to death and I don't want to part. Quite the contrary, I want to get married. But they'll laugh at me in court. They might even put me in jail for sex with a minor."

"Nonsense. We don't have to get married. And no one will know how old I am. OK?"

"Let me think about it. This is very important."

"All right, you think and I'll have a shower."

I left him and went into the bathroom. I stood naked in front of the mirror. My naked body looked back at me. I thought, *it might be a good thing that I don't look my age now, but what about when I'm twenty, will I look like an old hag? I'll think about that when the time comes!* I turned the taps on and leapt into the bath. I came out of the bathroom refreshed and happy. But Bo didn't look like that. I'd made that name up for him, and I liked it. He was lying in the same pose, smoking nervously.

"That's not good, smoking on an empty stomach."

Bo looked at me in surprise and lay there motionless for a second, then with a wild cry he threw himself upon me and grabbed me by the hands. He danced a mad dance around the room, laughing and groaning.

"Bo, are you all right?" I pulled myself away from him and burst into laughter.

"Yes, yes, yes! I'm mad about you and with you. My little magician, my little woman!"

We fell onto the bed panting and gave into that same intoxication again. The world disappeared. There was just him – with his boundless love. Late in the afternoon we went out. We took a walk through the town. We even went to the cinema. I didn't see or understand anything of the film. I was just in love. But worried as well.

"Ioana, we have to go home. I want to introduce you to my mother."

I was afraid of meeting that woman. But there was no way around it. I had to go with him!

"Bo, you won't tell her how old I am, will you, or anything else?"

"Darling, don't worry! Leave it all to me!"

When we got home, his mother was sitting in an armchair listening to music. She was incredibly beautiful. She looked like Bo. Or rather he looked like her. Her long hair fell over her shoulders like silk, and in her deep green eyes there was only tenderness and kindness.

She took my hand with both her hands and said to me with a smile, "Welcome, child! You are very beautiful!"

I sat in silence and didn't know what to say to her.

"Sit down next to me. Boiko, why are you standing there?" she told him off gently.

They sat me down in her armchair. The room was filled with music. It was something classical, which I have to admit I had never heard before.

"Would you like something to drink?" she asked us. "Tea, coffee, juice?"

"No, thank you!" I mumbled and I didn't know where to put my hands. I was so embarrassed.

"Mummy, leave her alone! I'll make something myself, and you get to know each other."

I cast an anxious glance at Boiko, which his mother also noticed. We sat there in silence.

"Do you like this sort of music, Ioana? If you like, I could put something else on."

"Oh, please, don't worry! I didn't realize that I liked that sort of music."

She smiled slightly and said,

"That's the Moonlight Sonata. There shouldn't be anyone who doesn't like it. But you're still very young, and I know what young people like. Tell me where you're from."

"Mummy, please!" Bo called out from the kitchen.

"Don't worry my little Ioana. Why don't you both come in here?"

The anxious expression on my face made Bo laugh.

"But darling, relax. You're home. Isn't she, mummy?"

"I have to admit that this is all just a bit unexpected," his mother said kindly, "but I approve of your choice."

We sat down at the table. Boiko had made spaghetti. I looked at him in surprise, not believing in his culinary abilities. But the dinner was delicious.

"I do think, however, that we need to know where Ioana's from, don't we?" She was looking at me kindly and smiled.

"I'm from Sofia."

"I understand."

"Mummy, you don't understand anything! But I can tell you, that Ioana doesn't live with her parents because she ran away from them and their way of life. She suffered things that would make your hair stand on end, if I was to tell you. That's why we can't get married at the moment, but we will live together, in a free relationship, until we can. I love her and she loves me. Is that enough?"

"Absolutely, my little girl! But won't her parents be looking for her?"

"And if they are, they won't find her!" my "fiancé" said belligerently. The conversation ended on this and we continued the evening.

After dinner his mother turned towards me.

"Darling child, you'll find the care and love you need with us. Once more, "welcome" to our family and good luck to you both!"

After that she wished us good night and went to her room.

I hadn't expected such an outcome, and I felt happy and reassured.

"Ioana, do you want to watch television? Or a video?"

"I want to go to bed!" I whispered passionately to him.

CHAPTER 3

Love Excitements

The days passed like a cinema film. I grew accustomed to my new life. It was just too good to be true. We slept until late, cooked, went out for a drive in the car, and sometimes on foot. In the evenings if we didn't go out somewhere, we made our own parties at home. I got on really well with his mother. I really admired her and even had grown to love her. I wondered how she could wait for her husband for months on end and look after her family by herself. Her husband still hadn't returned from his voyage and I was worried about meeting him. I had been living in their home for more than a month and had seen everything. It was clear that someone in the home was being paid in dollars. They had all sorts of things from the hard currency shop: furniture, jewels and clothes. Everything was so tasteful.

My relationship with Bo hadn't changed. He worshipped me and my love wasn't any weaker either. However, my happiness was overshadowed by the thought that he still hadn't given up his idea of going away to university. However young I might have been, I still realized that if he became a student, the gap which divided us would grow almost impossible. I hadn't even completed my secondary education. We had a few arguments about the matter, but he was resolute.

The summer was approaching and it would bring two unpleasant events with it: his father's return and his university entrance examinations.

One morning, when I least expected it, Bo said to me,

"My father's ship is at anchor in the harbour. Get yourself ready, we'll be leaving in a moment or two."

My heart quivered.

"Please, do I have to go with you? I'll go out somewhere and then I'll wait for you in the café in the Sea Garden. You can introduce me to him this evening."

"No, darling. My father must see you now. Not this evening."

"I don't like being told what to do!"

"Unfortunately, there's no room for argument. Get dressed, please!"

I sighed deeply and reconciled myself to it. What would it matter, a few hours sooner or later?

We got in the car, all three of us: Bo, his mother and me. She was excited and happy, while Bo was thoughtful and quiet. I assumed that he was as worried as I was. That was the reason for the argument in the morning.

There were a lot of people meeting the ship; mainly women and children, clearly the sailors' families.

I saw an enormous white ship with busy sailors going to and fro on deck. The children waved their hands and all shouted "Daddy, daddy!" I didn't know if the fathers could hear their children shouting. The people who had come to meet the ship were all very excited and I assumed the sailors were too.

Time passed slowly. I began to get more nervous. After about two hours waiting, I was eventually standing in front of a tall man with piercing, black eyes, greying hair and tanned skin, just like Bo. I could see that Bo had taken his dark skin from his father and his beautiful green eyes and chestnut hair from his mother. What a marvel of nature! To combine the best of two people in another – the one I loved until it hurt. I didn't even hear the introductions. I was deafened by the noise of children and seagulls, the thundering sea, nerves and anxiety.

I only saw his untrusting eyes squint and the countless wrinkles forming around them. A small, tired smile flitted across his tired face to greet me.

My intuition told me that he didn't like me.

We left the harbour. Bo and I walked ahead while his mother and father followed. She was probably in a hurry to tell him about me. And he was probably making known his own opinion about his son's romantic adventure.

We said nothing. I could see that Bo was confused. He didn't look at me. We got in the car in the same order. We sat in front and his parents behind. The music filled the emptiness between us. We got home quite quickly. I went straight up to my room, threw myself on the bed and burst into tears. I lay there for a long time like that. I finally calmed down. I listened carefully and could hear voices from downstairs. They were arguing, probably about me. *Why wasn't the Captain on a round-the-world voyage? It had been so good without him!* Of course, I was looking at things from my point of view.

Bo rushed into the room flushed and angry.

"We're leaving! Get up!"

"Hold on, Bo. Calm down. Tell me what's happened!"

"He doesn't want you here. He reckons you'll ruin my chances of a future. He called you…"

"What did he call me?"

"It doesn't matter. I don't want to think about it."

I quickly packed my things into my bag. He had more luggage.

Downstairs in the hallway, his father was waiting for us with an angry expression on his face.

"I want you to know Boiko, that if you leave now, you can never come back!"

"I hadn't even thought about it!"

"It's quite clear that you don't think about anything. You haven't got enough brains in your head to think about anything," his father said sadly and calmly before he retreated into his room.

The door of the house slammed shut after us.

"We're going to stay with a friend," Bo said curtly.

"Whatever you say, I love you and I will follow you anywhere. But are you sure you're doing the right thing?"

My question remained unanswered. A taxi took us to the outskirts of Bourgas. His friend was at home. After listening to Bo, he agreed to give us a room. It was so small that there was hardly any room for our luggage. It had only one bed, which looked like it was a relic from the last century. It had iron bedsteads with four brass balls on each corner. There wasn't a cupboard and the floor was bare. The small window looked as though it hadn't been washed for years and only a faint light could penetrate into the room. The atmosphere was very disheartening, but we tried to not to pay any attention. The most important thing was that we were together.

In the early evening, Bo and I went out. I tried to cheer him up, in every way I could think of. But he was gloomy. We went to have dinner in the same small restaurant which was filled with memories of our first night together.

That evening I hoped that I would succeed in cheering Bo up by taking him to that small, cosy restaurant. That's why I had insisted on going there.

He felt a little bitter, but there was still something wrong. In the end, I couldn't take it anymore.

"Bo, don't you think it's very unkind of you to sulk all day long and upset me as well? Anyone might think that I had dragged you out of your own home. I can't take it anymore! I asked you once and I'm going to ask you again. Are you sure you're doing the right thing? Because if there is any uncertainty, that means that very soon you will blame me for the situation you're in. And then we'll have to break up. And I don't want that..."

"Ioana, stop it! Be quiet! You don't understand anything! I love you infinitely. And I am absolutely convinced that I have done the right thing. But the world collapsed for me today. My father destroyed everything he had taught me today. Ever since I remember, my parents have brought me up to be completely independent. I have always taken my own decisions. My father always said to me, "Remember, in this life you take the decisions and you bear the responsibilities for your actions. That is the only way you will know what is right". And now when I took one of the most important steps in my life, he tries to tell me what to do. He doesn't care about my opinion. And I will never forgive him for that!"

And so, my Bo, my only one. And I had doubted his love for me. I stroked his hand silently as he nervously drummed the table. I looked at him so tenderly and loyally that he couldn't bear the tension anymore. Before the curious looks of the other visitors to the restaurant, he pulled me towards him and kissed me longingly. I wasn't reticent either. We forgot about all the other people and whispered vows of loyalty and love and kissed so passionately that we didn't see the manager of the restaurant come up to our table. We were startled by the sound of his voice,

"To the young couple! A bottle of champagne on the house!"

Our ears were deafened with a thunderous noise of applause and glasses toasting us. Bo and I looked at each other in astonishment. He reacted first. He took a glass and gave me the other. We toasted each other and drank the glasses to the bottom. It was just like a wedding! The applause didn't die down. I suddenly felt like a queen. They played a slow dance tune in our honour. There was no dance floor, so we danced between the tables, hugging each other tightly, as though merged into one body. It was an unforgettable evening. We left late. We were so happy and our little room was waiting for us...

A week passed, during which nothing happened to upset our happy solitude. However, one day came when Bo looked at me and said in a slightly anxious voice,

"Ioana, I have to go out today. I'll be home this evening."

"Where are you going to go, darling? I thought we might go and see that new film everyone's talking about. And then we could go shopping?"

"I'm sorry but I have to go out. And don't be cross with me. I have to rush now, but we'll go to the cinema in the next couple of days, all right? I promise."

"What am I going to do without you?" I protested crossly.

"It's important."

The door pitilessly slammed shut under my nose.

That's what he thinks, does he? I'll show him. I won't speak to him this evening, I thought, and thought of a plan to get my revenge. I got dressed and went out. First of all, I went to an open air café. I ordered a cola and lit a cigarette. I looked at the passers-by. It was the middle of May and the weather was great. The sun peered through the branches of the trees; a light breeze caressed my face and ruffled my hair. Brought outside by the good weather, mothers and their children had occupied the park opposite.

The little children ran around untiringly, some fell and cried at the top of their voices, waiting for their mothers to hug and comfort them. Suddenly, I felt a pain in my heart. What was my mother doing? She used to take me to the park and laugh at my fast little legs. She proudly told her friends about all the trouble I got into. They exchanged recipes for puddings and desserts. What was she doing now? She was suffering over the loss of a runaway, ungrateful daughter. And she wouldn't dare tell anyone. She hadn't dared protect me from the abuse of my father and other people. But most of all from my father. Why hadn't she divorced him, and then we might have lived normally and even happily? Who knows? And if we add to that my unclear present and future, we were in a right mess.

In stark contrast to the warm May temperatures, my mood dropped to below zero. On top of it all I was seriously concerned with another problem. I thought I was pregnant. I didn't dare think about it, but the regular throwing up every morning was a clear sign. I had kept it secret from Bo, but for how long? That was the question.

I went for a wander around the town. I wandered amongst the passers-by and didn't even feel them when they pushed me. Suddenly, I felt a hand on my shoulder. I stopped in surprise and turned around. It was Bo's mother standing in front of me. She was dressed very elegantly but she looked sad. There were deep wrinkles around her green eyes. I could swear that she didn't have them before.

"Hello, darling Ioana!" she said sadly. "How are you? Where are you living? How's Boiko?"

"Hello, Auntie Svetla!" I said in embarrassment. "Boiko's well."

"Where are you living?" She repeated her question and tears welled up in her eyes.

"We're renting a room from a friend of his, Stefan."

"Tell Boiko to call me. It wasn't fair to abandon me like that. I'm with you! I can't fight his father. He's irreconcilable and very bitter. Don't be angry, but he thinks he's right and he won't make any compromise."

"I'm not angry with him. I don't have the right to be angry. But Bo doesn't want to hear a word said about him."

"Let me come with you. I want to see my son."

"Bo will be back this evening."

His mother looked at me as though she didn't believe me. She said nothing and then after a few moments added,

"I understand. That's all right. Please tell him that I love him very much. And I'll wait for him to call me on the telephone. Tell him to phone at least."

"I'll tell him."

I stood there not knowing what to say. It wouldn't look good for me to leave first. I shifted my weight from foot to foot.

"Ioana, take this money. I'm sorry that I haven't got any more on me."

She put a handful of banknotes into my hand, caressed my cheek and walked away in tears.

I stood there dumbfounded. I looked at the money and thought to myself, *another weak woman. She hasn't got the strength to fight against her husband. She's no different from my mother, except that she's of a different class.*

I sighed deeply and continued along my way.

I spent all day walking around the town. I returned home in the evening, exhausted. Bo was waiting for me with an angry expression on his face.

"Where have you been?" He looked at me crossly.

"We seem to have left our good manners in the street!" I looked at him ironically. "Do you want me to spend all day sitting in this hole? And where have you been?" I raised my voice without realizing it. "If you think that's how it's going to be, you've got another thing coming! I won't let you push me around, do you understand?!"

I screamed the last words.

Bo stood there staring at me, as though he had never seen me before.

"Ioana, calm down! What has got into you? I would never think of pushing you around. I just didn't want you to worry about me. It's just we haven't got any money and I went to look for work today. But I didn't find any."

It was my turn to stare at him now. It had never occurred to me. We had never had to worry about money while we lived with his parents. But that was a problem now. I hurled my arms around him.

"Bo, darling. I'm sorry! How could I have been so silly! Forgive me! I remember there's something I have to tell you. That's what I should have begun with. I bumped into your mother today. She gave me some money and cried. She wants to see you. She looks really distraught."

I quickly told him all about my meeting with his mother. Bo said nothing; his face lengthened and his eyes took on the same expression that I saw on his mother. He didn't say anything for some time.

"I love her too, Ioana. But I'm not going to call her."

"Why?" I said downheartedly.

"Because she didn't say a single word to support me when I needed it."

"You don't have the right to hurt her like that. She's suffering so much. She loves you."

"And didn't you hurt your mother who you also love? Isn't that right? Why haven't you called her for so long?"

He had got me. I said nothing and thought to myself. He was right, of course. But I was right too.

"You know, Bo, there's a difference between your case and mine. My mother was a witness to the violence with which my father treated me for years. And she said nothing. She even took my father's side sometimes. And she preferred to say nothing. She would rather I ran away than stand up for me against my father or even get divorced from him. She chose her marriage over me. Perhaps out of fear. While your mother hasn't had the chance to make up for her mistake (if she has made a mistake). You just haven't given her a chance. Admit it!"

Bo followed my train of thought carefully, but suddenly grabbed me and closed my mouth with a kiss.

"My clever little girl! My sweet professor! You should be a lawyer! No daughter-in-law has ever defended her mother-in-law so well. And you did it, even though you have been cast out of your home and unwanted. I love you, my clever little one!"

Peace had been restored. We decided that he would call his mother and they would meet the next day. We had dinner quickly in a café and hurried to the cinema in the centre of the town. Promises had to be kept!

CHAPTER 4

Accident or The Finger of Fate

The meeting was arranged. I decided not to go. It was a marvellous day and I enjoyed a walk through the Sea Garden. I walked aimlessly, looking at the sea glistening under the bright rays of the sun and I was happy at the thought that I would soon be able to lie on the beach all day. It would be wonderful, of course, if it wasn't for that annoying sensation in my stomach which reminded me that I would soon be as fat and round as an Easter loaf. *Honestly,* I loved Bo madly but I didn't want a baby. I had seen lots of films where the woman, when the doctor tells her that she's pregnant, bursts into a smile and is very happy. I had read many books about girls who become single mothers and don't care about what other people think of them. But it wasn't like that for me. I hated that thing in my womb. Not because it made me feel sick, but because it was binding me down with some invisible chains and wouldn't let me be free. I probably wasn't a normal person. It was as though two different individuals were living inside me. One was saying to me that to hate your own child, which hadn't even been born yet, was inhuman, while the other person inside me was saying just the opposite. I was torn by contradictions. I even began to think that I was going mad. But the worst thing about it was that I didn't know what to do about the situation. If I told Bo, that would only make the situation more complicated. He would insist on us getting married. Given the situation, the consequences would be unpredictable. I was only 12 years old without any ID documents. His father was against me, we had no money, and then Bo was determined to go to university.

It was a complete mess. My head began to ache with all these serious and worrying thoughts. I was feeling uncontrollably nauseous and I looked at the thing hidden deep inside me which was causing me so much anxiety, with hatred. My other "I" was saying to me, that this little, helpless being which didn't even have a brain, or even a head, was completely dependent upon me, and I was the entire universe for him or her…and he or she already loved me, without even knowing it.

I sat down on a bench and started sobbing uncontrollably. I suddenly leapt up and jumped into the nearby bushes. A fountain erupted from my mouth and the frightened sparrows flew away chirping.

I looked around. It was a good thing that there was no one around. I could hear a baby crying but I couldn't see it or its mother through the trees. I felt a little better, but dizzy, and I sat down on the bench again. I sat there for a long time, unable to make any movement. I felt completely empty. I didn't know what time it was or where I was. I felt as though I had been sitting there for hours. I decided eventually to go home. I walked rather hesitantly, even swaying from side to side. I felt very ill. I wanted to go to bed as soon as I could. I decided to stop a taxi. I looked around. The traffic was very heavy but there weren't any taxis. I felt that I wouldn't have the strength to make it home. I noticed an empty taxi on the opposite side of the road and ran towards it. I was deafened by the noise of a horn and the screaming of brakes. At the same time something threw me up in the air with great force. Everything happened in the space of a split second, so quickly that I couldn't determine the course of events. Was I first thrown up into the air and then it started hurting, or was it the opposite? I didn't know. Then I lost consciousness.

CHAPTER 5

Hospital Woes

I found myself on a white, fluffy cloud. I was sitting in something like an armchair flying through the air. Beneath me there were beautiful landscapes and tall white skyscrapers. Everything was embraced by the light and the sun. Thousands of little suns seemed to be shining around me. It was warm and very light. I was as light as a feather and I was flying very quickly. Suddenly, one of the clouds, which were moving alongside me, bent down over me and said,

"I think she's coming to."

This cloud was clearly talking nonsense and I tried to laugh, but I couldn't. Something was holding my mouth. I was very angry and reacted.

"Who's holding my head so tightly?" But instead of the words, the sound that came out of my mouth resembled a groaning sound.

"Yes, yes, she's opening her eyes, doctor!"

Since I couldn't open my mouth, I decided to try and see if I could open my eyes. I blinked as much as I could and saw, albeit hazily, a man and a woman dressed in white pouring over me. I slowly looked around the room behind the two people and in front of them. Jesus, it was a hospital, and they were doctors. I tried to recall the events and somewhere faraway in my memories my attempts to fly appeared, the intense pain and the car horns. Jesus!

I was lying with bandages from head to foot and the two doctors were staring at me with expressions of hope and care.

"Doctor, do you think she will wake up?"

"Yes, yes. My little girl, if it's not too difficult, can you tell me how you're feeling? Where does it hurt?"

These questions were clearly directed at me. I tried to smile but I couldn't. A thought cut through me like a knife. I had no documents; I had run away from home; I was pregnant; I was living illegally with Bo. I was underage. God, what a mess! My head began to spin and I preferred to lose consciousness again.

When I woke up again after long and stupid nightmares, it was dark in the room and Bo was sitting next to my bed. His face was in shadow but I could feel his tense breathing. I mustered my strength and whispered,

"How did you find me?"

If the wall had suddenly collapsed, he wouldn't have been more startled. He leapt from the chair and fell to his knees next to the bed. He put his head next to my face and burst into tears.

He was sobbing like a child in a dark cellar, frightened to death.

"Calm down, it's all over. I'm alive." I tried to calm him even though I couldn't move. They say that a man's tears are priceless. If that is true, then Bo lost an entire fortune that evening. He finally calmed down and tried to hug me. But he couldn't, I was completely packaged in bandages. My left hand and leg were in plaster casts. My head was bandaged like a front-line soldier. Looked at from the side, I was a terrible sight.

He kissed me tenderly and asked me in a quivering voice,

"Does it hurt?"

"No!" I lied through my teeth and smiled gently.

The truth was that there wasn't a part of my body which didn't hurt.

"Darling, the doctor said that I should call him the moment you woke up, but before I do, I want you to know what I told him. I told him that you're my cousin, from Sofia. You've been living at home because your parents are in Libya. My mother will come in the morning to sign the necessary documents."

"Bo, you're great! I love you!"

"Shh! Don't talk. I'm going for the doctor."

While I was waiting alone in the little room, I thought about the baby. What had happened to it?

I carefully felt between my legs with my good hand and felt a sanitary towel. I didn't understand. As I tried to focus my mind, the door opened and the doctor came into the room. He was followed by a woman who seemed familiar to me. I remembered that it was the doctor who had been standing over my bed the first time I had woken up.

"Welcome back!" The doctor smiled at me. "Do you want to talk or do you want to rest?"

"What's wrong with me?" I asked quietly.

"My little girl, it would be better to ask what is not wrong with you." The doctor was quite young and had an anxious expression. "According to witnesses, you flew about three metres after the collision. You've got cuts and bruises everywhere, your left arm and leg are broken. You were concussed, only slightly thank goodness. I'm telling you everything, even though doctors are not really supposed to, because I want to get you on your feet. But before I go on, let me introduce myself to you. I'm Dr. Todorov and I'm your personal doctor. And this is my colleague, Dr. Pavlova. She's a gynaecologist."

A red light flashed in my brain. Something must have happened to my baby for her to be here. I tried not to show any reaction. I sighed softly and asked,

"What day is it today?"

"Wednesday. You've been here since yesterday afternoon. How do you feel?"

How did I feel? Everything hurt, but I was alive and that was the most important thing.

"Not very well, doctor. But it could be worse, couldn't it?"

"It could have been much, much worse. You were born under a lucky star. But if you're not too tired I would like to ask you some questions. What's your name, where are you from and how old are you? I have to fill in some forms for your admission to the hospital."

This is going to make things worse! I thought.

"My name is Ioana Peicheva. I'm from Sofia and I'm staying with some relatives here." I said all this very quickly and fell silent. Talking exhausted me. All the breathing in and out caused me sharp pain in my chest. My head hurt with a sharp penetrating pain. The doctor and his colleague looked at me very carefully. My face probably expressed the gravity of the situation of my body and soul. The interrogation stopped and was replaced by all manner of procedures. They took my blood pressure. A nurse gently gave me two injections, and constantly apologized that she couldn't find a healthy place to do them. Dr. Pavlova coughed in embarrassment and started explaining,

"Dear child, you've probably realized that there is a reason for me to be here. I have to tell you that when you were admitted to hospital yesterday, you were unconscious and you started bleeding, and you had a miscarriage. Believe me, the doctor who attended you was very worried because you were in a very serious condition. However, we did a fine job and we managed to prevent any complications, which we were worried about. I'm very sorry about the baby."

I said nothing and tried to take shallow breaths. It hurt less. There was silence in the room. Dr. Todorov had left the room and there was just Dr. Pavlova and me left in the room.

After a short pause she continued,

"Your auntie will come tomorrow. That's what that nice little boy, your cousin said. Do you want to tell them about the miscarriage?"

"No!" I whispered in fright. "I don't want anyone to know! Please!"

"All right. That's your business. By the way, how old are you?"

"16!" I said as confidently as possible.

"16 next birthday, probably?"

"Yes."

"All right then. Rest now and no sudden movements. Bye!"

"Good bye and thank you!" I said in a muffled voice and remained alone in the room.

A silence fell over me and struck me like a wave. I couldn't gather or arrange my thoughts. Too many things had happened to me in a single day. All right then. Let me think again. The Sea Garden. I felt sick. Then I went home. The taxi. The collision. Then a white blank. According to the doctors I had fallen in front of a car which had hit me and I had flown into the air. I had been brought to the hospital with a broken left leg and arm, concussion and a miscarriage. And all this had happened while I was unconscious.

God, thank you!

CHAPTER 6

The Disruption

I spent about a month in hospital. It was a nightmare. I couldn't move because of my plastered limbs. At least I hadn't lost my memory with the concussion.

The day came for me to be released. Flowers and sweets! Smiles and wishes for a speedy recovery. Then at last in the car. Bo, smiling from ear to ear, turned to me.

"Darling, I've got a surprise for you."

"I like surprises! What is it?"

"Wait and you will see!"

"Give me a clue!"

"No, no, no!"

"Just wait till I get these splints off and you'll have no peace from me!" I threatened him happily and we set off.

My surprise was a wonderful apartment in a huge, new block. It consisted of a bedroom, living room and kitchen.

"Bo, where did you find it?" I yelled out with pleasure.

"It was my mother. A colleague of hers is renting it to us. It's fully furnished."

"But it's wonderful! Just look how nice it is!"

"Let's not exaggerate. It's not exactly a present. The rent is quite high but my mother's going to pay it."

"I'm really grateful to her for everything."

"She loves you, Ioana. And I love you. That explains everything. I haven't given up on my intention of marrying you. And she's been helping us as much as she can."

Bo came closer to me, and put his arms around me carefully but insistently. A hot wave erupted in my stomach. My lips looked for his.

Making love when you're half in plaster is quite a difficult task, but we did a wonderful job.

Later, as we had dinner, Bo told me about his new job. He had started working for a design bureau which was constructing an atomic power station or something like that. He had a good salary and the work was interesting. I was pleased that Bo had given up on his dream of going to university. But I was shocked when he told me had taken the entrance exams for Varna university and had answered all the questions. He was waiting for the results and they came soon.

One evening when I was feeling irritated because of the boredom of sitting still for a month, Bo came home from work and ceremoniously put a shopping bag on the table.

"We're going to celebrate, darling! I'm a student!"

I didn't react at all. I felt a strange pain in my heart.

"Well, aren't you going to congratulate me? Aren't you pleased for me?"

How could I tell him how angry I was? I don't know why I was so annoyed by his plans to go to university. I was absolutely furious.

"I don't want to hear a word about your university. It's none of my business!" I said quietly and coldly.

Bo slowly went bright red, and then all the blood drained from his face and it turned the same shade of white as my plaster.

"Ioana, I think you should say you're sorry!"

"Sorry? Why should I say sorry that you're getting shot of me in such a tactful way? Never!"

"Say that again, you ungrateful little girl! Who's getting shot of you? Me? Do I have to tell you what I have done for you? Do I have to tell you about all the stress I went through with your accident? And what about me going to work all day and then studying in the evenings? I have had to give up so many things just so I could get you everything you wanted; I even gave up my own father!"

"There you are! You finally said it! I wondered when you were finally going to call me to account for your split with your father! And I didn't have to wait too long! You can go back to your father right now! I won't keep you!"

Silence. We said nothing and stared at each other. Bo spoke first, so quietly that I had to concentrate to hear him.

"Ioana, what you just said is very serious. I demand that you explain!"

"I'm not going to explain anything! You heard me very well. Leave right now!" I screamed and began sobbing uncontrollably.

"Ioana, you're getting hysterical! Shall I call for a doctor?"

"Go to hell! I don't want to talk to you ever again!" I screamed as I went into the bedroom, locked the door and threw myself onto the bed. I sobbed my heart out.

No one knocked on the door.

CHAPTER 7

Excruciating Breakup

The next day I got up late. Bo had already gone out. He went out to work before eight. I spent the day thinking. I tried to understand him and find an excuse for him, but I couldn't. I thought I was right and no one could have persuaded me of the contrary. But I still waited excitedly for Bo to come home. It was a rainy day and I was feeling even more frustrated. I hated the rain. I hated waiting. The hours passed by slowly, the evening came, then the night. There was no trace of Bo. I went to bed very depressed, listening all the time for the front door to open.

I woke up cross the next day. I checked the apartment and saw that Bo had not come home that night.

I was suddenly overcome by fear. What if something had happened to him? What if he had had an accident in the rain? No, nothing like that could have happened to Bo. He was just punishing me. But where had he slept? The worm of doubt began to crawl through my mind. Did he have someone new? I went to the telephone. I could easily telephone him at work to hear his voice. But my pride stopped me. *I'll wait for him to call first,* I decided.

Bo didn't call and he didn't come home. I realized that it was something very serious. I called his house. His mother hadn't seen him but he had called her to tell her that he was going away on business. And that he would be back tomorrow.

"Didn't you know that he was going away?" she asked me suspiciously.

"Of course I knew, but I thought that he might have come home early and gone to see you. Goodbye."

I was more than just angry now. He was playing tricks with me. My plaster was due to be removed on Monday. All right then. I had just three days left then I would be free.

Those last three days were difficult to stand.

Bo came home on Sunday after lunch. He hadn't shaved and his clothes were creased. When he came to me, he looked at me with a guilty expression and smiled sadly.

"Darling, forgive me! Please!"

I looked at him in silence. I waited to feel some sort of emotion inside me, whether it was love or anger. But I felt nothing. Absolutely nothing. I was empty and dry. I felt sick.

"Please, Ioana, say something. You frighten me when you don't say anything!"

"What do you want me to say to you?" My voice was so dry that it resembled a rasping sound.

"Whatever you want to say. You look awful! Are you all right?"

"That's none of your business! Leave me alone! I'm tired of waiting for you. It's late now. Leave me, and I'll leave tomorrow."

I dragged myself to the bedroom – my refuge. I locked the door and stayed there until the morning.

I didn't sleep a wink. I thought about this strange phenomenon. Of all the love I felt for him, there was not a single drop left. Where had it all evaporated to and how? I didn't know.

The night was damp and humid. I sat at the edge of the window looking at the sky. Somewhere amongst the glittering stars lay the answer to my enigma. In the next room lay a man who had been the meaning of my life for the last few months. And today when he begged me for forgiveness, I found him repulsive. Was I to blame or was it him? I didn't know. But I knew that I was leaving tomorrow. Forever.

In the morning I was dressed, bathed and ready to leave. The plan was to take a taxi to the hospital where they would remove my plaster casts and then goodbye to Burgas. But there was a problem. Bo.

When we met in the hallway in front of the bathroom, he looked at me seriously and said,

"Ioana, that's enough of this nonsense. I want to talk."

I decided that it would be better not to irritate him because his eyes were sparkling threateningly.

"OK!" I replied coldly. "Would you like coffee or tea?"

"Nothing, thank you."

"I'll have a coffee. Will you pass me the cigarettes please?"

I lit a cigarette. My mouth was dry and bitter. I put it out.

"What's happened to you? Has something changed? Don't you love me anymore?"

I thought carefully about my answer. Better to tell him the bitter truth than a lie.

"To put it bluntly, Bo, it's all over."

"That's not possible, Ioana! You're just angry!"

"No, Bo. I'm completely calm. I realized last night that I don't love you anymore. I'm sorry if that hurts you. But you have to know the truth. You deserve that."

"Ioana, I want one more chance. Please!"

"What exactly do you want?"

"I want you to stay a few more days. I want you to think a bit more calmly. I can't believe that the words which you just said so calmly are true. And think of your health. When the plaster's removed your arm and leg will need physiotherapy. You can't just put weight on them immediately."

Jesus, he was worried about my health!

"Just one week, Bo! Not a day more!"

"All right!" He sighed in relief. "And now let's go. It's nearly ten."

It didn't take very long at the hospital. I think I must have been born under a lucky star. Everything had healed well. I was "brand new" as my doctor said.

Bo took me back home, said goodbye kindly and went to work. I made myself a coffee and a sandwich and sat down to have lunch.

I felt very strange. I was happy that I was well and impatient to leave. There was nothing here to keep me anymore. But I wanted to keep my promise. One more week. I felt sorry for Bo. He was hoping for something. Perhaps a miracle. Miracles happen very rarely.

There was an unspoken agreement that I slept in the bedroom and he slept in the living room.

He was very attentive and quiet. I observed his efforts to try and make me happy. There were three days left until the end of the week.

Bo came home that evening with a large package. I could see from the bag that it was from the dollar shop.

"What's that, Bo?"

"Guess!"

"Tell me!"

"Have a look for yourself!" He smiled gently, almost imploringly.

I did my best to smile back at him. I unwrapped the parcel. There was a video recorder inside. I had been asking Bo to buy one for ages, but we had always put it off. This was probably the last tactic Bo had left in his psychological offensive. I decided not to disappoint him.

"That's great, Bo. Have you got any cassettes?"

"Yes, just the one. To begin with."

"Well, let's play it. I can't wait."

Bo smiled broadly. He fussed around with the video and soon the film was beginning. It was called "Ghost," a marvellous story about love, death and human morality.

I'm not normally sentimental, but I cried out loud. I couldn't calm down for a long time. The film had plucked strings in my heart which I didn't know I still had.

I have to admit that Bo knew how to fight, and he was winning on points.

He slept with me that night. We made love for a long time, to the point of exhaustion. In the moments when we reached the peak of loving intoxication, we held on to each other so tight that no one could have separated us.

Bo fell asleep with the first rays of the sun holding on to me tightly. I couldn't sleep. I was disgusted with myself. How could I have done it?

I carefully got out of bed and went into the kitchen.

I was just a little bitch.

Bo didn't deserve me playing him around like this. He was more than decent, from beginning to end. But I was just the most ordinary bitch. I had to get out of there, right away. I wouldn't be able to look him in the eyes now, just when he thought that everything was all right, and I was getting ready to leave.

I quietly crammed everything I needed into my bag and went to the door. I stopped, turned around and looked at him. Bo was sleeping calmly like a baby. He was strong and beautiful. Clever and intelligent. I would just have destroyed him and stopped him developing. "Run!" I said to myself. "Your affair is over!" Then, without knowing why I did it, I reached in to his jacket pocket and took his money and put it in my own pocket.

I closed the front door quietly. The morning outside was fresh and smiling. It was still early and there weren't many people on the streets. Most of the people in this busy port town were still asleep. Soon their alarm clocks would ring and the sleepy husbands and wives would start making breakfasts for themselves and their hungry children. I was in a hurry as well. I wanted to get on the next possible train for anywhere.

I sat thinking in the half-empty bus to the centre of the town. So I'm a thief as well now. I didn't actually need the money, because I still had a black purse in my bag with two hundred and fifty levs, the money that Krasi had given to me when we parted. "In case of emergency," he had said then, "keep it." And I had kept the money.

I shouldn't have taken the money from Bo. It would make matters even worse for him. He would be even more disillusioned with me. Perhaps he would forget me more quickly. Years later I would recall this day and realize that everything I did to Bo that day would hurt him very, very deeply.

However, at that moment I was aiming for the station. The ticket hall was empty. I sat in an armchair, since my leg was still weak and was causing me great pain. I wondered what direction to travel in. I finally decided.

"Could you tell me, please, when is the next train to Sofia?"

"The express is in two hours' time."

"Are there any tickets left? I want one first class ticket."

I paid for the ticket with my money. Bo's money felt as though it would burn my fingers. I hoisted my bag over my shoulder and walked slowly towards the station.

I looked at the windows of the shop on the way. It was still early and there weren't any shoppers up and about.

I walked along the streets and said goodbye to the town. The few months I had spent here were to leave an unforgettable mark on my life. But at the moment I felt completely empty. Love had suddenly disappeared in the same way as it had appeared. Now an emptiness had appeared in my soul, a cold void. Cold and irrevocable.

I decided to sit in one of the many cafés to kill a bit of time. I have always liked to eat. I hoped that my mood might rise by an octave if I had a hamburger. And I was right. The world never seems so black when your stomach is full.

It was time for the train.

I went to the station and headed for the platform. The train was ready to leave and .... Oh my God! My heart stopped beating. Bo was standing in front of me. Unshaved, unkempt, with trainers over bare feet. I stood motionless. He approached me. His eyes, oh those hypnotic eyes. The whole universe was contained in them. Grief, anger, fury, love and hatred flowed from them.

"Why did you do it?" I guessed the question, rather than heard it. At that moment I felt such a hard blow to my face that my ears rang. I looked at him in astonishment, unable to react. At the same time, I asked the question, "Is that really you, Bo? God, he hit me!" I couldn't believe it. The passers-by stared at us, enjoying the show.

"I want to know why!" He had regained his voice.

"What have I done?" I couldn't think of anything else to say.

"Why did you sleep with me last night, when you had already made up your mind to leave?"

He doesn't know about the money, I thought to myself.

"And I didn't know about your habit of stealing. How long have you been doing that?" His voice was as bitter as quinine.

I put my hand in my pocket hastily and pulled out his hateful money. I gave it to him in silence. A powerful blow to my wrist sent the money flying.

Bo looked at me hatefully from head to toe and said,

"I'm ashamed that I ever loved you!"

He turned around and walked away with his head held high.

The onlookers gathered up the money and walked away, disappointed that the show had ended.

I walked to the train humiliated and ashamed. My eyes were misty and I couldn't see anything. I managed somehow to find my seat and the train departed. I was experiencing grief and anger. I missed Bo, but I couldn't forgive him for the public humiliation which he had subjected me to.

I was alone in the compartment. I watched the countryside from the window and tried to calm down. I had to be calm to take the right decision. I was journeying into the unknown again.

CHAPTER 8

Again With Krasi's Gang

The train arrived at the Central Station in Sofia and slowly came to a halt in the midst of a crowd of people who had come to meet it. There was no one there to meet me, of course. I had decided in the meantime to look for Krasi. I hoped I would be lucky enough to find him.

I hoisted the bag over my shoulder and went to the café where his friend worked.

I had been away from Sofia for six whole months, and it felt as though years had passed. The Central Station – my second home – was even more filthy than usual. I didn't want to spend another night here, not for anything in the world, but I still looked around for any of my old acquaintances. I pushed open the door of the bar and stepped inside. I was hit by the odour of stale air, cigarettes and mould.

I boldly approached the bartender.

He recognized me and smiled.

"Where have you been, darling? It's been some time since you were here last."

"Hi! Have you seen Krasi?"

"No, I haven't seen him, but I know where he is."

"Where?"

"Hold on, little one! You're stifling me! Have you got any money?"

"How much?"

"A hundred..."

I counted out one hundred levs and elegantly placed them in the plate for change.

"Your boyfriend's in Sunny Beach, with some friends. He's getting a tan and girls and that sort of thing."

"What's the name of his hotel?"

"Sirena."

"Thanks. I'll remember you in my will." I gave him a crooked smile and left the bar.

Well that's really silly! I thought. *Why did I come all the way from Bourgas to Sofia? Just to find out that Krasi's in Sunny Beach?* I sat down on the first bench which appeared in front of my eyes and thought. I didn't have anywhere to sleep and hadn't got much money left, and Krasi was five hundred kilometres away from me. There was nothing to do but get the next train back to Bourgas. It was strange, but my life had become inseparably linked to the sea.

I bought a ticket for the train at 23.00. I had all the afternoon to kill and a bit of money. I was in Sofia and I could walk around the shops until it got late.

Should I call my mother? I thought. What would I tell her? That I was all right? And that I wasn't going to tell her where I was living. I had no intention of calling her.

I left my bag with the bartender in the disgusting café and went to the shops. I got bored of them after a while and my leg was hurting. I must have put too much weight on it. I sat down in a café and ordered a cola and a sandwich.

Someone tried to chat me up but I got rid of him quickly and managed to relax and enjoy my rest, when a man and woman entered the bar. They were arguing about something and went over to the till. My heart went cold. It was my mother and my father. They appeared to be quarrelling about something as usual. I leant over the table and turned around slowly. I crept out of the café and ran over to the tram stop. My leg was hurting but I ran as fast as I could. I jumped into the tram while it was still moving.

God, what bad luck! I thought as I tried to catch my breath.

There is a God after all! I concluded and went back to the station to wait for my train.

I arrived back in Bourgas in the early morning and immediately took the bus to Sunny Beach. I was dying of hunger and had no more money. All my hopes rested with Krasi.

I found his hotel and sat in the lobby.

I had been waiting for over an hour, when I saw him coming down the stairs with two other lads.

I straightened my hair and ran up to them. I stood in front of Krasi. He was completely taken aback. His killingly beautiful blue eyes stared at me in amazement and then sparkled with a smile.

"I can't believe my eyes! Baby! How much you've grown up! You look really great! Where did you come from?"

Two strong arms lifted me up to the level of his eyes and I received a deafening kiss. Then he put me down again.

"It can't be true! How did you know I was here?" He didn't give me the chance to open my mouth.

He was so happy to see me that all my fears disappeared. I felt very guilty when I thought about the circumstances of our parting, more than half a year previously.

"You haven't swallowed your tongue, have you?" he joked with me. "Let's go to the café opposite the hotel."

He took my bag, put his arm around my shoulder and we went to the bar.

We sat down and only then could I get a word in edgeways.

"Krasi, I've come all the way from Sofia. And I've travelled a thousand kilometres in twenty four hours. I'm dying of hunger, thirst and..."

"Ha, ha, ha!" he laughed. "You haven't changed a jot. Let's feed our little baby! Boys, get a move on, the baby's hungry. Let me introduce you first of all. I almost forgot, I was so excited to see her. Ioana, these are Chavdar and Svetlio. Two of my best friends. Boys, this is the sweetest girl I know. Ioana. And let me warn you right now. Hands off her! OK?"

His two friends laughed understandingly and went over to the bar. Krasi sat back in his chair. The umbrella cast a shadow over his face. His eyes and teeth flashed like glass. I could swear that he was happy to see me.

"What happened, baby?" he asked me tenderly.

"It's a long story, Krasi. To make a long story short, it's all over. I've got nowhere to go again, that's why I came to you... because... because..." I suddenly burst into tears and couldn't go on.

Suddenly, my whole life with Bo flashed before me like on a cinema screen, all the good and bad parts. I missed Bo, even though I had left him. I felt sorry for myself, for Krasi, whom I had abandoned for Bo, and now I was coming to him for help. I felt sorry for the baby whom I didn't want and who died before it was born. For everyone and everything.

Krasi hugged me tight. He stroked my hair and spoke to me.

"Come on, baby! It's all right now! Don't cry! It's all right! We're going to move on! I'll look after everything. Don't cry! You don't want those lads to think that all girls from Sofia are cry babies!"

I smiled through the tears.

"Snotty cry babies..."

"That's what they'll think." He laughed, pleased with himself and gave me a tissue. "Wipe your face, the lads are bringing your breakfast."

The table was filled with bread rolls, hot sausages, beer and coca cola.

"Come on boys, grab a sausage each, because once the baby gets going, there'll be nothing but beer left. I'm not joking, I'm absolutely serious. Come on, baby, show them!"

I laughed and my heart felt lighter. I tucked into the food.

Krasi watched me contentedly and chatted with the boys. I thought to myself once again, *I must have been born under a lucky star. Thank you, God!*

CHAPTER 9

The Smell Of The Seaside And Money

I had been living in the hotel with Krasi and the boys for two weeks. We had two rooms. Krasi and I were in the end room with a wonderful view of the sea and the beach. I already had a great tan and proudly walked around the hotel and the beach. Krasi was also very proud of me. He was head over heels in love with me and admitted it with a laugh.

The first night we were alone, I was embarrassed and shy. But Krasi was overcome by such an explosion of tenderness that I was astonished and overwhelmed. I gradually relaxed and the rest is self-explanatory... I was his Princess.

There were three big dollar shops in Sunny Beach and Krasi dressed me from head to toe in fine clothes. I don't know who enjoyed the shopping more, him or me.

"My Princess has to be the most beautiful," he would say tenderly as he took me to the next dollar shop. It was like a dream. A good dream, from which you don't want to wake up. I had already noticed that the group had a lot of cash. One evening, on the way home from the bar, my curiosity got the better of me and I asked,

"Krasi, where do you get all the money from?"

He gave me a meaningful look and said,

"I once said to you, a long time ago, 'People who ask too many questions...'"

"Grow old quickly," I interrupted. "But tell me, please. I'm not a child anymore and I can keep my tongue between my teeth!"

Krasi looked at me thoughtfully and hesitantly spoke,

"Here at the seaside, there are a lot of rich people. Their wallets are a bit too heavy and we help them get rid of some of the excess weight."

"How?"

"There are lots of ways of going about it, but that's not your business, Princess. You're here to have a holiday, and your faithful servant is at your beck and call." He turned everything into a joke.

"Krasi, I'm very serious. Listen! I'm fed up of lying on the beach or in the hotel. I don't want to spend your money. I'm just a parasite. I want to help you! Please!"

"You're mad!" he cut me off.

"I'm not! Just think about it and you'll see that I can be useful."

"Let's say no more about it, Princess!"

I got a bit cross and said no more.

This argument continued for a few more days. I could understand very well why Krasi wanted to keep me out of it. It was safer like that. But I was annoyingly persistent, and about a week later he gave in.

"All right, my darling! Light of my life! But just remember one thing: this is not a child's game and there is a great risk involved. And what's more I will tell you this and I will tell you it for one last time. From the very beginning I have been against you getting involved in our business. So do exactly what I say and no solo performances. You will keep absolutely to the script! All right?"

"You're the boss!" I smiled happily.

CHAPTER 10

Criminal Business

I will never forget my first job.

My task was to get to know a West German tourist and invite him to the disco. When we sat down at the table I had to put a little powder into his glass. After that it was easy.

Everything was perfectly planned. I was nervous, of course, and my hands were wet with sweat, but the operation went perfectly, and after Hans – that was his name and I had our "drink," he became as obedient as a little puppy dog. I suppose the powder affected his reactions and willpower. Or something like that. I told him to give me his golden bracelet and medallion and then his wallet, which he did without a second thought. Trembling, I put the things in my handbag and went to "make a phone call". I ran back to our hotel.

I was never alone. Krasi was watching me like a shadow from a safe distance. I was under guard all the time.

The result was two items of gold jewellery, 1800 German Marks and about two thousand levs. More than excellent. But Krasi was gloomy.

"I don't want you to do it anymore. I'm frightened for you... This sort of work is for people like me. I want you to remain clean and pure. I'll respect myself more if you do."

"No, Krasi. If it's a matter of your conscience, I want to tell you that I'm not the person you think I am. I stole Boiko's money without batting an eyelash. I'm not so clean and pure. And I want to ask you to let me keep on working! We'll be partners and everything will be OK!"

There was a long silence. I looked at this beautiful man in admiration. He really was in love with me and cared for me. Would fate always be so well inclined toward me? I asked myself, and threw my arms around Krasi's neck and covered him with kisses.

Things were decided in my favour. Chavdar and Svetlio accepted me unreservedly and we were like the "World Cup Team," in the words of Chavdar when he toasted me with champagne.

We were celebrating my 13th birthday. We were in a great mood. Work was going really well and we had accumulated a huge sum of money and valuables. I had a false passport showing that I was 17 years old. It had my photograph and all my details. I was really proud of it. It gave me the confidence of being older and I looked the age. And so everything was all right. The boys respected me and Krasi's word was law for them. Up to now we hadn't had a failure and we were celebrating my birthday wholeheartedly.

Krasi invited me to dance. We were in one of the biggest hotels in Sunny Beach, in the restaurant. I wasn't wearing a wig and was dressed very formally, as the event called for.

"Princess, you're very beautiful tonight! Allow me to tell you that I love you!"

"But I want you to tell me all the time, darling!" I laughed.

"Not all the time. You'll get bored of it!"

"I will never get bored of you!" I kissed him sweetly on the cheek, and froze.

Boiko was standing opposite us. My heart stopped. It missed a few beats and then rushed to catch up again. Krasi saw him after I did. He didn't lose control, however. He gave a restrained smile and offered him his hand.

"Hi, Boiko, long time no see!"

Bo was as white as chalk, trembling, and I expected him to start a fight. But no. Bo controlled himself, offered his hand as well and they shook. The music didn't stop and I felt very foolish on the dance floor with two men next to me. Krasi resolved the situation.

"I'm sorry, brother, but I don't want the lady to get bored. We'll finish our dance and then we'll have a chat. Our table is the second on the left. Come and sit with us."

Then he spun me around and led me to the centre of the dance floor. My legs were wooden and Krasi said,

"Calm down, darling, the worst is over. Trust me. Now take a deep breath because your eyes are glazed over and you're frightening me."

As ever at tense moments, Krasi managed to make me smile and feel better. I loved him very, very much, but from deep inside a memory, then a second and a third, floated to the surface of another man-boy who had loved me infinitely and whom I had loved. My heart felt as though it was being squeezed, and when the song finished I asked Krasi to take me back to my seat.

Boiko had disappeared as unnoticed as he had appeared. For the rest of the evening I was distracted, and I tried to hide my sadness with nervous laughter. Krasi noticed, of course, but he was tactful and a perfect gentleman. He caressed me gently and lovingly and I fell asleep without bursting into tears.

The days rolled on and our work with them. I was getting really good at my job by now and I worked without protection. One day at a meeting when we would normally discuss the next job, Krasi said,

"Friends and colleagues! I have to tell you that we're going to have to call a halt to operations for a while. I've got information that the detectives are on our heels. We'll have to lay low for a while. Chavdar and I are going to Sofia today. We've got quite a lot of compromising goods here. We're going to turn everything into green and we'll be back. Then we're going to Golden Sands and Albena. Svetlio and Princess are staying here. If you go to the beach, avoid the sectors with foreigners. Svetlio, you're in charge of security. No bars in the evening, have something to eat and go home. Any questions?"

Slightly concerned by the serious tone of his voice, I asked,

"Are they looking for me, or for you?"

"Princess, it breaks my heart to say this, but it wouldn't be a bad idea to go to the hairdresser's and cut your hair short. You could dye it blonde as well."

"But what's all this about?" I asked crossly.

"Don't ask any superfluous questions! Svetlio, you're her shadow until I come back!"

"OK, boss!"

Five minutes later they had left. Svetlio was a short fair-haired boy with a short temper. He was very intelligent and resourceful. He was a very good mathematician. I had often wondered what he was doing with the other lads. Krasi had told me that they had met at a police station. Krasi had been arrested during a mass action to check ID documents, while Svetlio had been taken in for attacking his mother's second husband. His fists were covered in blood, and Svetlio was in an uncontrollable rage. His stepfather got drunk every day and beat his mother and five-year-old sister. One day Svetlio lost control and attacked him. The investigator was an understanding man and let Svetlio go. Svetlio never went back to his home, and joined Krasi. Then Chavdar joined up with them. That's how the group was formed. Chavdar was a quiet shy boy. He carried out all his jobs to the very last detail. He was concentrated and inspired. He was from Plovdiv and everyone made fun of his accent. However, I have to admit that they were very honest with each other. There was no jealousy, no conflict over authority. I called them the "Three Musketeers."

So Svetlio and I went to the hairdresser's, and two hours later I left looking completely new and unrecognisable. I didn't miss my long hair. I was fed up with it. I had always wanted to see what I would look like with blonde hair. I had a wig, but it was black with a red nuance.

Even my parents would have a hard time recognizing me now.

It was a rainy day and Svetlio and I were packing up our stuff from the beach, when I heard a familiar voice talking in English. Without turning round I put my sunglasses on and tried to remember whose voice it was. Two fat Englishmen were standing just a few paces away from me talking to each other. I knew one of them. I had "enchanted" him just a few days ago and stolen a significant sum of money in Bulgarian levs and dollars from him. I trembled. Svetlio immediately realized what was going on. He quickly gathered the rest of the stuff into the beach bag, took me in his arms and started kissing me. The two men had been looking at me curiously, but when we started kissing, they laughed and left, so as not to bother us. I was sweating with nerves and surprise. But Svetlio didn't let go of me. He held on to me tightly until we arrived at the hotel. He only let go of me when we got to my room. Then he said,

"I'm sorry. It was a conspiracy! You know how things are! Anyhow, you're really pretty!"

He winked at me and went into his room.

I calmed down when I went into the bathroom. I laughed alone like a mad person. When I felt calmer, I got dressed and knocked on the neighbouring door. It opened and Svetlio was standing there, also dressed for dinner.

"Romeo, are we going to have dinner? I'm hungry." I smiled at him warmly.

"If just one kiss makes you hungry, what would happen if things went a bit further?" He laughed and we ran down the stairs.

The next day the whole team was back together and we departed for Golden Sands. We had to tell Krasi and Chavdar about the incident.

The boss said nothing for a long time and eventually responded,

"Princess, you're not going to do any more jobs!"

I wanted to argue but his categorical tone stopped me.

We got rooms at the "Chaika" hotel and the boys went out to look around. I stayed in the room. Someone had to look after the money. We didn't dare keep it in the hotel safe because we were Bulgarian and young, and would have aroused suspicion. It wasn't a small sum of money either. Krasi had exchanged everything – the gold, Bulgarian levs and German marks – into dollars. We had about thirty thousand. It was a fortune and we were carrying it around with us. We had some Bulgarian money for daily expenditure. I don't know what the boys were intending to do with the money. They were probably going to invest it into something.

The money was well hidden, but it was a risk to us.

I started feeling hungry and there was no sign of the boys. I waited for them for four hours. I couldn't stand it anymore. I grabbed my bag and a little money, looked at myself in the mirror and went out. I was intending to go to a small restaurant near the hotel for a bite to eat.

There weren't very many people in the restaurant at that time. Most people had already had their lunch and were either back at the beach or in bed.

It was a hot and stuffy afternoon. The sun beat down through the umbrellas. I was dressed in sandals, short denim pants and something like a vest – very short and cut out. Krasi thought I looked very sexy, because my shorts were tiny and revealed my treasures, not to mention my vest!

And so dressed like that, I was sitting eating cold tarator soup and a steak. I poured all this down with ice-cold Coca Cola, and I was enjoying myself. Suddenly, a middle-aged man came up to me. He had a pleasant appearance and was well dressed. He asked me in German, or rather gesticulated to me, whether there was a free seat at my table.

I shrugged my shoulders in irritation and invited him to sit down. The man sat down and quite arrogantly stroked my thigh. My first reaction was to slap him across the face, but my hunting instinct awoke within me and I said to myself, *It's your own fault!* I knew that I had a few powders left in my bag. He was asking for it and it was a sin to let it pass. Instead of striking him, I smiled at him enticingly and waited for the moment. Encouraged by his success, the German called for the waitress and ordered champagne. I prayed to God that he had brought enough money with him. I made use of the few sentences I had learned and he was hooked. When the champagne came, we drank. I was constantly thinking about how I would put the powder in his drink. I had already taken it out of my bag. I saw the salt cellar. I indicated at a table a few tables away from us and asked him to get it. I told him that no other salt cellar would do. He naturally went to get it for me and I managed to put the powder in his drink. We ate our meal calmly and drank some more. He was drinking quickly and thirstily. He finished the bottle off. I told him that I wanted to go. He paid the bill. I waited until the waitress was at a decent distance away from the table and asked him to give me his wallet. It was big and black, snakeskin, with lots of compartments inside it.

My magic powders had done the trick. He was looking at me like a little calf. He gave it to me and with a theatrical gesture invited me to leave with him. I went to the toilet first and from there ran back to the hotel. The boys weren't back yet. I took out the money. Jesus, he wouldn't have any money to get back to Germany with. There were two thousand German marks and almost four thousand levs. I was just happily putting the money back in the wallet when Krasi came in, followed by the boys. They looked at me in surprise. I was anxious and said nothing. Krasi spoke first. His voice rasped,

"Princess, have you been working privately?"

The two boys behind him giggled.

"Krasi, I can explain it!"

"Yes, I want an explanation."

"Krasi, I was waiting for you and you didn't come. I was hungry so I went to the Palma for a bite to eat and this German came on to me. I didn't want him, but he was really persistent and stuck on to me. And I..."

"You hit him!" Krasi finished the sentence for me.

"I wanted to count the money when you came in," I said in embarrassment, looking at them.

"Boys, you can go! Like we agreed to this evening."

Chavdar and Svetlio left. We remained alone in the room. I couldn't breathe because of the heat and tension in the room.

"Ioana, you must be very greedy!"

I almost died on the spot. He had never used my name before. Things were going to get really bad. I could feel it.

"Tell me, is there anything you need? Perhaps you need more clothes? Or shoes? Or make-up? Or... tell me! Tell me!" His voice had become hoarse and almost inaudible. I would have preferred him to shout out loud. I stood there silent, blinking and unable to open my mouth. Suddenly, bundles of dollars started flying at me. A rain which hurt. More and more. I thought that he must have lost his mind. I had been beaten before in my life, but never with money. I curled up on the bed and waited for him to vent his anger on me. He would run out of money soon, so I just had to wait.

The blows became more infrequent and stopped. I was covered in dollars, on top of me and all around me. Jesus Christ! If only someone could have taken a photograph of us. Me sitting on the bed with huge tears running down my cheeks, and all around me, on top of me and under me – there wasn't a free spot anywhere, and Krasi, white-faced despite his tan, looking at me like a wolf.

The picture was as comical as it was tragic. As I was sitting there sobbing quietly, I was overcome by laughter and the more I tried to suppress it the more I couldn't control, until I burst into mad, hysterical laughter. He looked at me in surprise and a moment later we were both laughing, fit to burst.

We were just shaking with laughter and couldn't calm down for a long time.

We finally gathered up the money, arranged it and counted it all. Then, like cultivated people, we apologized to each other.

"Please excuse me, Princess. But I was frightened for you. I don't want anything bad to happen to you, do you understand that? The cops might get hold of you and it will take a lot of effort to get you out."

"I understand! I want to say sorry as well! It was a childish thing to do. I won't do it anymore, I promise!"

Krasi looked at me tenderly and smiled.

"Princess, allow me to look after you while I am still free to do so."

His joke gave me the goosebumps. I suddenly imagined him in prison, with striped clothes and a beard. I groaned with terror and threw my arms around him. We made love for a long time, holding on tightly to each other.

There was a knock on the door. It was an invitation to dinner.

CHAPTER 11

Nostalgia

At the end of September, the weather turned bad. The sky went dark and a cold; biting wind blew in from the sea. The beaches were empty and only the seagulls dared to bathe in the crashing waves. There was no more work for us to do here. We had been to all the big resorts. The results were more than satisfactory. Without any problem, we had assured enough money to live on for the rest of the year.

At the end of the week we had decided to go to Plovdiv. I was surrounded by happiness and I was convinced that I had been born under a lucky star.

I had devoted friends who lavished attention on me. Krasi was a gentleman and deeply in love with me. I was young (too young perhaps), healthy (thank God) and pretty. I couldn't ask for anything more from life.

Sometimes I would think that this couldn't last forever and I shivered at the thought. However, for the moment, nothing seemed to be jeopardizing or threatening me or my life. I was happy and I tried to grab handfuls of happiness every day, to store it up in reserve for the day when I might need it. And so one cold October day, we arrived in Plovdiv. Chavdar, who was from Plovdiv, had gone ahead of us and had rented an enormous apartment for us.

Plovdiv is a wonderful city! If I could have chosen where to be born and grow up, I would have said Plovdiv without a shadow of doubt. It grabbed me and enchanted me completely. Since I had been released of any duties, I gave myself up the pleasures of walking through the Old City. I loved to go into the old fashioned shops and soak up the atmosphere of 80-100 years ago. I have never loved history, but what I touched there was living history.

79

I met an old man, Grandfather Zheko. He was a master craftsman. He was a member of the Association of Craftsmen. His speciality was working with copper. He could make anything out of this shiny metal, from a coffee pot to a coffee cup to the most impressive and infinitely beautiful candelabra.

"There aren't many of us craftsmen left," he complained. "Crafts are disappearing. Everybody's in business now, and there's no one left to make things. And I'll die one day and I've got no one to leave the shop to."

"Why, Uncle Zheko? Haven't you got any sons, grandsons to leave it to?"

"I don't know if I have or if I haven't any more!" His voice trembled, betraying a hint of a tear in his eyes. "They've all gone. They've gone abroad looking for work. And it's just me and the old grandmother left. I don't know if they'll ever see me alive again!"

I left Uncle Zheko's shop feeling sad. I bought a whole coffee service and a lovely bracelet. Uncle Zheko had convinced me of its magical properties. I had gathered quite a collection of weapons as well. Two pistols – huge and inoperable, a rifle which was so old it must have been used in the April uprising in 1878, and two daggers.

The boys were astonished by my passion for collecting such things – very unladylike. To top it all my collection cost me a lot of money, but wasn't I the Princess after all?

Krasi and the boys worked all day. Sometimes in the evenings as well. They kept their business secret from me, and I had no idea what they did. Krasi never let me know. He never refused me anything and was great in all respects. But whenever I tried to find out anything about their business – I couldn't get anything out of him. There was more money than enough. We usually went to the disco in the evening. We had wild parties and a great time. The only thing that spoilt my mood was that other girls hung on to Krasi like flies on a jar of honey. Of course, he kept his distance from them, but I was still very jealous and we often had arguments.

The weeks passed, one after the other. Sometimes I would get very bored, but the moment Krasi came home, everything changed. Every hour spent with him was exciting. He loved to dream out loud. He would love to describe the adventures we would have when we went to the Caribbean. He had promised to take me there. I believed him because his word was like iron. That's why he worked so hard. When I asked him what he did with the money he brought home, he would craftily screw up his eyes and reply ambiguously,

"I'm saving, Princess! For you and me to go the Caribbean. And that's a real challenge for my wallet!"

He would then caress me with the back of his hand. His character was a real mystery to me. I couldn't fathom how a man who was so severe and uncompromising in the criminal world, which he lived in, could store in his heart so much tenderness and love for the person next to him. This attracted me so strongly to Krasi and I would never have swapped him for another man.

But...

CHAPTER 12

Assassination And Breakup

There were two weeks left to the New Year and one week left until Christmas.

That evening we were in the Olympic discotheque, one of the biggest. The party was in full swing. Krasi, the boys and I were celebrating a particular event which slightly upset my equilibrium. After careful calculations, accounts and other such things, the boys had completed their financial year. The balance showed one million, two hundred thousand profit. I had had a lot of money in recent months, but the final figure astonished me. We were millionaires! The champagne poured freely, and the excuse for the party was "my birthday". The DJ dedicated song after song to me, and we looked at each other in happiness at our little secret.

At some time after midnight, the boys were getting excited. Krasi was drunk, but not very much. We danced tirelessly. But suddenly a girl appeared from somewhere. She was quite pretty, with long fair hair and even longer legs. She threw her arms around my friend's neck and began kissing him. I stood there, staring at them, and I could feel my anger beginning to well up, threatening to explode out of me with its entire force. To my horror, Krasi, instead of rejecting the advances of the strange girl, began to enjoy it. He didn't kiss her, of course, but he was holding her hand and talking to her tenderly. This was the last straw, and I approached them, shaking with anger. I pulled his hand away and asked him with a hissing voice,

"Excuse me, would you mind explaining to me what is going on?"

Krasi appeared not to like my behaviour, and he looked at me arrogantly and said,

"Go back to the table, please. I'll explain to you later."

I was overcome by fury. I took my aim and gave him an almighty slap. It resounded like a pistol shot.

The girl looked at me in fright and started to leave, but Krasi put his hand on her shoulder and turned her around to face him.

"Diana, don't pay her any attention. Stay here for a while."

"Is that right? OK!" Choking with anger, sadness and I don't know what else, I left.

I burst into tears when I got home. I sobbed so much that I was worried about getting dehydrated. I was alone in an enormous, strange apartment, alone in a huge, strange bed. Krasi had betrayed me. I couldn't believe it. I felt as though my life was over. Without Krasi there was no happiness. Life would be empty, grey and pointless.

I tossed and turned all night, and sometime towards the morning I fell asleep. I was woken up a little later by the door opening. It was Krasi, drunk as a lord. He managed to drag himself to the bed, fell onto it and immediately fell asleep. I didn't want to sleep any more.

I got up and went into the kitchen. I made some coffee, and as sad as the morning peering through the window, I sat down to drink it.

On the way past, I looked into the mirror. I expected to see some phantom with red eyes, but I saw something quite attractive, with the exception of the dark circles under my eyes betraying the nightmare of the past night. But they also gave me a spiritual appearance.

I didn't know how to treat Krasi. He was guilty, there was no argument about that. But what about that slap I had given him? I had made a fool of myself, there were no two ways about it. I decided to take a walk around old Plovdiv. The old town always calmed me down. The houses silently hugged each other beneath the foggy clouds. It was snowing and quite cold. I walked aimlessly but my feet took me to Uncle Zheko's shop. I hoped the old man would lift my mood with a story out of his life. He had an abundance of them and every one he told me had a moral to it. When I arrived, the first thing I saw was a small black ribbon over the door. I couldn't believe it. I stood in front of the shop and stared with vacant eyes at a small obituary notice, announcing that Zheko Nikolov Zhekov had suddenly died.

The small shop window seemed to be grieving for its owner. The cups in the coffee service no longer glistened, but looked sad. The coffee pot was leaning over almost on the point of falling. It seemed to want to die as well.

I stroked the glass and whispered through my tears,

"Rest in peace, Uncle Zheko! I won't forget you!"

With a heavy heart, I walked down the hill.

Everyone had got up. Chavdar and Svetlio were making soup and arguing about when to put the macaroni in. I said hello to them gloomily and went to the bathroom. Krasi was just coming out of it. When I saw him my heart fluttered. I looked at him and froze. He walked past me as though he hadn't seen me, and slammed the bedroom door. I hadn't expected the story from last night to continue. I followed him and slammed the door as well. My instinct told me that the best plan was to attack.

"Can you still explain your behaviour to me?" I asked in an icy voice.

"When you learn how to behave civilly," was the short answer.

"You weren't very civil when you left me on the dance floor and let that slut kiss you!"

"Don't you dare talk about her like that!"

"Oh, the little slut's got someone to stand up for her!"

"If you don't stop talking like that, you'll regret it!"

His voice had acquired a metallic tone.

"Why don't you just go and shack up with your slut?" I cried out and at that moment a blow struck me on the head.

For a moment, everything went dark and I felt a salty taste in my mouth. The pain was excruciating. I don't know how, but I was on the floor. I was sitting staring at the threads of the carpet beneath me. Slowly, I came to my senses. When I realized what had happened, I looked around and noticed that I was alone in the room. I stood up with some difficulty and went towards the door. At that moment it opened and the curly, fair head of Svetlio appeared.

"Are you all right?" he asked with some concern. Chavdar was peering in fright behind him.

I pushed them aside rudely and looked around trying to find Krasi. It would have been an understatement to say that I was furious. I was completely beside myself. I wanted to kill him.

Bastard! I thought to myself, *how dare he hit me! I thought he was a gentleman? Isn't that the way he was brought up?*

I looked in all the rooms, but Krasi was nowhere to be seen. He had gone out. *All right then! When he gets back, I'll be gone,* I decided and sat down exhausted in an armchair.

"Ioana, I want you to listen to me. I know that you're upset, but I want you to calm down and listen to what I have to say to you!"

The quiet low voice made me raise my eyes. Svetlio was bent over me, looking at me insistently.

I said nothing and looked at him with distrust, but I was calm.

"Ioana, there has been a serious misunderstanding between us. I know that girl very, very well. She..."

"Oh, is that right? She's slept with all of you, has she?" I interrupted him sarcastically and felt a wave of anger coming over me again.

"Ioana, please listen to me without interrupting!" Svetlio raised his voice slightly. "What I'm trying to tell you is that girl is Krasi's sister."

If Svetlio had suddenly sprouted horns and a tail, I would have been less astonished.

"What did you say? Say it again!" I whispered hoarsely.

"She is his sister. They're family! Do you understand now?"

"No!" I was even more confused. "He has never mentioned a sister to me."

"There was probably some reason for that. I don't know the answer to that either. But he's been looking after her and their mother from a distance. He often sends them postal orders. All I know is that his sister has created a lot of problems for him. All sorts of problems. Even in the summer he had to get her out of some mess she had got herself in to. I think it was connected with foreigners, drugs and other things like that."

I listened in amazement and I couldn't believe my ears. At the same time, I started to hate myself. *How could I have been such an idiot?* I thought. *I'm always making a mess of things at the wrong time! Now I've completely ruined everything!*

"Where's Krasi now?" I asked Svetlio bitterly.

"I don't know. The most important thing in my opinion, is to keep calm and just apologise to him when he comes back."

I reacted immediately.

"Of course! But why didn't he tell me?"

"Don't start again! You've got to do something about that stubbornness of yours!" Svetlio said instructively and tapped me on the forehead. "Come on, I'm starving! Come and have some soup with us. It's really good."

"I don't want any. I'm going to look for Krasi." I got up decisively and went towards the front door. I almost crashed into him. He was obviously in a hurry. He was sweating and panting. I hesitated for a moment, but recalled Svetlio's words, and I gulped and said,

"Krasi, I'm sorry! I didn't know that she was…" At the same time as I uttered the words, I held my arms out to hug him.

"I don't have any time for emotional outbursts," Krasi looked at me coldly and added, "We'll talk when I've finished work."

Then he went to look for the boys.

I went bright red with anger. I stood helpless, speechless at his vulgarity and coldness.

At that same moment, the three lads filed out one by one. Krasi passed first without looking at me. When Svetlio walked past me, he whispered a single word into my ear, "Job," and shut the door.

I slowly slipped to the floor, looking at the oak veneer of the door. I wasn't thinking, I was just feeling. I was a body without thought or soul. I must have been sitting there for hours; I might have fallen asleep. I don't remember. I was just sitting on the floor in the same pose. I tried to stand up, but I was rigid. I couldn't feel my legs, but managed to drag myself to the bedroom. Night fell and there was no sight or sound of the three boys. I hadn't eaten all day but I wasn't hungry. I lay in bed and smoked. I tried to think. *Since Svetlio and Chavdar aren't home, they must still be on the job. All of them. I must have really hurt Krasi, for him to treat me like that.* I was desperate and hurt as well. And when I'm hurt, I can get vicious. I wondered what would happen to us. I had seen him from another angle and it had really worried me. I didn't like that sister of his, even if he really cared for her. Perhaps I was just jealous? But what was taking them so long? The clock showed a quarter to three in the morning, when I heard the front door slam. I was half asleep, half-dazed. Before I realized it, Krasi had rushed into the bedroom. He looked terrible. His eyes were huge. He was so pale, he looked as though he was dead. I was frightened.

"Where are the passports?" he asked me in a harsh voice. "Quickly!"

"Wwwhy?" I stammered.

He had given me their passports to look after. I had one too, false of course.

"Where are they?" he asked me again, so adamantly and so frighteningly that I lost my power of speech.

I pointed to one of the drawers in the chest.

"Get dressed, what are you looking at? We're leaving."

"What's happened?" I asked almost inaudibly.

"Something very serious. Don't ask any more questions. It's better like this. Take only what you need. Put it in the red bag. I'll get the money."

He wasn't himself. I observed that completely objectively. Krasi impatiently took the chest apart. Between the mirror and the wooden frame there was a secret hiding place made of cardboard where our money was hidden to keep it safe. I looked at the wads of dollars and levs indifferently and my heart was filled with ice, sadness and something else. Something indeterminate which I couldn't get rid of.

His voice – sharp and metallic – cut into me.

"Why aren't you packing your bag? We don't have any time. We're going to Germany for a few years. We have time to sort out our relationship there. Don't look at me like a calf, pack your bag!"

I realized instinctively that the moment had come. The moment I had always feared.

"Krasi, whatever has happened, I'm not coming with you. I'm staying."

"Don't be ridiculous. Now's not the time for melodramatics. You can be as cross with me as you like later on. But you have to realize that we've only got a few minutes. We'll be using a reliable channel to get us across the border. There'll be no problem."

His voice was beginning to sound more human. He had got a hold of himself. Only his paleness remained. He approached me and he stroked my cheek. His touch made me quiver. I jumped back in terror.

"What's happened to you? You haven't gone mad, have you?"

"Don't touch me! You don't need to tell me; your panic has given you away. You've killed someone. That's what you're running away from. Whatever I might be, I can't forgive you for that. Get out of my sight!"

"Ioana, calm down! You're in shock. Yes, I really have killed someone, but it was in self-defence. I swear! Everything will be all right! You know how much I love you. How could I leave you alone here and go away? I will go mad without you! Please, darling!"

He approached me slowly, and I stepped backwards. My back pressed against the wardrobe and I couldn't move any more. Krasi was right in front of me now.

"If you take one more step, I'll scream so loud that all our neighbours will come running!" I warned him. "Now get out of my sight!"

Krasi looked at me with his tired eyes, sighed and said,

"Ioana, what you are doing is a mistake. I will never forgive myself for leaving you. But as God is my witness, there is no other way. If you want to betray me in this way, so be it. I don't have any more time to argue. But remember, this very night as soon as I cross the border, I'll get in touch with my people who will watch out for you, and if you need it, they will take care of you. If you have any difficulties or if your money runs out, and that will eventually happen, here are two telephone numbers." Krasi wrote something on a slip of paper and left it on the bed. "Learn the number by heart and destroy the paper. Just say your name. That will be enough."

I listened to him in silence, even indifferently. Krasi put the money in a bag, put it in the travelling bag together with his jeans and some underwear and turned to me, "I'm leaving. Will you let me kiss you?"

I shook my head in horror.

"All right! But remember. I will be back. I need you. It might be in ten years' time, but I will find you. I wish you luck, Princess!"

A quiet knock on the door reminded him that they were waiting for him.

The door closed behind him. I head the click of the lock almost immediately.

I was alone again....

I love you
When you touch me
And stroke me tenderly with your hand
You softly whisper
Secret words.
I love you
When you speak to me
With such deep warmth.
Your eyes –
So boundlessly blue
Embrace me entirely in their blueness.

Of course, the first days after each separation are painful. But these days were inhuman. I sat like a lone wolf in the huge, empty apartment, and I didn't know if I was still alive. I didn't sleep, I couldn't eat, I didn't even go near the windows. The days turned to night and then it was day again, then it was night again. I couldn't cry, I couldn't laugh. I couldn't even think.

I was devastated. It was terrible. I lacked the desire to live, but I didn't have the strength to kill myself. I just lay there waiting to die. But it didn't happen. I barely got up from my bed and completely lost any idea of time and space.

It was night. I was in a state of half-sleep and I might even have been dreaming. But my eyes were still open, I was sure.

Suddenly, the door of the bedroom turned into an illuminated screen and the figure of a saintly man appeared. I observed the manifestation completely indifferently. I was completely exhausted and powerless even to be scared.

The light emanating from the screen was milk white, the same colour as the man's long beard. The features of his face were youthful but his hair and beard were completely white. In his right hand he was holding a cross, the upper part of which was encrusted with diamonds and rubies. I couldn't tell which was brighter, the screen or the cross. But my eyes were affixed. It was as though some power were making me look at him. Suddenly, I realized that the man was speaking to me.

"Ioana, you are not going to die, even if you want to."

I was completely terrified. I sat up in bed and rubbed my eyes. I thought I was dreaming, but I wasn't. The "screen" was shining and the saint (at least that's what I called him) was standing there looking at me severely. He didn't open his mouth, but I could hear his words. I couldn't hide from his voice or from him. I felt forced, literally forced, to accept his message.

"You will suffer many more trials, Ioana! But you must endure them! You have a mission on this earth and until you achieve it, your earthly journey will not end."

"Who the Devil are you?" I whispered in astonishment.

Whether it was because I hadn't spoken to anyone and had forgotten my own voice, but I had no idea whether I had said it or someone else. At the same time, I felt a strong blow to the forehead. The man had struck me with the cross.

"Never mention the name of the Devil, Ioana!" the saint said to me.

Dumbstruck and completely overwhelmed with fear, I gulped.

"Why don't you have a drink of water?" The question resounded in my head like a command.

"And have something to eat as well!" he added.

I sensed that I would have to comply with the command, but that would mean getting up off the bed and approaching him and the "screen," which meant passing through him and the screen to get to the door.

That was too much for me. I was paralysed with fear. The connection must have been telepathic because he seemed to read my mind, and for a moment the screen moved onto the wall. They were now on the right hand side of my bed.

The path was free.

"Ioana, go into the kitchen and eat whatever you find there! Immediately!"

The words echoed through my mind, but as I watched him, I realized that at least I was free to see whatever I wanted.

Wobbling on my legs as though drunk, I went to the kitchen to look for something to eat.

A packet of biscuits, a piece of stale bread and a lump of mouldy cheese – that was all that I could find in the kitchen.

It was quiet, dark and terrifying. I could hear my own breathing.

I drank some water and took a biscuit. I couldn't hold the others and I dropped them onto the floor in front of me.

I managed somehow to eat the biscuit and stretched out my hand to drink some more water. My fingers were trembling and I knocked the cup over. It fell to the floor and smashed into a thousand pieces. In the dark and in my state of hazy consciousness it was like a gunshot.

Deafened and out of my mind with groundless fear, I ran back into the bedroom.

I crashed into the furniture as I ran but felt no pain.

I leapt back into bed and pulled the bedclothes over my head. I began sobbing and quivering with fear. I cried and gulped and a flood of tears welled from my eyes. But at the same time it had a therapeutic effect – slowly the pain, fear and stress disappeared, and I fell into a deep, restorative sleep. When I woke up it was light. I looked indecisively at the wall and then at the door of the bedroom. There wasn't a trace of the "saint". I tried to convince myself that I had never seen them and that this was just a dream, but at the same time the cross appeared in my mind down to the very smallest details. This could only mean one thing: "Don't forget!"

"God!" I mumbled in an uncertain voice. I coughed and said more confidently, "God!"

At that moment I sensed an overwhelming desire to pray. I didn't know any prayers. I didn't have time or the strength to look for a church.

So I knelt in front of the door where the "screen" had appeared for the first time and began fervently to pray.

The prayer was more like a story. I told him everything I had experience in life. The good things and the bad things. I prayed fervently and I sobbed again. I felt as though the tears and the words were being pulled straight from my heart or my womb. Or from somewhere inside. I began to feel the real sensation of lightness. I was becoming lighter and incorporeal. I suddenly felt, or rather received, the order to get up.

"Everything's all right! Everything's all right!" This phrase came to me from somewhere and I repeated it to myself. I was standing in front of the door, waiting for something. I suddenly felt pangs of hunger, incredible, inhuman hunger.

I have to go out, I thought. *Of course I have to go out. I don't know how many days I haven't been outside the flat.* A spark of joy crept into me.

"I'll have a bath! I'll get dressed and I'll go to have lunch somewhere. Or dinner? God, I don't even know what day it is! What's the time? I don't know anything. I'll find out. I'll get ready now." I said all this out loud and filled the bath. Everything was ready. I got undressed and was shocked at what I saw in the mirror. A thin creature with dishevelled hair and shadowed eyes was looking back at me. *That can't be me?* I thought. There was nothing left of my previously curved forms. I was just skin and bones. *I must have lost at least five kilograms.* I laughed. The state I was in was completely absurd and ridiculous. I stared back at my reflection and burst into laughter. *But that's amazing! I can probably eat cakes for five months without worrying!* I leapt into the bath happily. A little later I was ready to go out.

I started to like my new image. I was the shape and size of a model. I had a problem with my clothes, but that was a pleasant problem. I would go out tomorrow to buy a complete new set of clothes.

Krasi had left me enough money. *Oh!* A thought tore through my heart and stomach. Of course. Even the mention of his name caused me pain. "Come on, pull yourself together!" I ordered myself.

I managed somehow to dress and quietly left the apartment. It was almost evening. *So I'll have dinner,* I thought to myself and went to find the nearest taxi.

The driver measured me up approvingly and opened the door.
"Where to?"
"The Old House," I replied briefly.

The taxi drove off immediately, while I looked through the window, slightly anxious and shaking at the prospect of my first independent dinner out.

The town seemed entirely unfamiliar to me, even foreign and unpleasant. I wondered why I had come out of the flat. Yes, because I was very hungry. There was snow on the streets and not very many people.

I looked at the clock on the dashboard, 19:45. I checked my own. Krasi had given it to me for my birthday. It was expensive and elegant. "Oh!" I sighed, that familiar pain.

"God! Help me not to lose my mind!"

The car stopped, I paid the driver who looked me up and down again and clicked his tongue approvingly. I jumped out of the car.

"I forbid you to think about him!" I said to myself and went into the restaurant.

It was our favourite restaurant. Quiet and clean with an excellent menu. Everything down to the smallest details was familiar to me. There was our favourite table.

I sat down. I was completely overwhelmed by pain. When the waitress came over to me, I bravely fought off the desire to burst into tears. A sweet girl called Zhana, she had become a friend of ours. She looked at me in shock.

"What's happened to you!" She raised her eyebrows to her hairline. "Why?"

"You've lost so much weight! How did you do it? Let me in on the secret!"

This time I smiled sincerely, screwed up my eyes craftily and whispered to her:

"Sex, sex and more sex!"

"Is that true?" She smiled broadly. "Wait till I get my hands on that George of mine! Have you been eating?"

"Yes, all the time," I said confidently. "Now, for example, I want a double tomato salad, pan-fried bon-filet with butter, a portion of baked cheese and three pancakes for dessert."

Zhana looked at me in admiration.

"You're going to eat all that, and you're so thin!"

"Of course!" I smiled at her triumphantly and I was truly delighted at the gastronomic orgy I had organized for myself before Zhana's amazed eyes.

She went to the kitchen to place the order and I looked around the room. There were some familiar faces here and there, the wood panelling on the walls around the door was scratched from when Krasi had....

Stop! No more memories! I have to get on with life and not give in to depression.

Zhana appeared with a tray laden with all sorts of delicious delights.

"Darling, I told all the girls in the kitchen about your super diet. We're all going to start tonight. You didn't tell me how many times a night?"

I smiled cunningly.

"You have to do it during the day as well. I thought I told you, as many times as possible!"

The silly blonde completely believed me.

"I don't know if George would stand it...," Zhana replied uncertainly.

God, I giggled at the thought of Zhana exhausting her boyfriend with sex and him kicking the bucket.

"Darling, who said you have to restrict yourself to George? You'll kill him! You'll need backup. Get the idea?"

Zhana blinked her long eyelashes in astonishment and bright red with embarrassment whispered,

"But what if George catches me? He said he would kill me."

She served me dinner and, nervously swaying her hips, she went back into the kitchen.

My little joke might have marked the end for George, but it did me a world of good. I don't know how, but I ate everything. I even thought I could have eaten it all again, but good sense intervened. I lit a cigarette and looked in the direction where I had seen the young waitress last. She was standing at the bar deep in thought. I wondered what she was thinking about. I waved at her. She came over to me immediately.

"Zhana, don't be cross with me, if I tell you something."

"What?" she asked suspiciously.

"What I told you about the diet, wasn't exactly true. Sorry!"

"What do you mean? I thought you said…"

"I know what I said," I interrupted her impatiently, "but it wasn't true."

"But you really have lost a lot of weight," she protested.

"Yes, but I've been poorly. Very poorly."

Her beautiful eyes looked at me suspiciously.

"I'm not lying. It's true. Believe me if you want to. Here's the money."

I paid the bill and left a huge tip. Zhana was very upset. She began to collect the empty plates. She didn't even say thank you for the tip. She was clearly very disappointed.

"I really have read that sex is good for losing weight," I said as I was getting ready to leave, "but the dose is very individual."

I laughed cheerfully and left Zhana only half-disappointed and half-angry.

It was very cold outside. I walked along the narrow streets and gradually my cheeriness began to disappear. Where would I go now? What was I going to do? I was alone in an unfamiliar and cold town.

I went home. The huge apartment seemed strangely scary. Memories came flooding back to me. Krasi!

Wherever I turned, he was standing in my way.

I stood looking into the living room of the apartment which hadn't been cleaned for a whole week. No, it was far too big for one person. I went into the bedroom, our bedroom. Krasi hated dark colours. Everything in the room was white.

"Princess," he would say to me, "When we get rich, I will build you a house, completely white and gold. And it will face south and so it will always be sunny, bright and very, very happy!"

"Why, Krasi, why?" I sobbed, "Why did you leave me like this?"

It was silly to moan like that, like in some cheap melodramatic film, but I needed to talk. Even to myself. But I needed to talk. The silence was killing me.

The piece of paper with the telephone number appeared in front of me. He had written it on the night he had left.

I had to remember the number and destroy the piece of paper. If I had a problem I just had to call.

"My problem is that you're gone, silly fool! You destroyed my entire essence, my soul. Why? Did you need more money than we had?" I spoke quietly and stroked the piece of paper. "I miss you, I can't cope without you!"

"Ioana, I will never forgive myself for leaving you!" The words came back to me so clearly, that I turned to look at the door. It was almost as if he was still there saying them to me at the very moment.

"God! I'll lose my mind!" I sobbed, looking at the silent door in expectation. "Bring him back to me, God! I'll forgive him. He might not have killed that person."

"It was in self-defence. I swear!" The second phrase from our dramatic conversation that night crept into my ears.

"No!" I screamed. "You're a ghost. Leave me alone!"

"I'll find you again, even if it takes me ten years...! Ioana, darling..." His voice was so real and close that I almost collapsed into hysteria.

With my remaining particles of common sense, I realized that I should immediately get out of there. Otherwise I might very well go mad. I needed to run away.

I grabbed my jacket, bag and boots and rushed headlong out of the home where I had spent several reckless months of happiness.

The night which welcomed me outside was gloomy, cold and indifferent.

CHAPTER 13

Guests From The Afterlife. Shock And Reality

My first thought was to go to a hotel but I thought that it would be better just to leave the town. Everything here reminded me of him.

I was lucky. The express train from the Black Sea was about to arrive in Plovdiv en route for Sofia.

I bought a ticket and waited impatiently for the train. It was half-empty and there was almost no one in first class.

I got into the empty compartment without any luggage.

As the train slowly pulled out of the station, I cast a farewell look at the city and whispered quietly, "I hope my memories about you remain here as well."

I was turning a new page in the living book which represented my life.

I didn't know then but this was about to be the blackest page which anyone could imagine.

At the time I was just running away. I was fleeing loneliness and my memories which were so wonderful that they were causing me such indescribable pain and the impossibility of being part of my present.

The central station. My second home. My starting point for the world. My finishing line. Here I was again.

Unfortunately, it was getting filthier and more dangerous. Every time I came back, I was more and more disappointed.

The thronging masses of underage gypsy prostitutes, semi-naked gypsy children sniffing glue and thieves. My perceptive eyes could pick them out without any problem.

I got out of the Central Station as quickly as I could.

For a moment, I wondered where to go. I had a lot of money and I could go to any hotel I wanted. I had a good ID card, but I didn't want to be alone. I was afraid. I could go home. My mother would be pleased to see me. That would be an interesting experience! What was she doing? Torn between love, habit and drunken scandals with her husband. Should I call her? No!

I decided to go to a disco, and went to the taxi rank.

"Where to?" the driver was nervous and clearly not in the mood for sleeping. He didn't even wait for me to get into the car before he asked me.

"Which is the most popular disco at the moment?"

"Is that your problem, girl? Boredom? I'll take you to the best there is, and you can dance till sunrise. Have you got enough money to pay for the pleasure?"

"Don't worry about that!" I replied icily and got into the back seat.

Sofia at night was beautiful. The streets were filled with lights. Neon advertisements illuminated the shops. The centre was pretty, but in the suburbs I was sure that it was just the same filth and gloom as before.

I was happy to be there. It was interesting and exciting.

The taxi driver occasionally turned around, probably to check that I was still awake. We finally arrived.

"This is the disco, love. Need anything else?"

I kept my cool and gave him a 200 lev note.

I slammed the door demonstratively and left him staring at me, pleasantly surprised by the enormous tip and the sight of my pert bottom.

I paid the entrance fee and went in. The disco was full and the party was in full swing.

I noticed a free seat at the bar and headed in that direction. I felt the eyes from a number of tables looking at me, and following me until I sat down.

"What would you like?" The bartender was standing in front of me, measuring me up and down.

"Gin fizz with lemon."

"Lemon's compulsory here, love!"

I said nothing. I just took the glass and sipped. I hated alcohol but occasionally drank the odd glass. The dance floor was full but there was a huge gaping hole in my heart. I was sitting peacefully on my chair looking into the crowd dancing under the experienced guidance of the DJ.

I was just finishing off my second gin when a tall, well-built boy with a pleasant face sat down next to me.

"Will you let me buy you a gin, love?" he asked me, without a hint of shyness.

I hate strangers coming up to me and talking to me as though they know me.

"If I want a drink, I can buy my own, thank you," I said politely.

"OK. I understand. I'll try and be more polite. Would you permit me to introduce myself? My name is Boncho, but my friends call me Bruno. You can call me Bruno as well."

I looked at him. He was a good-looking man with an air of masculinity. He also seemed to have a sense of humour. If I had been completely sober I probably wouldn't have omitted seeing certain things in the expression on his face, but at that moment I had been drinking and my reactions and judgement were not precise.

"It's nice to meet you, Bruno! I'm Queen Ioana. But people call me Princess."

The last word almost brought a tear to my eye. The only person in the world who had used that name was now gone...

"That's what you call style. I'm impressed and would humbly ask your permission to buy you a drink, Princess!"

I drank my gin and something about Bruno began to remind me of Krasi. At one moment I even thought he was him. Naturally, this was a result of my intoxicated imagination, but it didn't seem like that on the dance floor. I danced with my head on a man's shoulder, imagining that it was Krasi. By now I was very drunk. I can't remember everything. I know that I told him something about my loneliness, about my love for Krasi and other such things. And he promised to do everything he could to help me forget all the men in the world.

We left the disco and he led me to his new BMW. I said that I liked his car and that I might like him as well, if he tried hard.

"I promise you that you will like me a lot."

"I can't like anyone apart from Krasi," I mumbled drunkenly as we travelled.

When we arrived, Bruno shook me strongly to wake me up. I had fallen asleep.

"Come on, come on, Princess. It's too early for sleep."

Still sleepy, I got out of the car. It was dark and I couldn't work out where I was.

We entered a block of flats where not a single light was working. It was as dark as hell in the lobby. Bruno was dragging me strongly by the hand.

We stopped on the third or the fourth floor. My host unlocked the door and only then in the light did I see where I was.

"Welcome, Princess! Make yourself at home."

We entered a room which was modest rather than impressive. One of the walls was fitted with black shelves and a wardrobe. There was a table, two armchairs and a mattress on the floor with a thick duvet.

I stood motionless and uncertain.

"Come on, relax!" Bruno threw his shirt onto one of the armchairs and began to caress me.

"Just wait a moment! Don't think that you can get me into bed the moment I come through the door!" I pulled myself away from him in indignation.

A sudden, powerful slap which almost removed my head made me sober up immediately.

The blow laid me out on the bed, but I got up immediately.

"Don't you dare strike me again, or I'll kill you!" I hissed.

A second blow, stronger than the first one, dazed me. Two powerful arms clasped me as though in a vice. He held my face directly in front of his and said very clearly,

"The games are over now. From this moment on, you listen and obey!"

I slowly began to realize that I was his prisoner. It was my own fault. I probably deserved it. I observed his expressionless face. Now I could clearly see the cold, even, cruel expression of his eyes.

"I don't think you're very hospitable," I said to win some time while I tried to recover.

Bruno was still holding me tightly close to him, measuring me up with his cold, grey eyes. My arms really hurt where he was holding me. But I wasn't going to give up. We were standing almost glued to each other, staring in each other's eyes. It was like a game of "who blinks first." I wasn't very good at the game and usually gave in to nerves first. Slowly, huge, salty tears began to flow down my cheeks. The effect was unexpected.

Bruno let go of me with one hand and slowly began to raise it. I was just thinking that I had won his pity, when a new, terrible blow struck my ears. Thousands of hammers pounded inside my head.

"What I hate most of all is cry babies! Stop it right now or I'll get really angry!"

I thought he must be mad and the only way out of the situation was to try and be good to him.

"What do I have to do to make you feel good?"

"That's how I like you, bitch! But without any games, because you know..."

His hands slowly released my arms and grabbed hold of my thighs. He dragged me down onto the bed and began to touch me.

"Take your clothes off!" he panted, in an aroused voice.

I already hated him from the bottom of my soul. I knew what was going to happen to me and I was reconciled to my fate. I slowly removed my jumper, jeans and socks. I was wearing only my pants, watching him.

He observed me carefully, examining me from head to toe. I thought that he just wanted to look at a naked, helpless girl. But I was wrong. Those minutes with that pervert were to seal my fate for years to come. But I don't want to get ahead of myself.

I was completely naked and he gave me the sign to lie down. He got undressed as well. I screwed up my eyes in revulsion when he began to touch me and examine my body.

He was completely perverted. He subjected me to such incredible pain that even I had no idea how I put up with it. When the morning came I was praying to die because I had no strength left. He was tired as well and we both fell asleep.

We must have slept all day, because it was already dark when we woke up. I woke first. I felt devastated, reviled and destroyed. I felt that I wouldn't last another night like that.

I got up quietly and looked for my clothes. Bruno was still asleep, or at least I thought he was. I dressed quickly and tiptoed to the door. It was just a matter of reaching the front door. I was already imagining freedom when a quiet, sarcastic voice stopped me in my tracks.

"You're not thinking of flying away, my little dove?"

I turned around. He was lying in his bed grinning contently.

"I... I was just going to the bathroom," I stammered, trembling with fear.

"That's right. Cleanliness is a very important thing!" Bruno nodded his head mockingly. "Go and have a shower and come back. I'll be waiting for you."

Everything went black before my eyes. I stood still like I was nailed to the floor.

"What are you waiting for? Get a move on!"

"There's something I need to tell you."

"Now what? Don't you want to have a shower now?"

"No, I just need to have a rest. Everything hurts and..."

"Stop playing games! Get into the shower and don't take too long, because I'm in a hurry!"

I went to the bathroom with the intention of slitting my veins or something. That sadist would never have me again! Never! But I was wrong. He caught me in the bathroom and subjected me to the same sexual terror. Two hours later Bruno let me get dressed, and to my great joy we left the apartment. I was broken physically and mentally. I wouldn't have cared if he killed me now. But he looked immaculate. Only his eyes, as cold as steel, betrayed the beast within him.

We got into his car, and as we drove off, he announced,

"We're going for a little drive."

I said nothing. I was completely indifferent by now. I thought that after the drive we would go back to the same gloomy flat and I would suffer again... The car softly whispered through the nocturnal streets of Sofia. I observed the landscape with complete indifference. Bruno turned the tape player on. He offered me a cigarette, and I accepted.

"What are you thinking about, doll? You're very quiet!" he asked half-jokingly, half-threateningly.

I decided to take a risk.

"I was thinking that I would rather die that have sex with you! Have you always been so perverted?"

"So that's what it's all about!" He grinned contentedly. "I'm one hundred percent man, not some Nancy boy. My sex is a real man's sex. But if you don't like it, all right then."

You're one hundred percent pig! I thought to myself but said out loud,

"What does "all right then" mean? Does it mean you're going to kill me now?"

Just then, as were talking, I noticed that the car was heading for Vitosha mountain. We had left the town.

"Where are we going?" I asked slightly nervously.

"I told you, we're going for a drive!"

I sighed submissively. I couldn't care anymore! If I was going to die, then die I would. We said nothing more. When we stopped I realized that we were somewhere around the "Golden Bridges".

Bruno stubbed out his cigarette and got out of the car. I got out too.

"What are we going to do?"

"We're going to the Bridge of Sighs," he whispered in a voice which made me tremble.

Everything was much more terrifying now and I was convinced that every step we took was bringing me closer to death.

It was freezing cold and I was shaking like a leaf, not just because of the cold. We walked in silence. The forest was silent in its white clothes. The snow crackled underfoot and in the silence I could hear my heart beating.

Somewhere in the distance I could heard the gurgling of water. *So there must be a river nearby,* I thought. We were going towards it. When we reached it, we stopped.

Bruno turned towards me.

"This, Princess, is the Bridge of Sighs."

I was frightened and said nothing, waiting for him to go on.

"Of course, you realize that our little drive is not without reason." His elegant speech was a complete contrast to the brutish slang he had been using up to now. "You're a clever, beautiful girl and I believe that you will justify my expectations."

I continued to not say anything.

"And so. After the test which I subjected you to, and which you passed successfully, I am offering you the chance of getting rich and perhaps even famous."

I looked at him with distrust and incomprehension.

"Yes, yes! Rich and famous! My colleagues and I select pretty girls to work as companions and sexual partners in luxury hotels. The nature of the work requires you to be skilled at these things. And sometimes, even frequently I would say, possess enormous stamina. You performed magnificently and I'm very proud that I found you. Now you have to say "yes" or "no". I hope to God you don't say no."

I slowly realized what this pig wanted from me. He wanted me to become a prostitute!

I was so furious I couldn't say a word.

He interpreted this as a hesitation, since he continued with threats.

"Now you probably realize that I will be happier if you agree. However, if you refuse then here at the Bridge of Sighs, you will take your last sigh. It's very cold, the snow is very deep and you will freeze to death very quickly. From a personal point of view, I will be very sorry, but business is business and I have to manage my business with an iron hand."

I thought fervently. I could take a risk and say no. But I wasn't sure whether he was bluffing or not.

He was concealing some duality within himself and he was unpredictable. He could quite easily have finished me off there and then. All that was left to me was to choose the lesser of the two evils.

"I agree. I just want to know where I will work and what I will receive for my work," I said quietly, decisively and in a business-like manner.

Bruno congratulated me for my wise choice.

"Well done, doll! You're a born business woman. As far as the payment is concerned, it won't be very much to begin with, but then you'll be on a percentage – 40 for you, 60 for us. You'll be living in the hotel, and you know how expensive that is, don't you? And we'll be looking after you. The other girls are happy..."

"What hotel?" I interrupted him nervously.

He listed three of the most expensive hotels in Sofia and offered me the choice.

I chose the one with the least number of girls. I hated prostitutes and I thought the fewer of them there were, the calmer I would be.

"Come on then, doll! Time to go! It's not fit to be out in the cold!"

I hope you freeze to death! I cursed him in my mind and followed him, deep in thought.

Whether it was the shock or the cold, it took me a long time to get warm in the car. He was cold as well, but I could tell he was happy. He even made an attempt to be nice to me.

"Do you want to go home and get something warm to drink?"

His motive was as clear as day.

"No, thank you!" was my categorical answer.

"Then let's go straight to the hotel." He sighed.

He drove wildly and it was making me even more nervous than I was before. I was more frightened of being injured and deformed in an accident than I was of being killed.

However, we arrived safely.

Bruno parked the car in front of the hotel and I got out of the car. I stood hesitantly.

"Come on, doll, don't be afraid. Everything will be OK." He took me by the hand.

However stupid this may sound, it reassured me.

Together we entered the well illuminated lobby and went towards the lifts. I noticed that all the hotel staff seemed to know him.

The porter made a joke about his BMW.

It seemed to take an eternity in the lift until we reached the top floor.

"Where are we going, Bruno?" I asked slightly concerned.

"To the bar, darling. The girls are already there. I want to introduce you and show you to the boys."

"What boys?"

No answer.

Before we reached the bar we could hear a song by Madonna coming from there. I stopped in front of the mirror in the lobby to tidy myself up, but he pulled me on.

"Come on, you'll have time to see to yourself later on."

When we entered, everyone turned to look at us. The bar wasn't full and there were only a handful of people inside. The "girls" were there and I recognized them immediately.

They were sitting at the bar, all of them looking towards us. (I was later to realize that this was a "professional deformation" and became an almost inborn habit).

I didn't know where to go, so I stopped and turned to Bruno, who impatiently pushed me from behind and said quietly,

"Come on, be a bit braver. You're the prettiest one of them all," and grinned contentedly.

I wanted to slap him across the face but I controlled the desire and went towards the bar.

We were being observed with distinct curiosity. There were six girls at the bar, a colourful bouquet of hair styles and shades, vivid make-up, all of them dressed in tight, body-hugging leggings. There were all the shades of blonde and red, but not a single black-haired girl. Oh, I was forgetting myself. I was to be the final addition to the colourful group for a "Magnificent Seven". My natural hair colour was coal black and stood out vibrantly from them. I instinctively realized that I won on all points.

We reached the girls.

"Hello, dolls!" Bruno stood in front of me, facing the girls with his legs apart in a sort of directorial stance.

"Hello," they all replied in a disorderly fashion. They looked at him timidly and tensely.

He noticed their reaction to him and he puffed his chest out even more. Like a cockerel in a henhouse, I thought and stifled a laugh, despite the wretched situation I was in.

"Dolls, this is the Princess! Say hello to her. You'll be working together. I want you to help her get started and don't try any tricks with her, because I know what you get up to..." The last few words were uttered in a threateningly quiet voice which gave me goose bumps. "You'll introduce her to the work and give her some clothes to get her started. She'll give them back to you in a couple of weeks. Natasha!" he commanded.

A tall, gentle, blonde creature jumped down from the last stool but one and came towards us. She had huge blue, thickly made-up eyes which looked at Bruno in fear. She was dressed in shiny black leggings with a glistening beige and gold unbuttoned tunic. Beneath it she was dressed in a black lace body. She wasn't wearing a bra but she had a fantastic bust, huge and taut. I liked her immediately.

"Natasha! I'm putting you in charge of the Princess. If there's any problem, you'll be responsible..."

"No problem, Bruno. Everything will be fine," she replied in a thick Russian accent.

Jesus, she was Russian!

"You still haven't learnt our language very well! You'll have to work on your accent! You're starting to annoy me. Get some language books and learn them!"

She bowed her head in fright and seemed to curl up.

The other girls sat in indifferent silence and even seemed to be pleased. They preferred the boss' anger to be vented at Natasha and not them. *Fuck you all. You just wait!* I thought, threateningly.

"That's it then. Down to work! What are you all doing here? Get a move on! Princess, come with me and I'll show you your room! Natasha, go with her and dress her up in something. Come on, get a move on!"

We went out of the bar and back into the lift; this time we descended.

In the lift Natasha looked at me and smiled timidly. I responded likewise.

Bruno was standing with his back to us, spinning the keys around his fingers.

The hotel was clean, quiet and luxurious. I liked the environment; if only the circumstances had been different...

We reached the middle of the corridor and stopped.

"Natasha, isn't this your room?"

"No, next one, Bruno."

"OK, give me the key then."

The room was in complete disarray. There were clothes everywhere, on the floor, on the bed, on the desk...

Black lace stockings, pants, bodices. Elegant ladies' underwear, blouses, skirts. The room was in unimaginable chaos. There was even a stocking hanging over the bed lamp.

"What's been going on here?" Bruno shouted.

Natasha blushed to the roots of her hair.

"Mihail was here. He made check."

I looked at him in disbelief.

Bruno looked at her severely and asked,

"Well, did he find anything?"

"No, I give you everything."

"Good girl! That's what I like. If I catch anyone concealing money, you know I can be merciless."

I still couldn't quite catch what was going on, so he added with a hypnotic stare,

"Everything you make goes to us. If the client is happy and pays more than the agreed amount, then that goes to us as well. You get 40%."

I was beginning to understand. In other words, if anyone gave me a present of money, I was obliged to give it to this blood sucker.

"That's all there is to it. Come on, get things sorted out. You'll be sharing this room. Good luck... Princess!" He winked and disappeared, closing the door behind him.

I stood in stunned silence for a few moments. "God, what have I got myself into now?"

Natasha looked at me sympathetically. She spoke first.

"Not worry yourself! I help you!"

She was touching and I managed to give her a crooked smile.

"It looks like you need my help," I said to her.

"Yes, yes." She nodded her head like a young horse, and smiled happily.

She came up to me and kissed me resoundingly three times on both cheeks.

She was so spontaneous that I kissed her back with pleasure. We were friends now.

We were the same height and about the same bust measurement.

"That's great!" Natasha shouted and pushed me into the bathroom for a quick shower.

Within less than an hour we were sorted out and ready. I chose a short black, lycra and lamé skirt from her wardrobe. I chose my stockings to match and put on a bodice decorated with black pearls and a silk blouse on top, loosely tied at the waist. I tied my hair back in a ponytail, raised high to one side, curled my fringe with tongs and put myself in the hands of Natasha who did my makeup. The shoes were a little too tight, but when I stood in front of the mirror, Natasha sighed with pleasure.

"Well, you a real Princess!"

I have to admit that I was very proud of myself. I really did look fantastic.

"Natasha, what do I have to do to get a client?" The joy at my appearance evaporated very quickly when I realized that Bruno was expecting me to make money this evening.

"Very simple. You must make impression!"

"On men?"

"Of course, yes!"

"Like dancing on the dance floor?"

"Exactly!"

I sighed.

"Let's go then."

Natasha nodded and whispered,

"Good luck, darling!"

I put my hand on my heart. It was pounding so hard I thought it might burst. "I don't care what happens!" I thought to myself, and left the room. Natasha locked the door quietly behind us and we went to the bar.

It was full and the girls were nowhere to be seen. Their stools were empty.

My new girlfriend and I sat down and ordered a whisky. I hated it, but I decided that I needed to get drunk quickly and get down to work.

"Cheers, darling Natasha!" I said, and downed the whisky in one gulp.

Natasha gave me a look of astonishment.

"No need to do it like that!"

"Yes there is, there certainly is!" I replied imitating her accent and took her glass as well.

"Will you permit me?" I asked and before she could react, I had drunk her glass as well.

I felt the effect of the alcohol making me dizzy. It was a pleasant and soft sensation, even pleasurable. Natasha looked funny the way she stared at me like I was an alien from outer space.

"Don't worry darling. I'm all right. It's just very warm in here. I'll take this blouse off. You don't mind do you?" I mumbled as I slipped off the stool. I thought I was going to fall, but I didn't. I was standing straight upright, almost sober. I slowly took off my blouse to reveal the bodice. It was very beautiful and fitted me perfectly. I had nothing to lose and a strange feeling of unhealthy curiosity from within was pulling me on. "What's going to happen now? What will happen later on?"

"Let's dance Natasha! I want to invite you to dance with me."

Natasha was looking really worried for me and we slowly walked up to the dance floor. The light fell on me and remained there.

Come on then! Look and faint! I can be yours if you pay for me! I thought evilly and danced and danced. The skirt and bodice hid only a very small part of my perfect body. I could feel the greedy stares of the men looking at me and I began to dance even more provocatively. Natasha was very close to me and looked very concerned, but I didn't pay her any attention. When the song finished, she grabbed me by the arm and dragged me back to the stools. However, before we got to them, a middle aged man stood before us and asked politely,

"Would the young ladies agree to come to our table?"

I spoke before Natasha and replied haughtily.

"Why not? As long as you're not very boring."

My words were greeted by friendly laughter from a nearby table.

Natasha cast me a conspiratorial glance and a devilish wink. The sweet young thing had no idea that her pupil was taking her first steps in a brilliant career, cursing the entire world and herself along with it. We sat down. There were another two men at the table. We were immediately introduced to them. The man who invited us to sit down was their translator, while the other two were Greek. They were businessmen who had come to Bulgaria for four days on business. They knew a word or two of Bulgarian but most of the time they used the translator, a very amusing person in himself, to communicate. We drank and danced.

One of them clearly liked me, while the other was a little uncertain about Natasha. The decision was finally made after a slow dance with my client. When we got back to the table they were no longer there. I sat tensely. The amount of alcohol I had drunk had not calmed me in the slightest. The moment came at last. Zlatan, that was the translator, asked,

"Ioana, Kostas wants to ask if you would like to accompany him to his room."

"Tell him that my fee is one hundred dollars for half an hour and no perverted stuff," I whispered and blushed despite my attempts not to.

While Zlatan translated, my eyes fell upon Bruno who was carefully observing all this.

Where did he appear from? He must have been watching me all the time.

Kostas smiled and stood up.

"Have a nice time, treasure," the translator wished me when I got up and he gallantly moved my chair away from me.

I gave him a crooked smile and went towards the door, watching for Bruno.

I had no idea where he had gone. My uncertainty didn't last long because I found him sitting in the armchair in the lobby in front of the bar. He got up and followed us to the door of the room.

While Kostas was unlocking the room, I turned around and looked over my shoulder. Bruno was standing a few doors down pretending to look for his own key. Kostas, who was quite drunk, finally managed to find his key, opened the door and we went in.

I was terribly anxious. Not that I hadn't ever seen a man naked, but this time it was different.

My heart was pounding in my chest. *Krasi, I hope you are swallowed up in Hell! I hope the Devil gets you!* These were my last thoughts before making the decisive gesture of removing my bodice.

The poor Greek man quivered so much when he saw me naked that he couldn't get his trousers off.

"Let me do it, fool!" I muttered through my teeth and pulled his zip. He watched me in utter amazement, as though I was going to violate him. But I gave him a reassuring slap on the buttocks and he laughed understandingly.

Everything happened so quickly that I didn't even feel Kostas come.

He lay down next to me exhausted and happy, while I ran into the bathroom. I washed myself long and hard. When I came out fully dressed, he was fast asleep with a smile on his face, and a one hundred dollar note on his bedside table.

I took it and looked at the sleeping figure. I looked at his trousers and thought there might be money in his pockets. I was almost tempted to rifle his pockets, but I refrained and quietly left the room.

I was now a prostitute. I repeated it to myself constantly. As I waited for the lift lost in wretched thoughts, Bruno appeared next to me imperceptibly.

"What's up, Princess?" he asked quietly.

"One hundred green backs," I replied in a muffled voice.

"Let me have it!"

I gave him the money in disgust. He was making me mad.

"All right then, Princess. Go back to the bar."

I obeyed and went back in. I looked around for Natasha. She wasn't there. I'd obviously finished before her. Two of the girls were sitting at the bar. I went over to them.

"How's the work going, sister?" one of them asked me in a harsh voice.

She had coarse facial features and a huge backside. Her hairstyle was reminiscent of Tina Turner, and was bright red. She was dressed in the obligatory black shiny leggings and red tunic. She was revoltingly vulgar.

"You have to learn that if you try too hard in the beginning, the bosses will get used to you earning lots of money. And then when you haven't got any jobs, you'll be in trouble with them..."

"Thanks for the valuable information," I whispered icily.

"And don't boast too much, sister, because you might get your feathers plucked."

"Go to hell!" I suggested and went back to dance.

My other "colleague," an unprepossessing creature with a pale face and colourless hair, also got up and joined me on the dance floor.

"Hi, my name's Katya," she offered me with a subdued smile, and danced around me in mincing little steps.

"You're not Russian as well, are you?"

"Ha, ha. No, I'm from Plovdiv."

As I danced my legs almost gave way under me.

"I hate Plovdiv," I panted and looked her up and down provocatively.

"So do I," she said as she slipped one of her bra straps down over her shoulder. She looked around the bar and said,

"Come with me love. We've got clients."

"Where are they?" I asked distrustfully.

"Come with me and you'll see."

Why not? Why not have a go with someone else? I thought and followed her.

"Good evening," Katya said to them. "Would you like some company?"

They clearly realized what we were asking them, because they nodded.

"Yes, yes."

They spoke English but I couldn't understand and said nothing.

Katya managed more or less with words and gesticulations to have a conversation with them.

She translated to me that they were both Arabs. I didn't like the idea very much. I felt indifferent towards them and looked over their heads.

"You are very nice," one of them nodded towards me and pinched my chin slightly.

"Take your hands off me, swine!" I pulled away from him sharply.

"Don't behave like that, darling!" Katya hissed at me.

"Why did he touch me?" I shouted at the table.

"Are you mad or what?" The girl looked at me in astonishment. "He's going to touch you anyway for one hundred dollars, isn't he?"

The two Arabs found the scene very amusing and laughed out loud. They even ordered champagne. I gulped a glass down. My tongue went numb, stung by the thousands of needles.

I had drunk so much alcohol that evening and I was still sober. That was amazing. It must have been a result of the incredible stress I was under. The night was progressing and it was probably after three o'clock when the Arabs decided that we would leave.

Katya bargained quickly with them. She knew what she was doing.

The charge was one hundred dollars for half an hour and they wanted us for two hours. So she agreed to five hundred dollars each. She winked at me cunningly and went off with one of them.

My client took me by the hand and confidently led me to his room. Bruno wasn't anywhere to be seen. He must have left. But there was someone else there standing in his place. He was tall and very fat. Enormous. He followed us almost to the door and waited for us to go in.

I had learnt the lesson by now.

I undressed at lightning speed, expecting the Arab to be amazed at my incredible figure.

However, he wasn't that sort of man. He pushed me face down on the bed and began to caress me. It was revolting, but I was at work, I repeated to myself. The Arab penetrated me and an incredible pain seared through my body. He was pounding me and thrusting into me at such speed that at one moment I thought to myself, *this is the end!* I suddenly thought of Bruno; the Arab reminded me of him. He was as inventive as Bruno, and as I was later to discover, even more perverted than him.

Even the memory of what that pervert did to me makes me feel ashamed.

It was terrible! But Bruno was right. I had stamina.

Two hours, or maybe an eternity, passed. I dragged myself to the bathroom. I filled the bath and lowered myself into it. I felt as though I was burning and certain parts of my body stung like hell.

I hope that pervert in the room rots in hell, I thought. He must have been taking tablets to keep him aroused. What he did was humanly impossible!

The pervert was still as fresh as a daisy and even tried to take me again when I came out of the bathroom.

I shouted out and pointed to my watch. He calmed down, paid me and I left his pit of a room as fast as I could.

When I reached the lift, I realized that I had no strength left.

"I have to go to bed and sleep."

The enormous man was waiting for me in the lobby. I gave him the money and told him that I wanted to sleep. He nodded his head in agreement and I even took a liking to him.

I dragged myself to Natasha's room and knocked. I had to wait for a little while, because the little Russian girl had just fallen asleep. She eventually opened the door.

"How was it?" she asked sleepily in her Russian accent.

"Don't ask!" I groaned and threw myself with relief onto the bed and fell into a deep sleep.

That was the end of my first working night. Bruno would be happy. 600 dollars wasn't to be sneezed at. I had earned it with my fragile body of a child with its wonderful figure and crippled soul.

CHAPTER 14

In The Clutches Of Trafficking Or Welcome To Hell

I woke up in the late afternoon with a heavy heart. I was as sad as doom and the entire world was to blame. The fact that I was now a prostitute in an elite hotel was driving me mad. I was particularly furious at the thought that it was all due to one silly little mistake of my own making. The disco, meeting the pervert Bruno and everything else.... I wanted to kill someone. My entire body was in pain. The revolting 48-hour sex marathon had destroyed me.

I carefully raised my head and looked around. I was alone. Natasha wasn't there. The room was immaculately tidy. On the bedside table next to me, my new girlfriend had left me a can of Coca Cola and two chocolate croissants. And a rose! How touching! The girl had a heart! And style! But what a life, Jesus! That beautiful creature had come from God knows what end of the Soviet Union to finish up here! I had to ask her where she came from. But where was she now? And what time was it? My watch, my beautiful watch, the one Krasi had given to me was carefully placed next to my head. Natasha had taken care of everything. She had undressed me and carefully tidied away my clothes, shoes and even my watch. I felt as though I might survive. The drink was pleasant, cool and refreshing. I took a fluffy, well-baked croissant filled with chocolate. Bliss! I don't know how, but I managed to eat both of them. Everything looked different after good food!

The fact that I was a prostitute wasn't the end of the world. There was probably a way of getting out of it. I just had to be careful and find my own way. The most important thing was not to hurry. That would mean remaining as a prostitute for a while. There was no other way. I had got myself into the situation and now I had to get myself out, with a lot of tact and cunning.

While I was considering my strategy, the door opened quietly and Natasha entered the room.

Her blonde hair was wet and had acquired the colour of copper. She was dressed in a pretty tracksuit and was carrying a towel.

The moment she saw I was awake, she smiled broadly and blew me a kiss in greeting.

"You woken up now! How you feel today?"

"Hello, my treasure! I felt awful before filling myself up with your nutritious and high-calorie food, which will make my backside expand to the size of a large family wardrobe if I eat too much of it."

I didn't know how well Natasha understood Bulgarian but she stood in the middle of the room and shook with uncontrollable laughter. She laughed until tears rolled down her cheeks. I was happy that she was with me at this period in my life. Anyone else's presence would have been intolerable.

Natasha calmed down and laid on her bed.

"Natasha, darling, where did you come from?"

"I was in swimming pool. Swimming. I regenerate myself."

"That's great! I'll go swimming too, if there's a swimming pool down below. But I'm asking you where you lived before you came to Bulgaria."

Her face took on a sad expression. She sighed and began her sad story. She spoke a mixture of Russian and Bulgarian, but I could understand her.

She came from Leningrad and she was 18 years old. She had two brothers. One of them was in prison for robbing a jeweller's shop. Her other brother was in the army. Their mother had died and their father had got remarried quite soon afterwards.

Natasha signed up to join a modelling agency. After signing the contracts, the girls were sent abroad... to Greece, Italy, Germany and Bulgaria.

In fact, this was no more than a legal channel for exporting young, cheap flesh for sale. Once trapped it was almost impossible to get out of it. The channel was excellently organized. They were under constant guard and if the bosses had the slightest suspicion of anyone concealing money or planning to escape, the torture and punishments were incredible.

Natasha showed me the scars on her body and legs. She had been "ironed" with a hot iron to force her into prostitution. They had extinguished cigarettes in her navel. After being tortured in ways which the Gestapo couldn't have imagined, she gave in to them and ended up here.

I listened in absolute shock. I thanked my lucky star that things had been different for me. I had been fortunate.

"Natasha, how many people are there in Bruno's group?"

"Oh, I think they must be more than ten of them."

"So many? Apart from running the prostitutes in the hotel, what else do they do? Guns, drugs?"

Natasha raised her eyes, put her finger to her lips and whispered,

"Mustn't talk about that. It's the same as talking about death!"

Her words chilled me. I decided that I had done enough information gathering for today. I had discovered the most important thing. Bruno was not just any old pimp; he was a link in a long chain in a much bigger organization.

This was not good, because it would be a complex and difficult operation to get out of here. However, I was an optimist with an adventurous spirit. So I tried not to get too worried about it and looked on the matter from a practical point of view.

"Natasha, how much money do you make for yourself in one night? Not from tips, but from a percentage?"

"It's different. 200-300 dollars."

"Sometimes more, sometimes less?"

"Yes, you get it now. It's a lot of money."

"Natasha, you and I are going to have a great time! We will go swimming together. We'll buy pretty clothes. I'll teach you to speak Bulgarian as though you were born here. You'll see! You're great and I love you!"

I ran around the room naked to get my body moving.

Natasha watched me and giggled at my nude gymnastics. She couldn't resist it either and joined in.

The whole room echoed with giggling and groans.

It was past six o'clock when Natasha and I finally calmed down. It was time to get dressed and ready for work.

That evening I put on a pair of white silk trousers which were almost transparent, with a red lace blouse with twirls and other romantic additions to it.

I gathered my hair in a high, tight bun. When I started doing my make-up, Natasha joked that from the waist up I looked like a Spanish noble woman. From the waist up... she emphasized.

"Which means that from the waist down I look like a prostitute, is that what you mean, you little pig!" I shouted out in pretend anger and we both fell about giggling.

That night I worked hard again and through my hands, so to speak, went two Bulgarian businessmen, a Japanese man and another Greek. I earned 800 dollars, of which Bruno with clear satisfaction gave me 320.

"You're a real treasure, Princess! I'm happy that I met you!"

Not me, you dirty bastard! I thought.

But in reality I said nothing to him. He realized that I hated him, but he didn't care. All he cared about was his profit from me.

The other girls, with the exception of Natasha, were beginning to dislike me. I could feel it. In the space of two evenings, I had become the hit of the bar and was "stealing" their best clients.

There was nothing unusual about that. I was young (still a child in fact). I wasn't even 15 years old. I was as fresh as a peach and beautiful. I was very beautiful. This might sound immodest, but I could see the stunned expressions on the men's faces, as well as the passion, sometimes even demonic, in their eyes. And I realized how strong I was with my female weapons.

At the end of the week I paid Bruno my rent for the hotel room and counted the money left to me. I had 1100 dollars. It was a lot of money, even though I had been spoilt by my life with Krasi when we had had much more money than that.

"Natasha, I want to go shopping."

Natasha was carefully varnishing her toenails and she stuck her tongue out at me.

"OK, why not?"

She had begun to express herself much better in Bulgarian and was very proud of herself.

"Would you like to go to dinner afterwards, in a small restaurant?"

She nodded, continuing to varnish her toenails.

"I agree."

"You always agree," I replied with feigned anger.

She raised her eyes and looked at me seriously.

"You're always right."

A little later we were on a hectic shopping spree. We visited a lot of shops and bought the most wonderful things. When we finished we could hardly breathe.

We sat down to have a rest and a drink in a café.

I lit a cigarette, inhaled the smoke and half-closed my eyes. A thought had been taking shape in my head. I was afraid of sharing it with Natasha, because I knew her well and knew that she was timid. Nevertheless, I decided to have a go.

"Darling, what would you say if we didn't go back?"

As she was sipping her coffee, she almost choked. When she stopped coughing, she went bright red and asked,

"Did I understand you correctly?"

"You understood me perfectly, darling. What if we decide not to go back to the hotel? What if we just get into a taxi and go to some faraway and nice town at the seaside? Have you ever been to Bourgas? Have you seen the sea? I'm in love with it!" I said quickly and excitedly.

Natasha shook her blonde hair and said,

"They'll catch us right away. They are everywhere."

I looked at her suspiciously.

"I know what I say. They killed one girl who ran far away to a big river..." Natasha was having difficulties finding the right words.

"The Danube?" I suggested.

"Yes. You know everything!" She looked at me. "They found her after two days. Then she was dead."

"Can anyone prove that?" I replied stubbornly.

"No one, but it is the absolute truth!"

I looked at her thoughtfully and smoked. I thought it would be easy to escape. But she was right. They were everywhere. Suddenly the memory of a very familiar voice came to me. "Remember this telephone number, and if you have any problems, call and say your name."

"God, why hadn't I thought of that? Krasi had thought of everything. What was the number?" I tried to focus my mind. I could only remember the number 4. *Come on! Come on! Remember!* Nothing came into my mind. The bad thing was that at that dramatic moment of parting, I hadn't made an effort to remember it. I had just glanced at the piece of paper with the intention of never using it. But now...

I tried for more than an hour, but I couldn't remember it. Natasha waited patiently. In the end I gave up. I sighed sadly and got up.

"Come on, darling. Let's go!"

"Aren't we going to eat dinner?"

"No. I lost my appetite." I looked at her with an expression of disappointment.

Natasha obediently gathered up her shopping bags and we left the café. Upset as I was, my perceptive eye couldn't help noticing the admiring glances of a group of boys standing in front of the café. They were staring at us, exchanging opinions about our natural gifts, while we proudly and haughtily walked past them. I heard approving whistles from behind us.

Natasha and I looked at each other and winked with silly grins on our faces. We took a taxi and went back to the hotel.

The room was packed with packages and boxes. We started unpacking and the disorder turned into chaos. We dressed and undressed, put on shoes and took them off. We were playing like little children with their mummy's clothes.

We eventually grew tired and lay down to rest.

"Natasha, how long do you think you will be a prostitute?"

Natasha wrinkled her beautiful little nose and said,

"Only God knows!"

"I'm going to get out of here. At the first opportunity!"

There was a knock on the door at that moment.

I went to open it. Stella was standing there. She was that ugly, plump girl who had threatened to pull my hair out one day. When I saw her leaning against the door frame, everything went black before my eyes.

"I came to see what you dolls have been buying," she said in a rasping voice. "But I overheard accidentally that someone wants to get out of here at the first opportunity. I won't tell Bruno and the boys this time, but I can't promise next time." She smiled maliciously and turned around to go.

The blood rushed to me head. Who did that slut think she was? Was she threatening me?

I ran after her and grabbed hold of her hair with one hand, while strangling her with the other. At the same time I pushed her into our room.

I was weak, but very quick and caught her by surprise. She fell onto the floor and began to bite my legs. That made me mad. I kicked her in the chest and winded her. She began to cough and went as red as a tomato.

"Ioana! Stop!"

Natasha was terrified. She was holding my hand, but I couldn't calm down and continued kicking that miserable bitch. She was now sobbing. Slowly my anger died down and I stopped.

Stella was lying motionless on the floor, groaning. I bent down to her, took her chin in my hand and said very clearly and slowly,

"This is only the beginning. If you don't behave yourself, the next time it will be much worse. Tell your friends as well. And now get out of here! Now!"

She couldn't get up and so she crawled out of the room on all fours, groaning.

I lit a cigarette and kicked a shoe box.

The chaos in the room was now unimaginable.

Natasha started tidying up quickly, casting meaningful glances at me all the time. I was leaning against the window smoking, watching her. I said nothing. Natasha broke the silence.

"You should not do that! She might be dead!"

"That's what she deserves. Exactly what she deserves!" I objected categorically. "She deserved to get it from someone. She's ugly, fat and smells! Apart from that she's envious and she's a grass! If she tries anything else on with me, I tell you, I will kill her!"

Natasha came up to me, stroked me with the back of her hand and said,

"These strong words. You must forget them!"

I pushed her hand away angrily.

"I will forget about it. But she must remember it well, otherwise she's in for a lot of trouble!"

It was close to seven. We had to get ready for work quickly because we had to be in the bar by seven. We were fined if we were late. At five past seven we were ready. I was dressed in a purple and black silk suit decorated with tassels on top. I really liked it the moment I had seen it in the shop. It was a super fit. I bought a pair of purple shoes with a twelve centimetre heel, especially to go with them. It took a bit of time to get used to standing on them. Natasha was wearing a black silk lycra dress, which was very short and had a plunging neckline. She put on her gold jewellery and looked amazing.

When we entered the bar, the other girls were already there.

Stella was sitting on the first stool and there was nothing I could do but walk past her. I was curious about how she would react. When she saw me, she went pale, her eyes opened wide and as I walked past her, she said quietly,

"I'm sorry..."

I smiled triumphantly and walked on. I had won! If that slut was apologizing to me, then everyone else had acknowledged me as their leader. When a tall, elegantly dressed young man entered the bar, I went up to him quite calmly and said to him,

"Good evening. Would you like me to make your evening a pleasant experience?"

The young man looked at me in surprise (whether because of my forwardness or my beauty, I don't know) and smiled politely.

"With pleasure, young lady."

He spoke Bulgarian with a foreign accent, which made him even more attractive.

"Oh, you speak such good Bulgarian," I praised him.

"That is because my mother is Bulgarian."

"Which means your father isn't?"

"No, he isn't. He's American."

"Oh, I love America! I've always dreamed of living there!"

"Bulgaria is also a wonderful country. I've had the chance to travel around and in my opinion it is quite like Switzerland, only more beautiful!"

This was a pure compliment.

"Thank you! It is very sweet that you like my country, which is actually also yours, even if only half. Since we're talking about geography, have you had the chance to visit the Black Sea?"

The dark eyelashes of my Bulgarian American furrowed and he shook his head.

"Then you haven't seen anything. The sea is the prettiest part. And... Bourgas!" I added sadly.

A lump came into my throat and almost choked me.

"You've upset yourself now! You shouldn't have!" He was very sensitive and immediately realized that there was something wrong. "Let me introduce myself. My name's Peter Redford. Unfortunately, I have nothing in common with Robert Redford. I live in New Jersey and I own a small fish restaurant. What about you?"

"My name's Ioana Petrova and I'm from Sofia."

Peter raised his glass.

"I know that the mother of your King is called Queen Ioana. So I drink to the Queen at my table."

"No, Peter, you're wrong! I am just a Princess," I said bitterly and drank my glass to the bottom.

He was beautiful. Dark, with dark brown, almost black eyes, dark hair and a high forehead. He had wonderful white teeth and the most attractive smile I had ever seen. His hands were large and strong, but he held his glass with such elegance. He was the epitome of cleanliness and freshness. He didn't smoke.

We spoke for a long time about all sorts of things. He told me about his mother. I said nothing about mine.

He tactfully avoided asking me any questions. We eventually got up. I looked at him questioningly.

"Come with me, Ioana. You don't have to do anything if you don't want to. I'll pay."

Tears welled up in my eyes. I followed him in silence. He also felt embarrassed. One of the boys walked after us. When we entered his room I couldn't hold my tears back any more and burst into sobs.

Peter approached me, raised my head in both his hands and whispered,

"How can I help you?"

The tears were pouring down my cheeks like a waterfall.

He stroked my head paternally and said,

"Ioana, there's something bad going on here. Tell me what it is and I'll help you."

"Shhh!" I put my finger in front of my lips. "Quiet, they'll kill me!"

"Ioana, no one's going to kill you if you're with me!" Peter explained with dignity. "I'm an American citizen and I want to know who would want to kill a little girl. You're still a child!"

I swallowed my tears and sat on his bed and began. I told him everything. I only concealed my age, so as not to shock him. I said nothing about Krasi. He gave me seven hundred dollars which I gave to the dogs in the bar. I told them that he had paid for the whole night with me and I went back to his room. He was lying on his back staring at the ceiling. When I lay down next to him, he moved aside to make room for me. This touched me and I stroked his stomach.

"Ioana, don't feel obliged... Just relax and go to sleep."

"I like you, Peter. I really do like you," I muttered and continued to stroke him. I could feel how my presence was electrifying him.

He bent over me and kissed my eyes, then my lips, my chin and continued down my body.

Such tenderness flowed from him that I suddenly cried out,

"Peter, I can't resist it anymore!"

His touch was so different from anything which I had experienced until then, that I didn't want it ever to stop.

Our bodies merged into one and moved together slowly and rhythmically, like in a dance. Everything was wonderful.

I could hear the music which was carrying me on its wings and I was travelling with it. Peter kissed me and caressed me. The ecstasy flowed from the toes of my feet into the rest of my body. Before it reached my brain, I heard the distant words through the music,

"Ioana, you're wonderful! I love you!"

It was Peter.

It was some time before I "fell back to earth."

Peter was lying on top of me, kissing my face, not leaving a single centimetre unkissed. He possessed the tenderness of centuries. I liked him. When I could at last speak, my first words were:

"You're wonderful too, Peter! And I want you to make love to me again!"

He looked me at happily and continued working on the unkissed parts of my body.

It was a happy night for me. For a long time, I had not woken up with such a happy heart. But I was fated always to be torn by contradictions.

I was already awake and Peter was still asleep. In his sleep he looked even more beautiful and virile. I was enjoying the opportunity to admire him when a strange and spontaneous feeling of guilt welled up in me. I couldn't initially comprehend what the feeling was, until it came to me in a flash. I had betrayed Krasi. Not physically. I had been doing that for a long time. But in my heart. I had fallen in love.

That was where my feeling of guilt was coming from. I knew that it was silly, but I couldn't get rid of it. I moved uneasily and at that moment Peter woke up. I smiled at him sweetly and he kissed me tenderly on the nose.

"Hello, darling!"

I experienced the absurd feeling that we had been married for a long time and our three children were sleeping in the other room. The feeling was as absurd as it was wonderful.

"Peter, I want to marry you. Do you understand?" I spurted out.

The words came to me unexpectedly. It was as though someone else was speaking instead of me.

Peter said nothing for a while and then asked hesitantly,

"Is this accepted in Bulgaria? For the woman to ask for the hand in marriage? God, how wonderful it is to wake up next to the most beautiful woman in the world, who doesn't want a diamond ring, but asks you to marry her!"

Silently and tensely I waited for the end of his monologue.

"Ioana, I'm astonished to say the least! Only..." he looked at his watch, "twelve hours ago, I had no idea of your existence. And now I'm a happy bridegroom-to-be!"

I interrupted him impatiently.

"Peter, say it, don't beat around the bush. Just say it straight out, that you don't imagine your future wife as a former prostitute, even though she is very beautiful."

He looked at me and laughed.

"Oho! My future wife's got some character! Darling, let me tell you something. I accept your proposal with pleasure and if there is anything I might regret, then it is not proposing before you did!"

With a cry of joy, I threw my arms around him and began to kiss him. That was enough for him. Peter didn't wait long for the invitation.

I was flying again, carried on the wings of the music, and the feeling that I was incorporeal was so intense, that I thought for a moment that I had died of happiness.

We were recovering in bed when there was a loud knock on the door.

I started to get up, but Peter pushed me back into bed and went to open the door. I shook when I heard Bruno's voice. In a tone which would countenance no objection, Bruno explained to Peter, that it was past 10.00 and that if he (Peter) wanted to hold on to me, he would have to pay.

When Peter came to get the money, there were sparks in his olive-dark eyes.

He paid the money and I was given to Peter for four days in return for 4000 dollars.

I was happy! I would spend four whole days with Peter. But it had cost him an entire fortune. It was a lot of money and he knew it, although he could still joke about it.

"Ioana, darling, in America for $4000 I could get a room filled with girls."

I looked at him with feigned anger and said,

"Yes, but the goods are better quality here!"

As I said these words I got out of bed completely naked and walked with dignity to the bathroom. I knew what his reaction would be. He followed me like a puppy dog. He was staring at my back. Knowing that he was behind me, I bent over to fill the bath.

Two hands grabbed me and a wonderful masculine body clung on to me.

"Ioana, you are impossibly perfect! I adore you! If I have to, I'll sell my restaurant and my house, but I'll save you. I'll get you out of here!"

"That's what they all say!" I joked. "You just want me all for yourself!"

We both leapt into the bath and the water overflowed, leaving hardly a drop in the tub.

CHAPTER 15

The Daily Life Of A Prostitute

The four days passed like in a dream. We didn't leave the room. Room service brought us food, but we almost didn't eat. The time passed in talking, making plans and love. Lots of love.

The final evening arrived. Peter wanted to have dinner in the Panorama restaurant, but I refused. I wanted him for myself. Here and now! I was nervous and burst into tears at the smallest thing. He tried in vain to calm me that everything would be all right and he would sort out all the necessary documents as soon as possible. I felt as though my heart was being squeezed in a steel vice and it hurt... it hurt.

Peter was very tender and attentive. The thought of our parting hurt him as well, but he behaved impeccably. He was worried that he was leaving me here in the hands of "those criminals," and swore on his mother, that if he had to he would speak to every single official in the emigration services until he arranged my departure. He went to bed early, because he had to catch his flight the next morning. I held on to him tightly and sobbed inconsolably. I had the feeling that I would never see him again and the thought was driving me crazy. He just caressed me and repeated,

"Don't cry, darling! Everything will be OK! You'll see!"

It was a dreadful night for both of us. He got up early and dressed. I sat in bed motionless. I was devastated. He was trying to be kind and even made a joke about something or other, but in vain. He gathered all his money, left a little for himself and gave me all the rest.

"Hide it well, darling! I hope it will be enough for you, until I come back."

I nodded silently. I couldn't talk. The vice which had gripped my heart was now clasping my throat.

The reception called to say that the taxi was waiting. Peter sighed and came over to me.

"Kiss me, darling!"

Two huge tears rolled down my face.

I thought I had no more tears to cry.

I stood on the bed and hung onto his neck. I clung on motionless and he stroked my back.

For a few moments we remained like that, then Peter pushed me gently.

"Come on, darling. I'll be late."

I let go of him in silence and remained staring at him, while he picked up his suitcases. He turned around at the door, looked at me tenderly and said,

"Look after yourself!"

The door closed behind him.

I lit a cigarette automatically and went over to the window. The car park resembled a handkerchief and the cars were like little toys. A yellow taxi was waiting for him with open doors. *It must be for him,* I thought and drew back from the window. I didn't want to experience the pain of seeing him off again. "God, why do I always have to be left alone? Is that my karma?"

Peter wasn't leaving me. He was going to get me out of here. But it was all so far away. Somewhere in the future. But what now? Oh, yes. I was now a prostitute and this evening I had to be at work.

I smoked my cigarette and began to get dressed; I had to go back to Natasha's room. I needed to sleep and get ready for the evening. God! The money! I counted it. Three thousand dollars. It was a lot of money. I had to find a good hiding place. I looked around fervently. My gaze fell upon a packet of sanitary towels. I got one out and started to unpick it. I took the innermost layer out and arranged the folded notes very carefully. Then I put the filling back in and sealed it. The "golden" sanitary towel had to be at the back of the packet. Now I could go.

I decided not to tell Natasha about what had happened. Not that I didn't trust her, but it was my insurance. There was no room for mistakes with Bruno and the others. One mistake might cost me my life. They didn't make jokes.

Natasha was out and I went to sleep.

I dreamed of Peter sitting on a cloud waving to me and saying something. It was something very important but I couldn't hear what he was saying. Then the cloud opened up and Peter disappeared inside it. I woke up bathed in sweat. The dream upset me even more. Although I'm an optimist by nature, the doubt that I might never see him again began to gnaw away at me again.

When Natasha came back, my spirits raised slightly. She was pleased to see me.

"Well, how was it with you?" She looked at me cunningly.

"Super!"

Laconic but true.

"I guessing..."

"What did you get up to without me? Looks like you've forgotten Bulgarian?"

"No, not at all," Natasha laughed. "I bought you a present!"

"Really? Sweet Natasha! Show it to me!"

With a theatrical gesture she turned around and a little box appeared suddenly in her hands.

I looked at it curiously.

"Please, this is for you!" She gave me the little box in her hand. I took it hesitantly. I slowly opened it and was stunned. Inside there was a little ring with a huge beautiful pearl. I sighed with astonishment. It was the most wonderful ring.

"Natasha! You're an angel! Where did you find such a beautiful thing?"

"That's my secret!"

"Wait, it must have been very expensive!"

"That's not important."

"Then you must know that I shall be forever in your debt!"

"Shhh!" Natasha closed my mouth and smiled.

"Natasha, if I understand you correctly, you've made a lot of money and instead of giving it to those slugs, you converted it into gold?"

"Shhh." She nodded and laughed devilishly.

"You're a genius. But we need to destroy the boxes."

And that's what we did. I didn't take my new ring off my finger. I had a lot of gold on my fingers but this ring was the most beautiful.

Then we took a shower, got dressed and went down to the hairdresser's. There was only one hour left to seven o'clock.

Thanks to Natasha, the evening passed relatively quietly. I only had two clients that night who didn't bother me with anything in particular and were very quiet and well behaved. I finished off early and went back to the room before daylight. Peter had arranged to call me in my room every morning at 8.00 Bulgarian time. I was sitting on my bed staring at the telephone. It was silent.

The telephone rang on my second cigarette.

"Hello?"

"Hello, darling, my distant Princess!"

My heart was pounding.

"Peter...," was all that I could say.

"I'm calling from my parents' house. I told them all about you..."

My heart stopped.

"They're happy that their future daughter-in-law's Bulgarian."

I began to breathe more calmly.

"My father has a friend in the Consular section for visas, and he promised to help."

"Peter, I love you!"

"And I love you too, darling. My mother and father say hello to you as well!"

"Say thank you to them for me!"

"I kiss you passionately and I'll call you the day after tomorrow. I'll be thinking about you."

"I'll be thinking about you as well. Come as soon as you can." I was crying already.

"Don't be upset! Everything will be all right!"

"I know! All right! I love you too! Bye!"

He sent me hot kisses and hung up.

Although I felt sad, my chest was filled with a strange joyous feeling. Somewhere over the ocean, somewhere in America a decent family and a beautiful man were thinking about me and worried about my problems. They wanted to sort out the confused life of a teenage prostitute.

Fraudulent Hopes

Three weeks had passed since Peter had left. During this time, we had spoken a dozen or so times and I was very happy, because despite the endless bureaucratic obstacles things seemed to be progressing. I was working less and Bruno noticed. One evening he called me over and said to me coldly,

"Look doll! If you don't get a grip on things, you'll regret it. I don't want to have to take steps!"

I said nothing and just stared at the ground. He went on,

"I don't like how you've been behaving recently. I think it's about time I taught you a lesson!"

I gave him a look of hatred.

"Go to your room!"

I knew what awaited me.

"Bruno, please don't. I'll sort things out. It's not my fault. It's just there haven't been any clients," I tried to make the excuse.

Bruno wouldn't listen to any excuses. He grabbed me by the elbow and powerfully dragged me to my room.

I don't want to recall anything else. It was disgusting.

Two hours later I went up to the bar. I could hardly walk, but I had to work.

Only the thought of Peter kept me going.

The next morning, I was still asleep when the telephone range. I was still asleep, but I realized it couldn't be him. We had arranged that he would call me on Friday and today was Wednesday.

"Hello?" I said quietly, because Natasha was asleep.

"Hello, I would like to speak to Ioana," I heard a trembling female voice with a slight accent.

"Speaking."

"Excuse me for ringing, I'm Peter's mother. I have some bad news."

The room started spinning in front of my eyes.

"What has happened?" I asked with a trembling voice. I thought I might have fainted or was about to faint.

"... an accident. Yesterday. On the highway... There was a fault with the engine... he...he's..."

"Is he dead?" It wasn't my voice.

"I'm afraid he is."

God, no, God!!! Why is God punishing me like this?

"It's not true, is it?" I screamed uncontrollably.

Natasha jumped in her bed and rubbed her eyes.

"It's very difficult for me as well. I thought that you were morally entitled to know as well. He was very much in love with you."

"Nooooo!" I screamed. I threw the telephone against the wall. "Noooo! It can't be true!"

Natasha threw herself at me. I was shaking crazily. She held on to me tightly.

When I had no strength left, Natasha let me go. She opened a drawer and gave me some pills. I took them obediently. Then I fell asleep.

When I woke up, Natasha was sitting next to me. She was dressed for work.

I opened my eyes with difficulty.

"Darling, are you all right?"

For a moment I thought it was Peter talking to me. I looked at her without blinking.

"Please say something."

I nodded slightly.

"I have to go to work. You stay here. You need to rest!"

"I want some water."

She didn't ask me any questions; she was just taking care of me. She brought me some water, hesitated for a moment and gave me two more tablets which I took obediently.

"Natasha, Bruno..."

"Don't worry."

"All right. I'll leave everything in your hands. I want to sleep."

"All right then. Good bye for now," she said with her Russian accent.

I closed my eyes and tried to sleep. I wouldn't be able to think if I slept. The pills hadn't begun to work yet.

Peter. What a stupid death! Why!!! Why did the people I loved all disappear one after the other? I must be cursed.

Tears of self-pity, warm and bitter dampened my mouth. I swallowed them and whispered in the dark, "Peter, come and take me!"

Then the pills started to work.

A few months passed since Peter's death. I wore black. No one apart from Natasha knew. She helped me in my grief and reassured me as much as she could.

I worked hard and the bastards were happy. I filled their pockets and there was a lot left for me as well. I bought myself lots of clothes and gold as well. I had become predatory, greedy and uncompromising. I hated all men and I stole from them whenever I could. I had become a one-hundred per cent prostitute.

I preserved a little corner of my heart for Natasha – my closest friend. I hated everyone else. I had to put up with conditions which were intolerable for most children in the world (I wasn't even fifteen yet), and I had developed a perfect sense of self-preservation. With one glance I could tell whether a man had money or was a sadist.

Thanks to my hard work and impeccable appearance, I had acquired a number of regular clients, including a handful of politicians, two bankers and a large number of foreigners. Little by little I conquered territories unknown to the other prostitutes in the hotel. I was twice hired to be a companion to one particular politician, about whom Bruno warned me that if I ever opened my mouth, "the Bridge of Sighs" would be my last home.

The girls in the hotel clearly hated me, but I was far above them by now.

I was accumulating money and valuables. It was a desperate act but carried out with the tenacity of which I was capable.

My acquisitiveness was to undergo its greatest test. Everything was normal that particular day. When we had woken up, Natasha and I went to the swimming pool. Then we went to the pedicurist, cosmetician and hairdresser – the complete programme. In the evening we dressed particularly carefully. Natasha was completely in white, and I was in black, as usual. My skirt had a side split which was attached to a belt. It was held together with two gold safety pins where my pants could be seen. I wasn't wearing underwear. I was naked with the exception of black silk stockings to the middle of my thighs. I looked really sexy. Instead of a blouse, I was wearing a black gauze shawl around my neck and crossed over my breasts then tied at the back. I had never dressed so provocatively before. I was completely naked, but dressed. I would even say scandalously dressed. But I didn't care. Natasha (who by now could speak fluent Bulgarian) and I (I had learnt quite a lot of Greek, English and Italian) walked proudly towards the bar.

There was a group of men in the lobby in front of the bar. When they saw us their conversation died down and we walked past them like Hollywood stars, convinced of our irresistibility.

"Ioana, do you think they lost their minds when they saw us?" Natasha whispered to me as we entered the bar.

"They fucking well did!" I whispered back.

"You should be ashamed of yourself!" she told me off. "You swear like a sailor!"

I grinned guiltily.

"I'm sorry, darling, I won't do it anymore."

"Not until the next time..."

"If you're so righteous, why don't you join a convent?" I joked.

"I'll give you such a slap on your made-up face and you'll see why!" she threatened me.

I replied by sticking my tongue out at her. In high spirits, we sat at the bar and ordered a whisky each.

I was used to whisky by now. I couldn't work without alcohol and cigarettes. I knew they were harmful to my health but I couldn't care less.

I had only one aim in life, to acquire money. Lots of money, and run away with Natasha.

I had just taken a sip of my whisky when one of the men who had stared at us in the lobby bar came up to us. He had a repulsive, shiny but obsequious appearance.

"Excuse me girls, would you like to spend the evening with us?"

I looked at him from top to bottom. He was garbage. He didn't have any money. I could tell immediately.

"I'm sorry, we're busy," I refused arrogantly.

However, he knew what he was doing.

"I omitted to give you the business card of our guest, Mr. Andropolus. He's a Greek billionaire, the owner of two ship building factories."

That was something else.

"Where's your billionaire?" I asked haughtily.

"He's outside in the lobby. We are thinking of going to the Casino in the Japanese hotel, so if you would like…"

"We charge by the half hour," I said. "One hundred dollars and one thousand for all night."

"No problem, girls," he sounded encouraged. (He was probably going to cream at least twice that amount from the billionaire). "Where's your boss, so that I can pay him?"

"I don't think you understood." I gave him a sarcastic look. "A thousand dollars each."

I could see him quivering in anger. He was probably cursing us three generations back. He managed to maintain his self-control. He gave a quick nod towards the lobby and said,

"Would you excuse me for a moment? I'll be right back!"

I waited for him to turn around and I smiled meaningfully. Natasha rolled her eyes and laughed sarcastically.

"He won't be back. You want to bet on it?" I suggested.

"There's no point, darling, because I agree with you," Natasha replied.

We lit cigarettes and went to play on the poker machines. We still hadn't sat down again, when the obsequious man returned.

"Everything's arranged girls. Our guest is captivated by you," his eyes eloquently stared at me. "Will you follow me?"

Natasha and I looked at each other. She left the decision to me.

"All right, then, let's see your billionaire!" I smiled condescendingly.

We took our handbags from the bar and followed Mr. Obsequious (that's what I called him). They were waiting for us.

Our man introduced us. The billionaire was a short, fat man of about eighty. He was completely bald with little mousey eyes. In short – repulsive. The other men of his entourage were younger, but no more attractive. In the entire group only Mr. Obsequious was Bulgarian. He was their interpreter. I was fed up with interpreters and had learnt to hold conversations in Greek, Italian and English. So I turned arrogantly to Mr. Obsequious and said,

"Please don't translate. I can have a conversation by myself."

He looked at me with respect and translated my intention to Mr. Andropolus.

The old man was delighted. He bowed to me gallantly, took me by the arm and led me to the lift. We stopped and I quietly turned to Mr. Obsequious.

"Go and pay the boy standing next to the mirror."

One of our "guards" was leaning against the wall.

Andropolus, who was watching every move I made, immediately understood my gesture and even before the translator could tell him, took a thick leather wallet out of his jacket pocket. He removed a thick wad of dollars, counted out two thousand and gave them to Mr. Obsequious.

He went over to Johnnie (I hadn't seen Bruno for two days) and almost imperceptibly gave him the money, saying something to him quietly. He nodded, smiled at us and we left.

Andropolus clung on to me and let the others know that he didn't want to be disturbed. I kept an icy silence. We got into his car driven by his personal chauffeur. It was a Mercedes. The other three and Natasha took a taxi which followed us.

After a short silence Andropolus asked me,

"Do you like to bet?"

I thought of my answer for a little while and answered slowly,

"It depends."

"It depends on what, young lady?" the old man asked.

"On the size of the bet. Did I say that correctly?"

"You speak perfectly. And you look perfect as well," he couldn't resist making the compliment. "And so, what shall the bet be?" he invited me to answer.

"I don't like playing for little amounts!" I replied.

He said nothing and the car drove almost silently towards the Japanese hotel.

How was Natasha getting on with the others, I wondered? The evening was promising to be interesting.

Before going to the Casino, we went for dinner. We took a large table, in the centre of which Mr. Andropolus and I sat. He ordered an abundance of delicacies including French Champagne which flowed like a waterfall. There were all the different types of sea food you could possibly imagine: crab, prawns, black caviar, octopus and all sorts of other Japanese delicacies.

Natasha and I didn't eat very much but drank champagne. When we were well and truly warmed up, we headed for the casino.

"Where would you like to play, my girl" he had asked me during dinner.

"Roulette, of course!"

"Wonderful!"

We were led to our seats and Spiros Andropolus gave me chips to the value of five thousand dollars. I asked him quietly,

"What will you say, if I lose it all?"

"Do I have to say anything?" he smiled.

He shrugged his shoulders and he placed his hand tenderly on my knee. I instinctively trembled. The sense of the touch of the old man's hand was repulsive.

"Rien ne va plus," the croupier declared.

With a decisive gesture I took all the chips and placed them on the number 17. That was my birthday. I turned around and looked at Andropolus provocatively. He smiled at me encouragingly. The roulette wheel spun quickly. When it slowed down and the ball began to bounce up and down, I felt as though my heart was pounding. I wasn't worried about the almost certain loss of the money. It was a like a flea bite for the old man. I was just excited by the thrill of the game.

The ball bounced a couple of more time and fell onto the number 17!!! Just like in a film! I didn't believe that it was possible, but it was a fact. Andropolus applauded when the croupier pushed a huge number of chips towards me. There must have been at least twenty thousand dollars.

"You're incredible, my child!" Spiros said with a deep sigh. "And you know how to play as well!"

"Nonsense!" I interrupted him. "It was pure luck!"

"Have another go."

"With all of them?"

"Of course. It's your money!" he said generously.

I looked at him in disbelief.

"I'm not joking. You won the money honestly and it's yours!"

The cursed old man was tempting me. This money, when added to the rest which I had hidden, would have provided a peaceful life in some quiet place for at least five years. *If I take the risk and continue to play, I might win more. The question is how will I hide it?* I was thinking to myself feverishly when my eyes fell upon Bruno. He was standing behind two men who were arguing about something. I felt an electric shock pulse through my body. "Go to hell, Bruno! And take the mother who bore you as well!" I muttered, putting all my chips of red. I wanted to lose. I wouldn't let the pig take all that money off me. The roulette wheel spun and the ball eventually came to a stop on .... Black! I was sincerely happy. I even laughed. Andropolus looked at me in astonishment.

"Let's go! I'm bored!" I got up.

He followed me. When we left the casino I turned around and looked at Bruno. But I couldn't see him. "I hope the earth swallows you up!" I cursed him with all my soul.

"You know how to lose!" Andropolus praised me and added, "Where would you like to go?"

"Anywhere, but not here!" I added in a spoilt voice.

The driver brought the car up and we got in.

"Where would you like to go?" the old man repeated.

"I want to drive around Sofia at night!" I said.

The driver nodded and we drove off. We drove for more than an hour. I was curled up in a corner of the car looking silently through the window. The Greek billionaire was concerned by my changeable mood but he tactfully maintained his silence.

When I was fed up, I told him I wanted to go home.

We went through the brightly lit lobby of the hotel and took the lift. We went back to his suite. There were two hours left until the morning.

"Have a seat; what would you like to drink?" He fussed around me.

"Gin and tonic, with lots of ice."

He fussed around some more, prepared the drink and gave it to me. He sat down next to me, stretched out his hand and untied the knot on my blouse.

Here it goes, I thought with disgust. *I wonder what he wants to do, he's so old.*

He seemed to be able to read my mind.

"Don't worry, darling. I'm too old for sex. I just want to caress you."

Jesus! That's even more disgusting! I thought.

"Do you want me to take my clothes off?" I asked in a business-like tone.

"I was hoping you would," Spiros Andropolus answered excitedly.

I pulled the end of the shawl and it fell off.

The old man groaned and sat down more comfortably on the divan.

I delayed taking my skirt off and took another sip. My breasts touched the old pig's face. He writhed with pleasure. With a slow gesture I undid one of the safety pins and the heavy silk fell to my feet. I spun around on my feet without taking my eyes off his face. He sat motionless like a stone and his eyes glistened unnaturally.

Jesus! If he kicks the bucket, I'll have to spend a week making statements to the police! I thought in horror.

I began to get dressed again, but he summoned me with a nervous gesture. I went over to him. He made me sit in his lap. I obeyed with a feeling of revulsion. His trembling hands touched every part of my body. His hot panting breath stung my neck. To deaden the feeling of repulsion at least a little bit, I drank my glass of gin and poured another one.

There was silence in the room. I could only hear his panting breathing. I sat there like a stone. It was disgusting and I prayed to God that it would end soon. When he grew tired, Andropolus gave me a tender shove. I was stiff with sitting on top of him, but I rushed into the bathroom, dragging my skirt with my foot. I took a long shower, and when I got out of the bathroom it was light.

He was waiting for me, lying on the divan.

"I have to go now." I impatiently paced the room.

"Yes, yes! Go now! Thank you. You were wonderful!"

I took my bag and said goodbye with a slight nod of the head.

I returned to my room before Natasha. I smoked a cigarette and got into bed. I tossed from side to side for a long time before I fell asleep.

Natasha woke me late in the afternoon.

"Come on, wake up! Someone wants to see you!"

I rubbed my eyes sleepily. Natasha was pulling me with all her strength.

"Don't pull me so hard. You'll pull my shoulder out," I muttered crossly.

"Come on, come on! The billionaire wants you!"

"I couldn't give a damn for his billions! I hope he dies with them!" I sat up in bed and looked for my cigarettes.

"Don't be vulgar, please!" my friend told me off.

"All right, all right! Just don't read morals to me!" I sighed submissively and I stood up. "What does he want from me?"

"He wants you to have a shower, get dressed and go up to his suite."

"Oh... the old man wants to have a nice view again."

Natasha looked at me crossly and said icily,

"You know very well that unfortunately we're not in a Carmelite convent."

"It's a good job I told you about convents!" I answered crossly.

Natasha chased me into the bathroom with a slipper and I squealed. The cold shower refreshed me and I looked on the world through more cheerful eyes.

"Come on, hurry up. You're like a headless chicken!"

The bathroom door shook with fist blows. I quickly wrapped a towel around myself and went out of the bathroom.

"What's going on? What's the emergency?"

"They want you for something very important. Please hurry up! You're beginning to annoy me!"

I became serious and business-like. I wasn't at work so I could dress more casually.

I pulled on a pair of jeans and a jumper. I tied my hair in a pony tail and went to Spiros Andropulos' apartment. I knocked on the door.

"Come in!" I heard his voice.

He was alone inside. He was holding a cup of coffee, dressed in a shirt and trousers. He was a perfectly ordinary grandfather. There was nothing to suggest that he was a billionaire. Only his diamond ring revealed that he had money. And perhaps his air of confidence.

When he saw me, his face brightened with a smile. He stood up and invited me to sit down.

"You wanted to see me about something?" I asked him simply.

He said nothing, and in order to give more weight to his words, he coughed and looked at me calculatingly.

"I imagine, dear child, that you have been informed that I am a rich man. I own some ship building factories and my name is known throughout Greece."

I nodded dignifiedly.

"I have a son who has not lived up to my hopes. He doesn't want to take over my business. He's given himself up to a life of orgies and doesn't even want to get married. His name has been mixed up in drug affairs and he has completely disillusioned me. His poor mother would turn in her grave, if she only knew..."

Andropolus fell silent. He sighed deeply and continued,

"I want to offer you a deal. Come with me to Greece. Marry me. I'm old and sick. I will only live for another two or three years. No more. Perhaps even less. I'll change my will and leave everything to you. All I want of you is to make my last years and days happy. You're ambitious. I can tell these things. You can take charge of everything and I will die calm."

Andropolus sat back and fell silent.

I said nothing too and thought. It was a difficult decision to make. He had just laid millions, no billions, of dollars at my feet. It could all be mine! In returned he wanted me to pose naked in front of a sick, old man and sit on his lap. That wasn't all. Somewhere in the orbit around the golden old man there was a waster of a son who, on top of it all, was a drug addict as well. Oh! He would fight to the last drop of blood for his father's billions, with all the resources available to him! They can all go to hell! Andropolus and his billions!

"No, thank you!" I said quietly and categorically.

"You don't have to hurry with your answer!" he begged me. "Think about it."

"There's nothing to think about!" I snapped. "You can't buy me with all the billions in the world. I don't have a price. I'm priceless!"

I got up to show him that our conversation was at an end.

Andropolus also got up. He sighed deeply and looked at me sadly.

"You're absolutely right. I'm sorry. However, if you change your mind..."

"I won't change my mind," I interrupted him and opened the door.

"Be happy, child..." The voice followed me as I shut the door.

CHAPTER 17

Indecent Proposal With The Taste Of Olives

When I got back to my room, there was a surprise waiting for me. Bruno was lying on my bed and there was no trace of Natasha. I stood dumbstruck at the door.

"Come in! Come in! It's your home!" He invited me in ironically. I closed the door but didn't take a step any further.

"You know, Princess, when I was watching you last night in the Casino, an idea occurred to me."

I said nothing and looked at him without blinking.

"I don't know if I got the wrong idea, but I got the impression that you lost the money on purpose last night. Just after you saw me."

He had realized the truth, the bastard. My blood froze.

"So I said to myself, go and have a chat with the Princess, because her loyalty to you has been a bit doubtful recently."

I had to act immediately, otherwise I risked everything. If they made a careful search of the room, they would find the money and then…. And I didn't want to think about that. I walked slowly towards him and smiled sweetly at him.

"Let me just take this jumper off. It's a bit warm in here."

I casually pulled the jumper over my head.

Bruno looked at me in surprise. He usually forced me to have sex with him. This time I was going to surprise him pleasantly.

"Bruno! Don't talk nonsense. It was the old man's money and he was really stingy. He made me angry, so I lost it on purpose. As you noticed quite correctly. Aren't you feeling hot as well?" I knelt down next to the bed and stroked him softly through his trousers.

This sex maniac was already aroused. I stood up, gave him a meaningful look and unzipped my jeans. They were tight and only opened slightly, just enough for him to see that I wasn't wearing any underwear.

I went up to him again, bent over and despite all the revulsion I experienced for him, I began to kiss him.

After his surprise, he began to give in to me, and because he was very aroused by now, he grabbed me and pulled my jeans down.

He undressed in a flash and in a grating voice he said to me,

"I've always known that you were fantastic! You could seduce the Devil!"

Then he forced me to kiss him on the mouth.

A few hours later I was lying in the bed exhausted. Bruno left happy, happier than ever before, and had completely forgotten the reason for his visit.

However, I noticed that although the sex had lasted much longer than normal, he had been a bit kinder than before. His bestial instincts seemed to have become a little more dignified. I was particularly impressed when he turned to me just before he left and said,

"Princess, you're looking a little tired. Why don't you have a rest tonight? You've deserved a little holiday!"

I looked at him as though he was an alien from outer space. He was an idiot! Had he lost his head over me? I stayed in bed quite happily. Natasha, tactful as ever, didn't ask me anything. She got ready for work, smiled at me and left. I fell blissfully asleep.

Nothing in particular happened over the next few days. I worked well and earned well. The other girls didn't have many clients, but I always found them whenever I wanted. Natasha laughed at me.

"You attract men like a magnet. You must have some secret! Tell me!"

I invented all sorts of nonsense and presented them as tried and trusted recipes. We both laughed our socks off.

To top it all, Bruno began to hang around me more persistently. I noticed, however, that he was waiting for me to seduce him. It seemed that he didn't like forcing his sexual advances on me. After a slight hesitation on my part, I decided to enter the game. *So what?* I thought to myself. *What if I do make him fall in love with me? He is quite an attractive man, that's why I noticed him at the disco in the first place.*

Moreover, he was the boss here. If I were to become his girlfriend, then I would have unlimited power over him and everyone else.

We were at work and there was hardly anyone in the bar.

I popped out to go to the toilet and met Bruno. He was just arriving. I decided to act. I smiled charmingly at him and kissed him softly on the cheek.

He stood there embarrassed, not knowing how to react.

"Bruno," I chirped, "where were you last night? I waited for you all evening!"

"Why?" he asked foolishly.

"Don't you know? I'll give you three guesses."

My hand was stroking his chest.

He looked at me and I imagined him as a piece of soft, shapeless plasticine. I decided to mould him into just the shape I wanted.

"I wanted to make love! You're so good and you're strong! I... I'm worried I might fall in love with you..." I attacked him. "Let's go to the toilet, Bruno!" I panted. "I can't wait and it's too far to go down to the room."

He followed me obediently, captivated.

I attacked him with so much sex and passion that when we finished, he caressed my leg and looked at me with the devotion of a puppy, and I said to myself, "It's all over now! I've got you in my grips!"

While he waited for me to wash and arrange my clothes, his role as a man took over from his role as a businessman. Hesitantly and with slight embarrassment, he said to me,

"Why don't you go to your room? There's not much work tonight, is there?"

I wanted to kiss him. That's what I was waiting for. But not to make my crafty plan so evident, I said,

"There might be some clients later on. I'd better stay for while."

A nervous tic flitted across his face.

"If I say it's all right, you can go. Off you go then."

"Bye bye, honey! Ciao!"

I spun around on my heels and walked towards the lift. I knew he was staring at my back. When I turned around suddenly, I saw him. He was staring so much that his bottom lip was drooping. I was triumphant: he was jealous. He didn't want me sleeping with other men. I went back to the room happy. I was out of the habit of sleeping during the night, but I read a book and fell asleep.

The next morning, I told Natasha everything and she was stunned.

"You're a real devil, darling!" she whispered conspiratorially.

I said to her importantly,

"You don't have to whisper! We're the bosses now!"

We laughed out loud. Then we went to the swimming pool.

My birthday was coming up, so Natasha and I decided to go shopping. I wanted to buy some new clothes, but first we would have a swim. To my enormous surprise, Bruno appeared from somewhere and called to me. I got out of the water and went up to him.

"Hi, Bruno!" I smiled slyly. "How are you?"

The arrogant Bruno had disappeared. In front of me there was an anxious young boy who, if I was not mistaken, blushed while he looked at me in my clinging, wet bathing costume.

"I have to talk to you. Right away!"

I was confused.

"All right! Just wait for me on the terrace. I'll be there in a minute. I'll just go and get dressed."

Bruno turned around and left nervously. While I dressed, I tried to guess what he wanted, but nothing came to me.

I found him on the terrace. The warm sun was pleasing to the eyes and I felt light at heart.

"Would you like a drink?" he asked me attentively.

"A grapefruit juice, please."

When the juice and Bruno's coffee arrived, he took a sip, choked, coughed for a long time, lit a cigarette and finally said,

"Ioana, do you want to live with me?"

I pretended not to understand.

"How do you mean, live with you?" I repeated his question.

"I mean leave the hotel and come and live with me. I'll take care of you. You know I've got a lot of money and you won't want for anything. And what's more, my company's expanding its activities and I'm going to get even richer."

I said nothing. I hadn't expected this outcome. I thought that our relations would remain as they were for now, which was fine by me. But what Bruno was offering me now was serious.

The only positive aspect of it was that I would be leaving the hotel. Everything else, however, scared me.

"Bruno, you've caught me a bit by surprise," I started hesitantly.

"I know that you didn't expect it. Believe me, I didn't expect it either. I don't know how it happened, but I've fallen in love with you. I have never been in love before. It was just technical sex. I've fallen for you, that's it. I've changed. I can prove it to you. I'm a different person now. I'm not who I was."

But I don't love you, darling! I thought to myself. *And that's very important. You've completely ruined my life and now you want me to love you. Well, you'd better think again!*

"I've noticed a change in you. And a change for the better. I also have feelings for you, but it's too early. Let's leave things as they are for the moment and time will tell..."

"No, no!" he interrupted. "I can't stand the thought that you're sleeping with other men, now that..."

"You love me?"

"Yes!!!"

"Who said that I would sleep with other men? I just need a little more time. I have money. I won't work, I'll just live with Natasha. Give me a chance to forget..."

"I know. I behaved like an animal with you. I'm sorry. All right. I agree to that. But not for very long."

"It won't be. I promise." I hesitated a little and said, "Do you want to go upstairs? Natasha's still in the swimming pool."

Bruno looked at me with an expression of gratitude and followed me.

As he left, he made me promise that I wouldn't work anymore. I swore happily that I wouldn't.

I couldn't wait to tell Natasha. That same evening, I openly demonstrated my relationship with Bruno. His colleagues grinned meaningfully, while my "colleagues" went yellow and then green with anger. Natasha, of course, was happy, but a little scared.

"What will happen, when he stops loving you?" she asked me with an air of concern.

"By that time you and I will be a long way away from here," I said with conviction.

Natasha looked at me doubtfully and shrugged her shoulders.

It was the beginning of wonderful days for me. I couldn't recognize Bruno. He changed with every day... He began to resemble the soft plasticine which I wanted to turn him into.

I played along with him very carefully, trying to convince him that I was falling irresistibly in love with him. He passionately responded to my "feelings," which was a great cause of amusement for me. It was a very interesting but dangerous game. If he suspected anything, then that would be the end of me. I tried to surprise him every time we had sex. The poor man! He really had swallowed the bait. I was having fun with him, but it had never occurred to me that I might fall in love with him. I despised him. And I was planning to destroy him. I had learnt a lot about his work. Natasha was right. They were everywhere. It was terrifying and worrying. But at least I wasn't threatened by anything. Quite the contrary. I had been treated with such attention and care as I could never have imagined. I have to admit that it was not unpleasant. My birthday came and I spent all day undergoing cosmetic procedures – sauna, swimming, hairdresser and cosmetician. Bruno arrived at 7.00 and I was ready. He asked me to wear the same outfit I had worn to the casino. He had admitted that I had aroused him for the first time that night. My hair was raised to accentuate my long elegant neck. Bruno arrived with a bouquet of fiery red roses and a small package.

"Happy birthday, Ioana!" He greeted me ceremoniously and gave me the roses and the package.

"Thank you, darling!" I replied in a spoilt drawl. "What beautiful roses! And what can this be?"

"Well, open it then! Don't be so lazy!" he said with feigned irritation.

I pretended to scold him with my finger and pulled the ribbon. There were two little boxes inside. One was long and narrow. The other was small and square. I held my breath and opened the long box. Thousands of glittering sparks shone from inside the box.

"God! What is this?" I was really surprised.

Inside the little box, lying on a bed of black velvet, there was a gold necklace encrusted with small diamonds. Each one of them reflected the light of the lamps and I had the feeling that sparks were flying through the room. It was incredibly beautiful. Bruno was laughing.

"Do you like it? Well, take it out then! You're such a coward!"

I didn't pay him any attention. I was staring at the necklace in enchantment.

Then he took the box out of my hands, removed the necklace from it and put it around my neck. He fastened the clasp from behind and kissed me tenderly.

"Thank you, Bruno! It's wonderful!" I said to him sincerely.

"I love you! And look at the other one!" he presented the smaller box to me.

I opened it. Earrings. It was a set of two small diamonds, like two tears about to drop from my ears.

"Bruno! You're impossible!" This was beyond my wildest dreams.

"Do you like them? Put them on!"

"I can't. My hands are shaking with excitement. They must have been so expensive, Bruno!"

I really was touched. But I couldn't love him. Not for all the diamonds in the world. He carefully attached them to my ears.

"Ioana, just look how beautiful you are!"

"Do you like me?" I smiled at him happily.

"So much that I want to marry you!"

I didn't think I had heard him correctly. I stopped dead in my tracks.

"What did you say?"

Bruno was kneeling at my feet, repeating passionately,

"Ioana, my love, please marry me!"

I realized that I had gone too far. Too far. There was no way back now. What could I do? Could I say no? My heart wouldn't let me. Should I say yes? I would hate myself to the end of my days. What then?

I knelt down in front of him. I hugged him and kissed him tenderly.

"Bruno, darling. I'm too excited at the moment. I can't think at the moment, and I need to. It's a very serious step getting married. If we get married, you have to know that it'll mean the end of many things.

"Until death do us part," you know. Are we ready for that? What about my age? And the profession I used to have until recently? One day you might hate me for it... although..." I hesitated awkwardly.

"Although it was me who forced you into it?" he helped me out. "Ioana, I've changed. Before I fell in love with you, I was an animal, a real swine. I thought that love was pure idiocy, spoilt nonsense. Now I know that it's not true. I've become a man now. And my conscience pains me day and night when I think what I did to you, and not just to you. I have to make up for it somehow. I've even started hating my work. All of this filth. I want to get out of it all. We'll get married and we'll go to France. I've had an offer of work there as a coach to a wrestling team. You'll look after our children and I'll go to work. And everything will be all right..."

I listened to him and couldn't believe my ears.

Was this really Bruno? What had I done to him? And what was I going to do now? I had got myself into another mess, and that was a fact!

"Bruno! Please, don't talk! Give me some more time."

"That will be wasted time! You don't understand! I'm in a hurry!" He looked at me with an expression of devastation on his face.

"I don't want to have to understand anything more today. It's been too much for me."

"All right then," he conceded. "We'll talk about it tomorrow. Is that all right? But no later."

I nodded with a heavy heart. I had won a postponement of 24 hours.

The evening was wonderful. I was the centre of the universe. Everything revolved around me and everyone was captivated by me. Bruno was a little depressed but very much in love.

The evening ended in the casino. I asked for it. We played a little, lost and we left.

I decided to give him a pleasant surprise.

"Bruno, would you like to go to your flat? I haven't been there for ages."

He frowned (probably at the recollection of my first visit) and said,

"Won't you find it a little unpleasant?"

"No, otherwise I wouldn't have suggested it."

"Let's go then."

Bruno helped me out of the car. He was silent and engrossed in his own thoughts.

"Do you live alone?" I asked him.

"No, I've got a whole harem in the other room," he joked gloomily.

"Will you introduce me to them?" I joked back haughtily.

He carefully picked me up like a fragile object and carried me into his room.

"Don't switch the light on," I whispered lovingly and tickled his ear with my tongue.

When I took my clothes off in the darkness of the room and my naked body glinted for a moment in the moonlight, Bruno groaned in pain.

"Ioana, where was my mind when I saw you for the first time?"

"Forget about that!" I said to him nobly and I bent over him.

His hungry lips touched my cold hands. Then I realized that his face was wet. God, he was crying!

Kissing my hands silently, he was asking forgiveness from me!

I HAD WON AGAIN!

CHAPTER 18

Sex, Money, And Diamonds

I slept until lunchtime. Bruno wasn't there when I got up. I looked for a cigarette. The cigarettes were gone as well. So Bruno must have gone out.

I jumped up quickly and went into the bathroom. I was still there when the door opened and Bruno showed his head.

"Hello, darling. How did you sleep?" I called out cheerfully from the shower.

"Not very well. What about you?"

"Great!"

"I've bought something to eat. Are you coming?"

"I'm as hungry as a wolf. What are we going to eat?"

"Surprise!"

I ran naked into the kitchen.

Pancakes with chocolate and ice cream.

"Bruno, you're wonderful!" I cried out in delight and gobbled one.

"No. I'm just in love," he responded pensively.

I grabbed one of his shirts and put it over my naked body.

I was eating pancakes, chattering happily. I looked at Bruno and stopped.

"What's wrong Bruno? Why aren't you eating? You look worried."

He stared pacing the kitchen nervously.

"Ioana, I've got problems. I can't tell you any more than that. It's better you don't know." (That was a familiar phrase. Words like that were always followed by something unpleasant). "You'll have to go back to the hotel now. I'll get a taxi for you. I've got some work to do.

I'll call you this evening. And no more clients, like we agreed to, all right?"

I looked at him suspiciously.

"Bruno, I won't ask you what the problem is. But if there is anything I can do to help you..."

He looked into my eyes and I could see the pain in them.

"You promise, don't you?"

"Yes! I already told you! No more!"

"I'll get you a taxi. It's time to go."

While we waited for the telephone to ring, Bruno disappeared and came back a moment later with a small envelope.

"Ioana, darling, take this money. There's 5000 German marks in here. Hold on to them and spend them if you need to."

This was a familiar scenario as well. God, there was nothing new under the sun. It looked like he was leaving me as well.

"Bruno, what's going on? This looks too much like a parting to me."

"Please," he groaned, "just not that..."

"Will you at least tell me something?"

"No," the answer was clear and categorical.

The telephone was ringing insistently. The taxi was waiting in the street below. I pulled on a pair of his jeans, which were too big for me. I put my clothes in a bag and looked at him.

His face was grey. He pulled me towards him and kissed my face passionately and anxiously.

"I'll call you tonight. At all costs!"

Who knows? I very much doubt it, I thought to myself.

"I'll be waiting!" I waved at him and went down the stairs.

CHAPTER 19

Hell's Door Is Opening Slightly

It was quiet in the hotel. Natasha was cleaning the room.

"Hello, darling!" I greeted her with very much enthusiasm.

She was as sensitive as a barometer.

"What's happened?" she shot her question at me instead of a greeting.

"I don't know. If it hasn't happened yet, it will happen any moment now."

"Well, I hope it won't be too bad," she sighed. "Oh, I'm so tired. This cleaning is really tiring."

I lay on the bed and lit a cigarette. I was nervous and expected something to happen, but didn't know what.

To try and calm my nerves, I decided to go for a swim.

"Natasha, do you want to go for a swim?"

Natasha shook her head negatively.

"I want to have a rest. I'll have a little sleep, but you go. Off you go, you need it, just look at your backside!"

I looked at her in horror.

"Do you really think I've put on weight?"

Natasha was laughing like a drain.

"Tell me! You're like the inquisition!"

"No, of course not, I was joking!"

I stood with my back to the mirror. I couldn't see anything. It all seemed to be in the right place.

Reassured, I took my robe and swimming costume, stuck my tongue out at Natasha and left the room. From the corridor I could still hear the laughter of my loyal friend.

The swimming pool was full of people. I didn't like it when it was so busy. But the swimming pool was for everyone after all. I got changed quickly and jumped with a splash into the water. It was clean and pleasantly cool. I turned onto my back and relaxed. I was trying not to think about anything. Suddenly, I felt a powerful blow to my head. As a result of the surprise and pain, I began to sink. I was really scared. I began to wave my arms and legs, trying to reach the surface. I didn't have to struggle for very long. Two attentive masculine arms grabbed me and with two powerful strokes of his legs he brought me to the surface.

I gasped for breath and looked around. The frightened face of the same man was trying to smile at me with the guilty expression.

"I am really, very, very sorry," he said in Italian.

I nodded my head to show that I accepted his apology, and paddled towards the edge of the pool. I climbed up the steps and looked for my towel. My head was hurting from the powerful blow. It clearly wasn't a good day for me.

I was startled by a soft tap on the shoulder. I turned around. My Italian rescuer who had sunk me like a torpedo a moment ago was now standing in front of me.

"I am very sorry, miss, are you all right now? Can I do anything for you?"

I said nothing and looked at him crossly. He was tall, with an attractive face, big stomach and an open, honest face. He hesitated and smiling politely, he asked me,

"Do you speak Italian?"

"Yes," I answered hesitantly.

"In that case, please let me make up for my mistake."

I thought about Bruno. If he was to see me with this kind gentleman, he wouldn't be very happy. On the other hand, it was too early for Bruno. He had told me to wait for him this evening.

I nodded my head and smiled shyly.

"You're not entirely to blame."

"No, no," the Italian man protested. "I don't agree with you. Would you like to have a drink and argue about the question of blame?"

While I dressed, my thoughts turned to Bruno. Although I didn't love him, my heart felt heavy with uncertainty. What was he so worried about? Or rather who was he so worried about?

I shook my head. The kind Italian and his unsuccessful "assassination" attempt upon my person came back into my mind. Bruno and his problems would wait for a while.

I looked around. The Italian was obediently standing by the door. I waved at him and walked towards him. When he saw me, his face lit up with a smile.

"Let me introduce myself," his eyes laughed happily. "My name is Sergio Severini. I live in Milan, Italy."

"Pleased to meet you," I smiled at him charmingly. "My name is Ioana, and I'm from Sofia."

"Your city is wonderful. As are you!" He bowed slightly to me. "Where would you like to go?"

"Let's go up to the terrace bar. I don't have a lot of time."

"Oh, I understand," he nodded. "All right. Let's go to the terrace then. How do we get there?"

I smiled. He was easy and pleasant to talk to.

"I'll take you there with pleasure."

"The pleasure will be all mine." He stood back and let me pass. "You lead me."

The terrace was brightly decorated with multi-coloured umbrellas. The sun's rays shone through their bright awning, reminding me of a village fair. We sat down at a small table with two chairs.

"What would you like?" Sergio Severini asked me with a smile when the waiter came.

"Just a juice, thank you."

"Then I shall have the same. Would you ask the waiter for two juices? Your language is quite difficult."

I gave the order and smiled contentedly. It had been a good idea to buy the textbooks and phrase books. I didn't have a problem learning foreign languages. I spoke them quite well and the nature of my work required it. My stomach turned over. Work... Bruno... problems.

I ordered myself to calm down.

"Do you know..." I turned to Sergio and said politely, "I learned your language in only a few months. I really like it."

When I said this the Italian beamed a smile.

"And I love the songs of Toto Cotunio, Eroz Ramazotti and Adriano Celentano."

"You surprise me, young lady. I am very pleased to hear that such a young lady as you has found the time to learn my native language."

I don't know why but I suddenly spurted out,

"I have always dreamed of seeing Rome. As they say, 'See Rome and die...'"

Sergio Severini laughed loudly and said as he gasped to take breaths,

"Oh, Italy is much more than Rome. It's Venice, Naples, Florence, Pisa and Milan."

"Oh yes, and the leaning tower of Pisa. I've read about that. Italy must be a wonderful country."

"Yes. I really recommend that you see it."

I rolled my eyes sadly and replied in a dreamy voice,

"I don't think I ever will."

"You never know, young lady," Sergio Severini reassured me philosophically. "Anything might happen."

"You are so right!"

My thoughts turned to Bruno. What was happening to him? I became anxious and began to fidget. I shouldn't stay here any longer. I had to go. Bruno might come back earlier. "Anything might happen!"

"I have to go. I have had a wonderful time, thank you!" I gathered my things and stood up.

"Wait for a moment. You haven't told me the most important thing," he looked at me anxiously.

"And what is that?" I frowned.

"When will I see you again?"

Oho! What's going on here? I thought. It sounds like a pick-up.

I decided to rebut the attack.

"As you said yourself, 'anything might happen,' including bumping into each other again."

I got up to leave, but he stood in my way.

"Please, Ioana. I still haven't had the chance to apologise properly. Don't leave things like this. Please!"

I looked at him from head to toe and back again. I hesitated.

"All right, since you insist. Tomorrow morning at 10.00 at the swimming pool."

He was disappointed but concealed it. The poor man probably was thinking of dinner.

"You're an angel and I'll be waiting for you."

"Ciao!" I said goodbye and hurried to disappear. I didn't want him to see that I lived in the hotel.

Natasha was still asleep and I decided to do the same.

I lay down, and hadn't fallen asleep when there was a persistent knocking on the door.

"Who can that be?" I wondered. When I opened the door I found myself standing in front of one of Bruno's boys. A nervous knot appeared in my stomach.

"Hi, what's up?" he asked as he panted. "I want to come in."

"Come in then." I stood aside for him to pass. "Where's Bruno?"

He fidgeted nervously.

"Hold on a moment. I've got a job to do, then we'll talk. Have you got somewhere to put these things, somewhere safe?"

I looked and saw he was carrying a sports bag.

"What's inside?" I asked not very politely.

"A little ironware and some powdered sugar."

I took the bag and opened it. Guns! Different types and calibres. What else was there? It wasn't powered sugar, of course! I looked at him furiously.

"Is that drugs?"

"I don't know." He shrugged his shoulders arrogantly.

"And you want us to keep all that here?"

"You're going to have to."

"Does Bruno know about this?"

He shook his head silently.

"Where is Bruno?" The interrogation was beginning to make me angry.

"He's not around. We're waiting for him to call."

"Where from?" I almost screamed.

"I don't know anything," he replied laconically.

I thought quickly. Things were getting pretty serious. The police were mixed up in this now. They were clearly expecting a search and he had brought the guns and that other stuff here. But what if they came to our room? So what? We weren't registered here. I don't know how but Bruno had managed to arrange it. He had connections with the hotel managers. He might even be paying them.

So we weren't officially residents in this room, and none of the stuff in the room was officially ours either.

"All right, we'll take it," I informed him.

Only then did I look over at Natasha. She was lying in her bed wrapped up to her neck in her bedclothes, staring with wide-open eyes.

The boy was getting ready to leave.

"Hold on a second. You said we were going to talk. Come on then, out with it!"

He looked at his hands and said,

"Some of our boys messed up an operation with lots of money and other things. The cops got wind of it and searched our office. Some of them were arrested. The bad thing is that they've got evidence against them."

"Who's been arrested? Bruno?"

"I don't know. He hasn't called from anywhere yet. He wasn't arrested with the first bunch. He's just disappeared."

"Tell me as soon as you find out. I'll be here. You know that I'm not working now, don't you?"

He nodded silently and left. I stood in the middle of the room thinking. Where could Bruno be? God, after everything I had been through, I was worried about him! What was the name for that? Lack of character? Or perhaps a kind heart? I didn't know. Where could I hide all this stuff? It wasn't money. Why had I agreed?

For Bruno's sake, of course. If the cops got hold of it, and him as well, it would be serious evidence.

"Natasha, darling, give me an idea!" I begged her.

She thought hard.

"But it's very big..."

"Yes, that's obvious...," I said and gave her an acidic smile.

"I don't know. I'm scared."

"And I'm just a little bit scared as well." I added, "The less we show it, the less suspicious we'll look."

Natasha looked at me questioningly.

"Have you got any dirty clothes? Underwear? Towels?"

She laughed in embarrassment.

"I can find some."

"I can find some as well. We'll fill the bag with dirty underwear, clothes and everything else we don't need. Nice and smelly. That'll be best. And we'll leave it in the wardrobe under the clothes hangers. If the cops come, all they'll see is dirty pants..."

"Ha, ha, ha," Natasha laughed out loud.

So that's what we did. It was quite a good idea. Of course, in a more careful search it would be discovered. That didn't worry me too much. I loved the risk!

I was more concerned about Bruno. I couldn't get yesterday's scene out of my head, here in this room.

He was on the verge of giving it all up. He wanted to turn over a new page and get an honest job. And now what? Handcuffs! And farewell to France! Destiny had a finger in all this! Perhaps everything has a price sooner or later. I had a bitter taste in my mouth.

"Natasha, darling, what's happened to the good manners you used to have? In the good old days when I woke up I would find chocolate croissants, Coca Cola and roses next to my head! And now, nothing of the sort!"

She was writhing in giggles.

"Don't laugh! I'm dying of hunger. I've got a bitter taste in my mouth, and you're laughing!"

"All right! All right! We'll go and have something to eat!" she said hurriedly.

"Where?"

"In the restaurant, of course!"

I pictured a huge tomato salad, fried bon-fillet and thousands of other delicacies. I was feeling ill with hunger.

"Come on then! I'm dying of hunger!" I shouted and rushed to get dressed.

Half an hour later we were in the restaurant. The waiter, who was a good friend of ours, brought us a whole trolley to choose from.

"Ladies," he said with a tone of concern in his voice, "you'll explode if you eat all that!"

"Don't worry about us, friend!" I replied quickly. "Don't forget to bring us another Coca Cola. It helps to wash it down!"

In the middle of our feast, as I was cheerfully eating, I sensed that I was being watched. I turned around and saw my Italian friend from the swimming pool sitting at the next table watching me with a smile on his face.

My stomach turned. I took a large gulp of Coca Cola, to calm it and nodded towards hm. In response he raised his glass to us and took a sip. He was with another man and they were observing us openly and persistently.

Natasha noticed this and whispered,

"Ioana, looks like we've got clients!"

"You're probably right," I muttered.

I finished off my dinner quickly. We paid and were just about to leave when they came over to our table.

"Good evening, Ioana!" my friend greeted me. "I'm happy to meet you unexpectedly."

It was my turn to say something.

"Good evening!"

"I hope I won't be too intrusive if I present my friend and colleague?"

His colleague kissed our hands in turn.

"Mario Bertoldi."

I introduced Natasha.

What now? It was obvious that they were going to the bar from here. What were we going to do?

"Would you care for a drink with us in the bar?"

I knew it.

"I'm sorry but we're in a hurry," I replied hastily, nodded to say goodbye and dragged Natasha after me.

We left the two of them staring at us in disbelief.

"What did you do that for, Ioana?" Natasha asked, me out of breath, when we had reached the lift. "They both look very nice."

"Yes, they're very nice. But what did you expect? To show ourselves up in the bar when Bruno arrives?"

"Bruno's not going to come back," she said quietly.

I looked at her in shock.

"How do you know?"

"I feel it."

"I hope you're wrong!" I sighed deeply.

Natasha looked at me in amazement. She raised her eyebrows almost to the level of her hairline, but said nothing.

We went back to the room without talking. It was past seven o'clock.

"Ioana, I have to go."

"You're not going anywhere," I ordered her.

"What do you mean?"

"You can't go to the bar. The Italians will be there. They'll realize immediately."

"But who cares?" Natasha said crossly.

"I don't know. I just don't want them to know that we're prostitutes." I lit a cigarette angrily.

"I just can't understand you today. They might be staying here for a week or two. Does that mean I have to take a vacation for the whole time?"

"Yes!" I shouted back.

"But what about the boys? Won't they..." Natasha made a gesture of a knife across her throat.

"Leave that to me!"

"Then I give up. I just don't want to argue with you. I'm going to bed to read."

"So will I."

When we were in bed, my head was filled with thoughts spinning around like a hurricane. I couldn't read. Not a single line entered my head. I was nervous because I expected one of the boys to turn up at any moment with news of Bruno. But I was certain, like Natasha, that he wouldn't be coming back. I waited for a long time and finally fell asleep without any news.

I woke up early in the morning. The day promised to be wonderful but I was feeling depressed.

I took a shower, dressed and paced around the room nervously. Natasha was sleeping like a baby with her hands above her head curled into fists. I smiled as I looked at her. She looked so innocent as she slept, if you didn't know her profession. To fill the time, I took out one of my Italian textbooks. I wanted to revise a few things. I wanted to improve it for when I met Sergio Severini again...

A little before 10.00 there was a knock on the door. I ran to open it. Two of the boys were waiting outside. They came into the room, and I closed the door quickly.

"What's up?" I was impatient to find out.

"They've got Bruno," one of them reported and looked at me with respect. (They all knew about my special relationship with Bruno).

I felt as if I was going to be sick, but managed heroically to stifle the sensation.

"When?"

"Yesterday afternoon."

"Where?"

"Anything else?"

"He's in police custody now. He managed to smuggle out a note for you (my legs felt wobbly) and instructions for us."

I couldn't control myself any more. I ran into the bathroom and barely managed to slam the door before I threw up. I felt better immediately. I washed and went back into the room. There was an uneasy silence in the room.

"That's about it. We're leaving now." They shifted their weight from foot to foot.

"What about the note?" I shouted.

One of them slapped his forehead.

"Oh yes! The note!"

He took a crumpled piece of paper out of his pocket and gave it to me.

"Come on, we'd better be going."

I unfolded the note impatiently. The note was written in small, surprisingly neat handwriting.

"My darling Princess. Things have taken a turn for the worse, but I sincerely believe that everything will work out fine. I have influential friends who will get me out of here. I just want you to know that I love you very much and that the plans I had for you and me will come true. Even if I have to go through hell! I hope you are thinking about me. I hug you warmly and kiss you. Bruno.

PS. Remember you promised me something."

The note ended with this.

I stood staring at a single point. How could everything be so messed up? Why had I started this game? I didn't love him. I hated him and now I was feeling sorry for him. But he had changed. He really had changed. And that's why I wasn't so indifferent towards him now. That was why I was trembling, vomiting and crying. Yes, I was crying! Hot tears were flowing from my eyes. For Bruno? I couldn't believe it!

"Ioana, calm down. Come and sit down." Natasha pulled me down gently. "Don't cry!"

"I can't stop!"

"But why? Do you love him?"

"I don't know," I sobbed. "I changed him. I turned him from an animal into a human."

Natasha smiled slightly.

"Don't you believe me?" I replied crossly.

"I do believe you. I really do!"

"He wasn't capable of feelings, but I taught him how to love. I was playing a game with him. What now?"

"What now?" she repeated.

"He has to learn the cruel truth now."

"And what is it?"

"That I never loved him and I can't love him. I feel sorry for what I am about to do to him."

"What are you going to do to him?"

"I've been waiting for this moment for a long time and now it's come. This afternoon, you and I are leaving this hotel. Forever!"

"What did you say?" Natasha stared at me with a stunned expression.

"You heard me very well! Now's the moment. Bruno's been arrested and everyone else is scared. The cops are on their heels, and it's either now or never."

"I'm frightened." She looked at me indecisively. "Won't they catch us?"

"They won't."

I was suddenly in a hurry.

"Where's my swimming costume? And my towel?"

Natasha looked at me in disbelief.

"You're going for a swim? Now?"

"Why not? Wait! Come with me! Quickly!"

"Why are we in such a hurry?" she rushed.

"You'll see," I said enigmatically and I slammed the door decisively.

It was past 10.30 but Sergio Severini was still waiting for us. As I imagined, his friend Mario Bertoldi was there as well.

As soon as they saw us, they jumped up and waved their hands.

We rushed up to them with the grace of gazelles.

"Ciao!" I greeted them. Natasha only nodded.

Sergio covered his eyes with his hands and sighed.

"What's up with him?" I asked Mario.

"He's gone blind!" He looked at us expressively.

"Aha!" I understood and laughed. I translated for Natasha and she giggled.

"Come on, let's get into the water!" I called out and elegantly leapt from the board into the water. Everyone else watched me and laughed. We swam for a while and chased each other in the water. There weren't many people in the water and it was great. When I grew tired, I gave a sign that I was leaving the game and got out of the pool.

Sergio and the others followed.

"Girls, would you like something to drink?" He turned to me.

"Yes, and we're hungry as well."

"That's great. Then we'll go to the restaurant to have lunch."

"We'll go and get dressed first and then we'll come down."

Sergio looked at me sadly.

"But why? You're so pretty like that!"

I grinned meaningfully. My wet swimming costume emphasized everything which could not be seen.

"See you soon!" We said goodbye and left them.

The Italians remained behind staring at our backs.

"You crafty little thing!" Natasha shouted when we got to the room. "You're so clever!"

"Wait, it's too early to say yet. Let's get dressed. I really am hungry."

Half an hour later we were ready.

When we arrived they were already waiting for us. We sat down with them and called for the waiter. We ordered huge amounts of food and Sergio smiled as he watched us.

"I don't know where you get such huge appetites from, and you're so...." He couldn't quite find the word.

"... perfect," I helped him.

He laughed out loud.

"Exactly!" And he added, "You're not short of self-confidence! But that's not a bad thing."

Mario joined in the conversation.

"I wonder what the ladies would like, if they came to Italy and had to encounter our culinary temptations every day?"

"Tell us about them," I begged him, translating to Natasha at the same time.

"Our national cuisine includes a lot of pasta products."

"Yes, we know. We also love pizzas and spaghetti," I said.

"That's just a small part of the huge variety which we have. But it has to be seen to be believed. And tasted. It's too hard to describe. Ravioli, tortellini and many other things."

At that moment the trolley arrived and we forgot all about Italy.

During lunch I noticed that Sergio, instead of eating, was staring at me and smiling expressively. He grinned at me.

"What are you planning to do this afternoon?" he asked me, when I finished eating.

I thought. We had to do something very important and dangerous. We were going to leave the hotel.

"We're leaving," I spurted out.

"Where are you going?" Sergio Severini looked at me in surprise. "I thought you said you were from Sofia?"

"Yes, we are. But we're going to Borovets." I don't know where that came from.

"Oh, yes. Borovets. I've been there. It's very nice," Mario intervened enthusiastically. He turned to Sergio.

"It's your first time in Bulgaria. Why don't we go as well? You will be very pleasantly surprised. What do you think about that, ladies? Shall we come with you?"

What had we got ourselves into now? I quickly translated for Natasha. She rolled her eyes to the ceiling, which meant, *'Sort it out yourself. I'm having nothing to do with it!'*

I hesitated, and as always decided to take the risk.

"All right! We'll leave at 15.00."

I had calculated that this was the time when most of the other girls were either asleep or in the town. And the boys came in the evening.

"Sergio, can I ask you for a favour?"

"Of course!" He was ready to do anything for me.

"Would you come in an hour's time and get our luggage? We're in room 914."

"That's the least we can do for you. Mario's got a rented car from the airport, so we've got transport. We'll sort things out right away and as soon as we get our luggage, I'll come for you."

I smiled contentedly. Things were working out fine.

"So, we'll leave you for now. I have to get things together. We'll be waiting for you!" I smiled at them radiantly and kicked Natasha. We stood up and left the Italians to enjoy their good fortune.

"What's happening now?" Natasha asked me excitedly on the way back to the room.

"Well, if you hadn't been too lazy to learn Italian, you wouldn't be asking me now," I admonished her and Natasha slapped my bottom. "We're going to Borovets!"

"I've never been there. Where is it?"

"You'll find out. It's one of the best mountain resorts."

"Are there any snakes there?" Natasha asked in horror.

"It's full of polar bears!" I joked and hurried to pack my bags.

We had a lot of clothes and couldn't pack them all. So we restricted ourselves to the most necessary.

"Ioana, it's a real pity that we have to leave all this stuff!" Natasha was almost crying.

"And I feel sorry for it as well, darling. We spent so much money on those clothes, but there's nothing we can do about it. Come on, get a move on. Let's count our money. And where are the jewels?"

Natasha gathered her money from countless hiding places. I had trained her well. I gathered mine as well.

"Check that the door is locked," I said to her in a scared voice.

"Yes, it's locked. I locked it as soon as we came in," she reassured me.

We put all the money together and counted it. We had 19000 dollars and about the same amount in levs. Then there were the four thousand German marks Bruno had given me.

"Darling, we're rich. I had no idea we'd got so much money."

"What about the jewels?" Natasha reminded me.

"Yes, there's the jewels as well!"

"Where are we going to put it all?"

"I'll carry the money and jewels in my bag," I said.

"All right, but be careful. Jesus, I'm scared!"

"Pull yourself together!" I said to her sharply. "We'll be fine!"

Half an hour later, we were ready.

"Ioana, what about this?" Natasha was holding the bag with the guns and drugs.

"Oh! I don't know what to do with that," I exclaimed. "Listen, they won't notice we're gone until tomorrow at the earliest. When they come looking for us, they'll search the room and they'll take it. I don't care what happens to it."

"What about Bruno?"

"What Bruno? That's all over!" I sighed. "First it was me who suffered, now it's his turn! But I'm still sorry for him."

We said nothing after that. I lit a cigarette. I tried to put things into perspective and simplify everything. But just externally. Internally I was torn apart by contradictions. He would turn every stone to find me and when he did... I didn't want to think about it! Natasha was also lost in her own thoughts. I looked at her tenderly. She had also suffered. But that was history now. We now had a future... What future? Time would tell. The minutes passed. We both examined our lives over the past few months. In my thoughts I bade farewell to the profession which had been forced upon me in such a cruel way and which had turned us into real warriors. We had learnt to fight with all possible means, in order to protect ourselves and achieve what we wanted.

A cheerful knocking on the door aroused us from our thoughts.

Sergio was standing at the door, smiling kindly, and behind him I could see Mario.

"Are you ready, ladies?"

"Yes!" I answered in a business-like manner and began quickly to hand them our bags. They took two each and headed for the lift. I was dying of terror at the thought that someone might see us...

"We'll be waiting for you downstairs," Mario shouted out.

"Shhhh!" I hissed and shut the door quickly. "Those fools will wake the dead!" I hissed.

"Calm down, darling! No one heard anything!"

"I hope so," I said through my teeth. I looked around. "Have they taken all our luggage?"

"Yes, just our bags left."

I looked through the window. I could see them putting the luggage into a white car. I couldn't see what make it was from above, but it was big.

"Natasha, put your sunglasses on. It's not much of a disguise, but..."

"All right. Let's go!"

Natasha was first at the door.

I crossed myself three times (something I had never done until then) and we crept out of the room like thieves.

In the lift my heart was beating like the church bells of St. Alexander Nevski. The lobby was half-empty, apart from the two Japanese men standing in front of the lift. God, I would have preferred a group of noisy Greeks. We crept out through the front door. The concierge was dozing lazily in the heat and didn't pay us any attention.

We reached the car. It was a Volvo.

"There you are!" said Sergio happily. "Who's going to sit in the front?"

"You!" I said quickly and pushed Natasha into the back seat. I sat next to her, slammed the door and hid my face with my hair. It all happened in the space of seconds. The two Italians were astonished.

"Are we going?" I shouted impatiently and nervously.

"Yes, yes!' They fussed around. Mario sat in the driver's seat and Sergio next to him.

"We're leaving!"

The car drove off and a sigh of relief came from my chest. I looked at Natasha. She was as white as a sheet. There wasn't a drop of blood in her face. I felt Mario looking closely at us in the mirror. We were all silent. I needed time to calm down. Darling Natasha was half-dead and half-alive.

The car sped confidently along the sun-filled streets of Sofia.

"Do you know the way?" I was the first to speak.

"I've been coming to Bulgaria for a few years and I've been to Borovets a few times," Mario Bertoldi boasted, and turned on some music.

I lit a cigarette and could feel a calm overcome me. My plan had worked. I could feel a tiny hand pressing mine. I raised my head to look at Natasha. She was smiling timidly and I could see gratitude in her eyes.

CHAPTER 20

The Glow Of My Lucky Star

We rented a Finnish lodge in Borovets. We chose it because it was independent and we wouldn't have to bump into people in lifts and lobbies, bars and restaurants. It had a cooker and a fridge, everything we needed.

Natasha and I took the room on the second floor, and the Italians took the room on the ground floor.

We told them we were tired and went up to our room.

I really didn't feel very well. I had a terrible headache and I wanted to get straight into bed. Natasha couldn't take any more either. I threw myself into the bed and immediately fell asleep.

I was woken by an insistent knocking on the door. I opened my eyes. To begin with, I had no idea where I was. I looked at Natasha. She was lying next to me like a dead body. I touched her because she looked very red. She had a high temperature. The knocking on the door continued.

"One moment!" I shouted sleepily and covered Natasha with a blanket.

I got up and stumbled towards the door. I opened it to see Sergio standing there.

"We thought that you might wake up hungry. I sent Mario out shopping and I stayed on duty in the kitchen. Would you like something to drink?"

"I want a bowl of water with ice. Natasha's got a temperature."

"Mamma mia!" sighed Sergio with a concerned tone. "Is she very poorly?"

"I don't know yet. Bring me some water and ice," I instructed him. "And if there's any tea?"

He turned around obediently to fulfil my orders.

I went back into the room; Natasha was a red as a tomato.

"How are you, darling?" I called to her.

I had to wake her up. I remembered that my mother wouldn't let me sleep when I had a high temperature.

She moved and groaned.

"What's wrong?"

"Oh, my head's aching and my throat and my whole body," she complained unhappily.

"Come on, come on! Pull yourself together! We'll get you better. You've got the flu."

"What do you mean? Flu in the middle of the summer?"

"Silly, haven't you heard of summer flu?"

There was a knock on the door.

"Come in," I said.

The door opened and Sergio entered with a pan in his hand. It was full of ice cubes. He had a handkerchief over his hand.

"Here I am. I've got everything you wanted. Do you want to give her some of our medicines?"

He was being very helpful and familiar. Misfortune brings people together.

"What have you got? Something combined against headache, temperature and flu symptoms?"

"Yes, I've got just that."

He rushed down the stairs and I wet the handkerchief, wrung it out and placed it on Natasha's burning forehead.

She fidgeted uneasily.

"Keep still, darling. I'll give you some medicine now."

Sergio rushed in with a bag full of medicines.

"Hey, that's a lot of stuff you've got there! Which one of you two needs so much medicine?"

He smiled triumphantly.

"It's not me. It's Mario. He always brings everything he might ever need."

He rummaged in the bag and gave me some tablets.

"Give two of these to Natasha. I'll go and see if Mario's back."

"Come on, darling! Lift your head up to take these tablets." I raised her head carefully. She swallowed them with difficulty and fell back on to the bed.

I continued to swab her head with cold compresses.

I heard Mario come back. They were talking in muffled voices. Then there was a soft knock on the door.

"Come in!"

Mario entered.

"How's Natasha?"

"Just the same."

"Shouldn't we get a doctor?"

"No, no! She'll be all right," I said categorically.

I didn't want any strangers here. He paced around the room indecisively.

"I can stay here and take over from you. If you want to, go downstairs and get something to eat. I've brought some food from a nearby restaurant."

I looked at him slyly. He seemed to read my thoughts and smiled at me.

"I'll be the most faithful nurse." I laughed.

"All right. I give up. But when Natasha starts sweating, call me to change her clothes." I gave him a friendly and familiar smile.

"I promise." He looked at her tenderly and I realized that I was leaving my friend in capable hands.

I went downstairs to look for Sergio. I found him in the kitchen.

"What are you doing?" I asked curiously.

"I'm making dinner. Are you hungry?"

"Very. But I want to have a drink before that."

"What would you like?"

"I'd like a gin and tonic, with ice and lemon."

The fridge was filled with everything we could possibly want. We made ourselves a drink each and sat in the living room.

I lit a cigarette and looked at Sergio.

"We've caused you a lot of trouble."

"Not in the least! On the contrary! When I'm with you, time flies without realizing it."

"Thank you! Cheers!"

"Cheers!"

We raised our glasses and drank. Sergio looked at me and smiled calmly.

"Tell me something about yourself," I asked him.

"I'm 32 years old. Not married," he emphasized his status. "I live with my mother and father. I have a brother and sister who are married with children. I have a timber business which seems to be going well, thank goodness."

He said nothing else.

"Don't you have a girlfriend?"

Sergio looked me straight in the eyes and replied,

"No. I don't. But I think I might find one here in Bulgaria."

That was more than a gentle hint. I pretended not to understand.

"What about Mario?"

"He's in the machinery business. Fork lift trucks. It's big business and he's got connections everywhere, even in the government."

"Is he married?"

He hesitated for moment but replied honestly,

"Yes."

I took a large sip in silence.

"It's your turn now. Tell me something about yourself."

I looked at him carefully.

"What do you want to know?" I tried to play for time.

He asked quite simply,

"Why did you run away from the hotel?"

So, I thought to myself, *they know everything. They're not so silly. They could have worked it all out.* I drank my glass and began to tell him everything. I had lost count of how many times I had told my life story. Who cared? I hoped it was the last time I would have to. That was the most important thing for me. I stopped occasionally to light a cigarette or for Sergio to pour me a drink. I told him everything. I didn't even hide my age or anything else. I finally finished.

There was absolute silence in the room. I looked at him. He was staring quietly at me in disbelief. He wasn't even blinking. I stubbed out my cigarette in the full ashtray and asked him,

"What do you think about that?"

"I think it's absolutely incredible. It's impossible! I don't know what to say!"

"Don't you believe me?"

"I believe you absolutely! But I can't believe that you've survived all this crap!"

"Yes. I've survived so far. Natasha too. But what happens now is very important, because if they find us, we're dead."

Sergio wanted to say something, but couldn't.

Mario came in and called to me.

"She's sweating. I think you need to change her."

I smiled.

"OK, I'll go. You can lay the table while I'm upstairs. I'm dying of hunger."

Natasha was sweating profusely. I changed her clothes, wrapped her up and left her sleeping calmly. Her temperature had fallen. When I went back downstairs, I realized that Mario had been informed of the most important details. However, this hadn't changed our relationships in the least.

When he saw me, he smiled pleasantly and said,

"I'll go up and see how our patient is, and you and Sergio have dinner."

I didn't argue.

As we sat at the table, Sergio was thoughtful but attentive.

Finally, before going upstairs, I wished him good night. He took me by the hand tenderly and said,

"Ioana, I have been very moved by what you told me and I shall think about you all night."

"Don't," I advised him. "Leave that for tomorrow. Don't you know the saying that tomorrow is always wiser than today?"

"Good night, then!"

"See you tomorrow!" I ascended the stairs with a lightness in my steps.

Mario asked in a slightly disappointed voice,

"Didn't you like the dinner?"

"On the contrary. Why?"

"You've come back very soon."

"No, I'm just tired. The day was filled with emotions. I just want it to finish!"

"Well, good night, Ioana!"

"Good night." I closed the door behind him and quickly got ready for bed.

I was woken by the sound of birds chirruping. I opened my eyes and looked for Natasha; she wasn't there.

I leapt out of bed and ran downstairs. The three of them were sitting there. Mario had bought a Bulgarian Italian phrase book and they were trying to converse in fits of laughter. I felt a sense of relief in my heart. They didn't see us as prostitutes any more but just ordinary girls.

"Good morning!" I greeted them.

"Here's our angel of salvation!" Mario called out. "Please Ioana, ask Natasha how she is today?"

I looked at him and burst out laughing.

It was such an absurd situation...

They had been there for perhaps an hour, maybe two, trying to talk to each other, sitting next to each other, and he didn't even know how she was feeling! I burst into laughter and the others started laughing too. I couldn't stop. Every time I tried to ask Natasha how she was, I burst into uncontrollable laughter again.

When I felt exhausted, I calmed down a little. The others stopped too. In the ensuing silence, I looked at Natasha seriously and asked,

"How are you?"

"I don't really know. I've got a sore throat."

"It'll get better."

I wiped the tears of laughter from my face and went into the bathroom.

When I came out, they were already waiting for me impatiently.

"Come on, darling! We're going for a walk," Sergio shouted.

"I don't think that's a very good idea."

"Why?"

"You know why," I replied quietly.

Mario approached me and said,

"Ioana, don't be cross, but Sergio told me everything."

"I assumed he would have."

"We've decided to look after you."

"How?"

"We'll work that out this evening. Now let's go for a walk. We'll choose the quiet paths where there aren't any other people."

He sounded serious and respectable.

"All right," I agreed.

We had a wonderful walk. Mario and Natasha walked in front of us with their phrase book, while Sergio and I followed behind them. We stopped from time to time to admire the view.

It was a wonderful summer day and Mother Nature seemed to be singing the "hymn of life". We talked a little about insignificant things. We eventually grew very hungry and decided to go back to the villa.

The men got down to work in the kitchen, and like typical Italian gourmets, they brought us a delicious lunch.

We ate our lunch with a lot of laughter and games.

Natasha felt tired and decided to go to bed. I unfolded a deck chair and put on my bathing costume to sunbathe. It was very sunny outside the villa and I wanted to get a bit of a tan.

Sergio and Mario came outside as well.

"Do you want to play a game of cards?" Mario asked.

"Why not?"

"Shall we bet?" Sergio asked.

"Yes!" I replied quickly and rushed back in to get some money.

They watched me in astonishment. We played until late in the afternoon. They lost all their money to me and I won 1600 levs.

"It could have been much worse," I said, happily gathering my money up.

"You must have been cheating!" Sergio laughed.

"Never! You just don't know how to play!" I responded and went into the bathroom.

The pleasant aroma of roast chicken was coming from the kitchen. I had a bath and went back to the room. Natasha was awake.

"Where have you been?" she asked me.

"Outside, getting some sun."

"Goodness, you're as red as a tomato!"

"Rub some cream on my back!" I turned my back to her.

Natasha rubbed my back and then I got dressed and we went downstairs.

"Come on girls, time for dinner!" Mario shouted out happily.

Sergio had cooked an incredibly delicious dish of chicken with mushrooms and cream.

"Hey, you're a fantastic cook!" I shouted out with my mouth full.

"I do everything fantastically!" he said ambiguously and grinned.

"Time will tell!" I replied to his insinuation.

When we had eaten everything and cleared the table, Mario lit a cigarette and spoke,

"I'll talk first because I'm the oldest and I assume the most sensible."

I translated quietly for Natasha.

"So. Sergio told me everything. I can't tell you what feelings I experienced when I heard his story. I will say only that I have decided to help you whatever it may cost. Sergio too. What is the problem, however? The problem is in my opinion that you are frightened of being pursued and eventually caught by the Mafia. Am I right?"

"Yes," was my short answer.

"But you can't spend all your lives in hiding. Can you?"

"No."

"Then there are two options. One is to go to the police, tell them everything and ask for their protection."

"No!" I almost yelled out. "That's not possible."

"Then, there's the other option."

"What's that?"

Silence followed. I even forgot to translate for Natasha.

"And that is to get you out of the country."

I looked at him in stunned silence. His entire body emanated power and authority.

"Where to?" My short phrases revealed how anxious I was. Our destiny was being formed at that very moment. I was certain of that.

"Italy. We will help you get on your feet there and you will live a normal life."

"What do you want in return?"

Mario looked at me coldly.

"I want nothing for myself. I am just helping two children in trouble." He fell silent, then added, "I have a daughter myself, who is almost the same age as you. I feel responsible. Even if only for her sake, I shall help you."

I stared in shame at the ground. Sergio rescued me from the embarrassing situation.

"We're not angry with you, Ioana. You were right to ask. You have lived such a life where everything was reduced to sex, money and violence. You're not to blame, that the environment you lived in was devoid of concepts like honour, morality and humanity. You are free to choose. Do you understand?"

I nodded because I didn't have the strength to say anything.

The room was silent. I was trying to overcome the grief which seemed to be stifling me. I quickly translated everything for Natasha. When I had finished, Mario continued,

"If you agree, we shall have to discuss the details."

I translated this for Natasha and in fine old tradition she rolled her eyes. "Whatever you decide. I leave it all to you."

I sighed and said the fateful words.

"We agree!"

There was no way back now.

"I congratulate you. You have made the right choice. Now for the details."

The first sentence which he uttered froze my blood.

"You will have to leave the country with false passports."

I went pale. This was a bad beginning.

"That's impossible. We'll be caught!"

"That's my problem. Leave it to me. You will need to have photographs taken. Tomorrow we'll go into Sofia to get photographs taken. After that I'll bring you back here and I'll go back to Sofia alone.

I have friends in the Embassy who will sort the visas out for you. I will need another three days or so for the passports. Sergio will stay here with you. I will do everything else."

It sounded like a fairy story. Natasha prodded me to translate everything for her.

"Oh, yes, and there's something else."

I looked at him inquisitively.

"Ask Natasha how she is today?" He winked at me and we all laughed.

I couldn't sleep all that night. I flayed around in bed like a fish out of water.

Everything seemed so complicated, frightening and dangerous. I imagined us getting caught at the airport, and arrested and thrown into prison. They were horrifying thoughts! I even imagined Bruno and the boys arriving in their cars and kidnapping us. Those thoughts were even more horrifying.

When the morning came I had huge black rings under my eyes and a look of torment on my face.

"Oooo, I look like my grandmother!" I cried.

"Who cares? You'll look older on your photograph," Natasha reassured me.

"That's easy for you to say," I complained. "You slept like a log all night long!"

"Well I'm sick. I have to sleep." She stuck her tongue out at me and ran down the stairs.

Mario and Sergio were waiting for us.

"Come on, ladies. I don't want to be late. We've got a busy day ahead of us."

Mario was extremely business-like.

We arrived in Sofia in no time at all, got our photographs taken in a photo studio in one of the suburbs and headed straight back to Borovets.

The moment we got back to Borovets, Mario left us and drove back to Sofia. Natasha went back to her room to rest and I went out to sunbathe on the deckchair.

Sergio came to talk to me. It was a quiet, calm and sunny day.

"Are you all right?" he asked me softly.

"Yes, why?"

"Last night you looked scared."

"Yes. I was. And I still am, and I will still be scared tomorrow. I'll only be calm when this nightmare has ended."

"You don't need to be afraid. Mario knows what he's doing."

"I hope you're right."

"What will you do when you come to Italy?"

"I don't know yet. Let's get there first. I think I want to study. You do realize that I've hardly been to school at all?"

"That's marvellous that you want to study. You speak Italian very well already. And when you get there you'll learn it perfectly. I'll help you..."

I looked at him carefully. He was a very nice man. Who knows, I might even.... Stop! It was too early to think about anything like that!

I smiled at him encouragingly.

"I'm sure that you'll help me!"

He nodded his head excitedly. The sun warmed me and I fell asleep. When I awoke the sun was still high in the sky. I was covered in a sheet, so as not to burn, and I had a newspaper hat on my head. Sergio was lying next to me reading.

"You're such a wonderful, attentive man and I'm so grateful to you."

He said nothing and just looked at me, but his eyes said,

You're wonderful, perfect and I'm very much in love with you!

We remained in Borovets for eight days. I shall remember those days with particular pleasure. They were filled with silence, sun, Italian lessons, laughter and dreams. Mario only came twice during that time. He was serious, business-like and always in a hurry. No one, not even Sergio, knew where he slept in Sofia when he wasn't with us.

He arrived one evening exhausted but smiling from ear to ear.

"We're flying tomorrow!" he announced, and my heart leapt and began to pound.

We got busy packing our bags. We collected up all our textbooks and phrasebooks. We saw our passports. They were just like real ones. I looked at Mario seriously and asked,

"How much did all this cost?"

He frowned. And then replied tenderly,

"Two happy smiles, ladies."

The night was endless. I didn't go to bed, because there was no point. In the morning I was serious and scared. Natasha too. Mario warned us to act natural, and we looked at each other, checking on each other to see if we looked normal.

We arrived at the airport early. I saw some telephones and suddenly decided to do something.

"Mario, will you give me a coin for the telephone?"

He looked at me in surprise but gave me one.

I went to the telephone and with a trembling hand, dialled the number. The phone rang a few times then a voice answered,

"Hello?" It was my mother.

"Mummy!"

Silence.

"Mummy, can you hear me?"

Sobbing.

"Mummy, how are you?"

"All right, how are you?"

"I'm all right as well. Are you still living with my father?"

"Yes. We got divorced, but we're back together again now."

"Together again?" I couldn't believe it.

"Yes. We couldn't cope without each other."

"Mummy. I'm all right. I'm leaving. I'll call again."

"Ioana, I love you!"

"And I love you too, mummy! I wish you happiness!"

I hung up the phone. I didn't have time to cry. We had to check in. I felt as though I was dreaming. Customs declarations, monitors, passport control. Everything was like in slow motion. The stewardess, the airplane. We were flying. I thought I had fainted. Or was asleep? I came to when I heard the announcement, "Please fasten your seatbelts, we shall be landing shortly." Beneath us was Milan.

Life wouldn't be so interesting from now on, because the problems and the hardship were over.

Natasha and I rented a flat which we paid for ourselves.

Mario had arranged for our money to be taken out of the country as well.

I registered as a student and Natasha opened a small hairdressing salon. She learnt Italian very quickly but retained her love for Bulgaria, and whenever we were together we spoke Bulgarian. Her business started to do well and she was very proud of it.

"I'll support you, you study!" she told me one evening.

I had decided I wanted to study sociology and become a social worker. First of all, I had to endure many years as a student and work very hard. I wanted to help protect children. I was absolutely convinced that this was the most important thing in the world.

Our friends visited us often. Natasha would sometimes go out with Mario but never told me how far their relationship had gone.

As far as Sergio Severini was concerned, he finally decided to tell me that he was in love with me. We decided that we would get married when I graduated.

"Ioana, that's so long!" he said with dissatisfaction. "That's seven years at least!"

"Well, that's the best way to test our feelings for each other," I laughed.

"There's nothing to test! I'll burn up and die like a flame with my love for you!" he complained.

We walked along the bright streets of Milan at night. Sergio held me tightly in his arms, as though protecting me from the entire world. We arrived home. We stopped for a moment in front of the entrance and I raised my head to kiss him goodnight. I saw a star shining brightly above me. It was my star watching over me. I could be calm now. It was a guarantee of my happiness and success. My heart was filled with happiness and pride. This time I really had triumphed!

* * *

Part 2

The happy, almost idyllic life of the Severini family is suddenly turned on its head. The twins, Julia and Roberto, disappear. The young mother knows the kidnapper. He is a sinister underground figure who played an important and negative role in her past.

Ioana is a woman with a strong spirit and character. She is determined to do whatever it takes to get her children back. In the entire horrific story, destiny gives her the advantage in the person of the noble Krasi. He is a key figure from her past and has long been in love with.

In the eternal struggle between good and evil, destiny is on the side of good, although the means are not always ethical. Nevertheless, as they say, "All is fair in love and war."

The sun playfully and sneakily danced upon my face, and I pulled the blanket up over my head. I didn't want to wake up yet. I was dreaming of something important and I wanted to see how it ended, but there was nothing I could do about it now.

The door handle clicked softly and I heard the tapping of bare feet coming confidently closer. Then the blanket was pulled down and two little bodies cuddled up simultaneously on either side of me.

"Mummy, Roberto's broken Barbie's leg and..."

"That's not true. It wasn't me. She broke it last night."

"You're lying!"

"You're lying!"

"Stop it!" I frowned without opening my eyes. "I'm still asleep! I don't want to listen to your ugly arguments!"

"That's not true," the two little heads both said amicably and started kissing me.

I smiled a happy smile and opened my eyes. My dream had gone and my children – my twins Julia and Roberto – were here with me, and that automatically made me the happiest person on earth. Two wonderful creatures of six years, ten months and twenty-two days.

Sergio and I had married the moment I finished college, and only seven months later they appeared – two tiny bundles upon whom all my love, energy and attention were focused.

During the first year I got up constantly throughout the night, just to check that they were still breathing and weren't suffocating. To begin with, Sergio laughed, and then got angry, but eventually accepted my maniacal maternal love and even did his turn of duty in the nursery, to let me get a couple of hours of sleep.

Initially we lived with his parents in Milan, but subsequently his work took him to Locarno and we had to move. It was a beautiful resort town in south eastern Switzerland on the northern shore of Lago Maggiore.

I was charmed by the beauty of the Alps, the lake and the town itself. There were palms everywhere, on the lake shore, the coastal road, the parks and even the narrow streets. Everywhere. They were always fresh and marvellous, even during the winter. The lake, with its crystal pure water, its cosy shoreline covered in exotic and abundant flora, was the pearl in the crown of Locarno. Standing high above this paradise was its guardian, the Lady of the Rocks.

The villa in which we lived was situated on the surrounding mountain slope to the north of the town. It was a quiet, luxurious and very sunny spot.

"Come on, mummy, get up! We're going to the lake today, aren't we?" Julia was tugging at me impatiently. "We'll go on the lake in a boat."

She had a little round face, with olive black eyes and chestnut hair. Her brother was half an hour older than her. They looked like each other, but not so much that it was hard to tell them apart. Roberto was clever, calm and wise. He amazed me with his thoughtful questions. His eyes and hair were identical to Julia's, but his face was longer and he had a high, intelligent forehead. They were my pride and my happiness. They were my life!

"Oh, all right then!" I said. "Have you had your breakfast?"

"No, papa's making pancakes downstairs."

"Ohh!" I exclaimed in delight. "I'm coming! You go down now, I'm so hungry I could eat them all!"

The children squealed with delight and ran clattering down the stairs. I got out of bed and went into the bathroom. I looked at my reflection in the mirror and smiled at it. I was inordinately happy.

But at that moment, the anxious thought that something terrible, dreadful and indeterminate was about to happen caused a lump to rise in my throat. I looked in the mirror and had the feeling that It was about to come. The Nightmare.

The Nightmare from the past. I mustered all my strength and tried to cast the thought out of my head. I shook my head and splashed my face with ice-cold water. I tried to wash It away. But no, it didn't want to leave me.

It stubbornly and arrogantly crept into my subconscious mind and tried to grab at my heart.

It is me; I was a prostitute. A child without a childhood, a girl deprived of her youth. I had been spiritually crippled a long time ago, when as a child my father would regularly beat me. I had no upbringing at home. Then I ran away and lived on the streets, entered into early sexual contacts and, as could be expected, ended up being trafficked.

I had lost count of the number of times I had been sexually abused, and had lived with the constant uncertainty of whether I would live to see the next day. All this had crippled me psychologically forever. If it had not been for Sergio and Mario, neither I nor Natasha would not have survived. God alone knows whether we would still be alive today, if we had not escaped from that country.

"Everything's fine, everything's fine. I'm safe." I repeated these phrases to myself like a mantra and waited for the wave of panic and terror to subside and retreat inside me again. I held my breath, poised for my heart to calm with every beat.

"Mummy!" Julia shouted out impatiently from downstairs. "Come on!"

Sergio was standing in the door frame. He came up to me, and I felt his strong arms carefully and tenderly embrace me. A warm kiss.

"Darling. That same thing again?"

I nodded.

"Don't be afraid. Everything's fine. You know it, don't you? Calm down. Look at me."

I looked at him.

"I will never let anything bad happen to you. Never!"

He hugged me and held me tightly in his arms. I stood there with closed eyes as I gradually returned to my normal rhythm.

"Come on, darling! Let me see my little girl's smile! That's right! Bravo! You can see for yourself – there's nothing wrong!"

I smiled gratefully. My wonderful husband. The crisis was over, for the moment.

***

It really was a wonderful day. The lake glistened like a huge aquamarine and its surface reflected the deep blue of the vast sky. In the distance the high Alpine peaks filled the background with their exceptional beauty.

We had been invited to the yacht of our good friends, Giovanni and Romina. There were rich; they owned the chain of hotels which were managed by Sergio's company. Just as Julia had said, we were going to go on the lake in a boat. For her, boat and yacht were the same thing.

"Ciao, Sergio! Ciao, Giovanna!" Our hosts waved to us heartily from the deck of the yacht. "Hurry up, we're going to be late!"

They called me Giovanna. Ioana was difficult for them to pronounce.

He was short, plump and balding, bursting with kindness and his Italian was like a waterfall of sounds, laughter and melody. His wife, Romina, was over 50 and filled with vitality and spirit. She must have been very beautiful when she was young. They had no children. Perhaps that was why they delighted in ours.

Our children ran into their arms with whoops of joy. Julia told Giovanni how they were going to catch fish and he laughed joyfully, spinning her around the deck. Finally, Sergio and I managed to get close to our hosts.

"Wonderful, beautiful children! Bravo! Bravissimo!"

"Oh, Giovanna, you are the light of my eyes! Madonna mia, Sergio, you're so lucky!"

"How are you, Giovanni? Hello!" I was in a good mood and my smile was radiant and captivating.

He pretended to flirt with me in front of Romina and she laughed until her sides were fit to burst.

"Come on, that's enough," she said. "Leave the girl alone. We'd better get going before midday." There were gold flames in her dark red hair and her eyes glistened like the water of the lake.

As much as Giovanni was short and plump, she was tall and slender.

"Very well, my love! Aye, aye, Captain," he saluted precisely and turned on the engine.

Leaving the men and the children on deck, Romina and I entered the elegant dining room where she served me coffee, biscuits and ice cream. Romina smiled cheerily.

"Relax, darling, and take it easy," she said. "The children exhaust you. You're beautiful, but you look tired."

"No, no. I'm not tired. I just had a bad morning." I shook my head energetically.

She looked at me tenderly.

"We can take the children with us for a couple of days, and you and their father can have a rest."

I could not imagine for a moment that I would not be by my children's side, and refused the gesture.

"I wouldn't be able to relax without them. Thank you, but no."

Romina nodded understandingly.

"You are such a devoted mother. At least get a woman to help you with the housework."

Sergio was constantly suggesting I did this, but I stubbornly refused. For so long I had neither home, nor family, and now when I had all that, I could not imagine letting anyone else in! It might be a primal instinct, but that was what I felt; that was the situation.

"Mummy!" Julia cried out in excitement. "Giovanni's caught a fish. Come and see!" Everything excited her, and she squealed in delight even when she saw a worm in the garden. She discovered the world in the most astonishing ways, sometimes bringing tears to my eyes.

Romina and I ran up onto the deck. Roberto was proudly holding a huge perch with an exceptionally beautiful dorsal fin.

"Mummy, Giovanni's caught a fish!" Julia was jumping up and down like a spring.

"It's a perch," Roberto said proudly. Sergio and Giovanni looked at each other and winked.

"That's right, my boy, it's a perch."

"Mummy, it's going to die!" Julia said, desperately.

I looked at the men questioningly.

"No, it won't!" Giovanni grasped the perch, released it carefully and threw it back into the water. Julia was the most impressed of all of them.

"He's going home now, isn't he, Papa?" She pointed vaguely to the water, which shone enticingly and brought a sense of pleasant coolness.

"Of course, darling." Sergio picked her up. "He's already home."

She looked at the blue surface of the water and sighed with relief. She said nothing for a moment and then added, "I'm hungry!"

We all laughed and went to have our lunch with the best of spirits. Romina had prepared the most wonderful meal.

"I don't trust anyone else in the kitchen," she said quite sincerely. "Cooking is my hobby and I relax when I cook."

"To my greatest pleasure," Giovanni interrupted her contentedly. "Will you give me a little more pasta, darling?"

The yacht was sailing towards the Borromean islands. This was the final point on our journey; Isola Bella, to be precise. A little corner of Paradise, the most beautiful of the three Borromean islands. I had never been there and I was curious. Sergio had told me about the archipelago many times, and we had even seen films about it, but it was a completely different thing to see them before my very eyes. I was captivated the moment I stepped onto the island, with its palace, gardens and ten terraces. I was captivated by the splendour and beauty of this corner of Paradise, and I was grateful to Sergio for looking after the children to give me a little bit of peace and quiet. Romina and I walked ahead and she performed the duty of guide.

"Look, Giovanna, the island was once a bare rock, and now it's the pearl of the archipelago. The palace was built by Count Carlo III Boromeo to honour his wife, Isabella. The greatest architects and sculptors of the time created this splendour..."

The tour around the palace filled with works of art was quite exhausting and even Roberto, who was normally so patient and curious, admitted that he was tired.

"Papa, let's go into the gardens," he said. "There's some beautiful peacocks there."

"Yes, really, what are we doing stuck inside here?" Giovanni replied. "Roberto's right. Sergio, leave the women by themselves, and let's take the children to see the terraces. I've got an idea of doing something like that for our new hotel. By the way, you haven't forgotten about the arrangements for tomorrow? We'll be leaving early. Make sure the workers get everything loaded."

This was a business conversation which did not interest Romina and me, so we walked away. Before we parted, we agreed to meet half an hour later in the café. The children were kneeling in front of a peacock which played with them. It approached them and regally unfurled its feathers. The sight was indescribable. In the midst of this beauty of flowers and greenery, elegant statues and fragrant flowers, my children stood opposite the white ethereal creation with its huge outstretched fan, and they stared at it as though enchanted. The picture could have come straight out of a fairy-tale and was almost unreal.

Romina nudged me. "Giovanna, let's go and see the amphitheatre. There's a wonderful statue of a unicorn."

"Yes, yes," I said, completely overwhelmed by the beauty and splendour around me.

"Do you like it here?" She smiled kindly at me.

"It's wonderful!" I said sincerely.

"You know that many famous people have been captivated by the magic of the Italian lakes. Stendhal even said, 'If you have a heart and a shirt, sell the shirt and visit Lago Maggiore,' and he also said, 'What can you say about Lago Maggiore and the Borromean islands, other than to feel sorry for the people who have not visited them?'" She laughed and prodded me to carry on walking.

It was such a wonderful day. The sun, the wonderful journey, the pleasant company, my life. However, somewhere deep inside me, my heart was sending signals. I knew those signals. They spoke to me of something imminent, and the worst thing was that they were growing stronger and I felt trapped. Who could I speak to? How could I explain it? They would think I was mad. Sergio had already suggested that I speak to a psychoanalyst but I refused categorically. Why did this have to happen today of all days? And it was such a wonderful day. We approached the colourful umbrellas with their small, pretty tables. There were tourists sitting all around and the air was filled with so many different languages. Julia saw me from afar and ran towards me carrying a cornet of ice cream.

"Mummy, what took you so long?!"

She stumbled at that very moment, tripped over and landed in the lap of a man, coating him all over with ice cream. I dashed over and Julia burst into tears. The man stood up and sympathetically stroked her head in an attempt to calm her. Roberto also ran up to me and we found ourselves standing in a circle. My children, me, and the man with the ice-cream-stained trousers.

"I am so sorry," I said, looking at him anxiously.

He really was covered in ice cream. At that moment, I felt as though I had been struck by lightning. I stood frozen to the spot, unable to think or to breathe. My heart seemed to stop beating. Perhaps time had stopped. My nightmare was standing in front of me. It was Bruno! My whole world suddenly collapsed into dust. Nothing existed any more. Nothing! Nothing apart from Bruno!

His eyes stared into mine and burned me up. I stared speechlessly at him for several moments unable to react. I was paralysed by terror. He was the first to come to his senses from the astonishment. Somewhere to my side, Roberto's voice echoed in response to something Julia was saying. She was quietly sobbing. I tried to turn around to look at them, but I couldn't. I was completely immobile. My eyes could do nothing but follow the movements of Bruno's eyes. And his lips. His lips opened into a shining smile. Then they moved.

He was talking to me. Very quietly. Or perhaps I was imagining it? I concentrated all my powers just to hear him.

"I'm sorry, I didn't mean to frighten you. She's so sweet. Are they both yours?" He was speaking Italian and bowed down.

From afar it appeared as though we were apologising to each other for the inconvenience. He was respectful and polite, smiling and magnanimous. His last words before I lost consciousness were barely perceptible.

"Don't worry! I will find you!"

Then I fainted.

When I came to, Sergio and Giovanni were bent over me. Romina was calming the children and Julia was sobbing at the top of her voice. The people around us were stretching onto their tiptoes to see what was happening, while I was lying on the ground drenched in water.

"Don't move, darling!" Sergio was bent over me, holding my head. "There will be a doctor along in a moment."

His words were unnecessary. I couldn't move if I had wanted to.

"The children, look after the children, not me..." I wanted to say, but I couldn't.

My tongue was numb and I couldn't move my jaws. Sergio looked at me with terror. But he understood.

"Giovanni, hold her, but don't shake her. It's serious. It's more serious than I thought."

Giovanni dropped to the ground next to me and took my head in one hand, and poured water over me from a bottle in the other.

"Jesus Christ!" He called out as loudly as his voice would allow. "Won't that doctor ever get here!"

A young, handsome man bent down over me and looked carefully into my eyes. I was lying helpless on the ground, unable to inform Sergio of the imminent danger. I could not move, I could not speak and my brain would not work. After my initial shock at the meeting, my thoughts reached fever pitch. I knew Bruno very well and it was quite clear to me that this would not be our last meeting, and the worst was still to come. I lost consciousness again when this thought occurred to me.

***

"Darling, did you think you might have been wrong? It's been so long! Are you sure that it was him?" Sergio was sitting next to me on the hospital bed. He had brought the children to see me.

I had been undergoing treatment for twenty days already and there was always something in my condition that the doctors were unhappy with. I sobbed and sulked and insisted that I felt well, but the intense nervous shock which I had experienced at meeting Bruno and the long-term psychological disability after years of sexual slavery with the very same Bruno were now taking their toll.

The neurologist was categorical that I was not well and could not go home. The panic attacks which overwhelmed me were so powerful that they could barely be controlled with medicine. I had no way of explaining to them that I had been in this state for years, and that a chance encounter had knocked me off the rails. Most importantly, I was anxious about my children. I knew I wanted to be with them. I felt ill for them and there was no medicine in the world which could replace them. I said as much to Sergio.

"While I'm in here, there's no way I will get better, do you understand? I have to come home to you. I want my children. They're in danger!" I raised my voice and Sergio looked at me anxiously.

"Calm down, darling. Shall I call for the doctor?"

"I don't want any doctor," I almost shouted. "I want to go home. Or do you want me to die here? Is that what you want? Tell me!" The children looked at me apprehensively.

"Ioana, calm down." Sergio was on his feet and walking towards the door to get the doctor.

I suddenly imagined what might happen after this scandal. I might perhaps remain forever in some psychiatric clinic. Incurably ill. I froze in terror. I leapt out of bed and grasped his hand.

"If you do not swear at this very moment that I will come home tomorrow, I will kill myself tonight. And that is a cross of shame you will have to bear until your last days on earth. Do you understand?" I was resolved to do everything. Even that.

Not that I didn't want to live: quite the opposite. But I could not imagine a moment of life without my children. But they were struck dumb, and looked at me in terror. Roberto ran over and clung to me. Julia stood like a little statue and huge tears rolled down her face.

"Mummy!" Roberto gripped me tightly around the knees in his childish arms. "Mummy, you're not going to die! If you do, then I will as well!"

Sergio looked at us, and I stared back stubbornly and resolutely.

"Did you hear me? Go on! I will not give in this time!" I was in an exceptionally aroused state of mind. I felt as though a huge wave of energy was coming towards me and pouring into me.

I was prepared to wage war on the entire world for the sake of my children. Even against Sergio, if necessary. He nodded silently and went towards the door. The children hugged me and at that moment I realised that God was sending me the strength I needed.

We were standing in the middle of the room, me and my two wonderful children. The three of us frozen in an embrace; that is how Sergio found us.

"Ioana." His voice was muffled and worried. "I've arranged everything. I shall come for you tomorrow at lunch time. I just have to fix up the documents. The treatment will continue at home. We shall come back here for examinations."

"That's what you think," I said to myself angrily. Yet I nodded in agreement. I even tried to smile.

"I can't wait to get home!" I said as I stroked the heads of my children.

Sergio looked at me pensively.

***

We were in the garden of our house. I had been home for a week now. The children were playing in the small swimming pool while I trimmed the rose bushes near the fence.

It was the middle of the summer and the sun was seriously making its present felt. There was not a single cloud in the sky and only the shade of the trees offered any sense of coolness. The children were splashing happily in the water, and their laughter for me was like magical music. I was waiting for Natasha. I had already spoken to her and I couldn't wait to see her. A car stopped on the street outside. I knew it was her and I ran to meet her. I opened the door and cried out with joy.

"Come on in! What's taking you so long?"

"Do you want me to park on the drive? It's in the way here."

"Oh, all right then."

She was like that. Very obedient and precise.

She parked carefully on the drive in front of the garage, got out of the car, smiled broadly and shook her head in delight.

"It's so beautiful here, Ioana! You're so lucky! Every time I come here, I go back to Milan with a sinking heart."

"Auntie!" Julia ran up to us in her wet bathing costume and bare feet. She threw herself into Natasha's arms and began kissing her.

"My darling little doll! How grown up you are! Let me see how much you've grown." Natasha carefully put her down on the ground, measured her with her eyes and said in delight, "Well, you really have grown!"

Roberto approached.

"Hello, Auntie! Have you got a new car?" he exclaimed, and hugged her tightly.

She raised her eyebrows and smiled.

"You're a mister know-it-all, aren't you? Let me give you a kiss, my little man." Then she looked at him carefully.

"Can you tell the different makes apart?"

"Of course I can. Daddy and I look at car exhibitions on the computer. That's a Lancia, Delta, the latest model."

Natasha gulped.

"Goodness, he really can. You're a little wonder child. Come here and let me give you a kiss! Hey, you're going to grow up into a big man!"

She chatted with the children and looked at me as she laughed, and only when she had given them their presents and they had gone away to look at them, did she come up to hug me. We remained in each other's arms for a long time.

I loved her more than if she had been my sister. In a certain way she really was my sister. My sister of destiny. Human trafficking had taken her far away from her home. Our fight for survival had made us comrades-in-arms. After Sergio and Mario had managed to smuggle us away from the traffickers and out of the country, we had begun a new life.

I had a family, and Natasha, with the help of Mario, had established her life in Milan. She had opened a beauty studio which had become so popular that clients needed to book ten days in advance for any procedure.

Mario had helped her a lot. They were very close, but he hadn't got divorced. She had accepted her role as lover, but she felt lonely at weekends and during the holidays. That was when he was with his family and she was by herself. She wanted at least one child, but he didn't want to hear of it. That was the drama of her life. She loved someone else's husband and longed for a child.

These two facts had turned her into a desperate workaholic with excellent income, but a very, very lonely one. Only when she came to visit us did her heart relax, and she would play with the children to her heart's content and she loved them as if they were her own. She had brought a huge pile of presents for them, as well as a bottle of expensive French champagne, which she gave to me.

"This is for your wonderful husband, the proud father of these two angels."

"And what did you get me?" I asked half-jokingly, half seriously.

"A couple of slaps for you!"

I looked at her in amazement.

"Why? Are you mad or something?"

We were strolling over to a small summer house. The garden wasn't very big. On one side of the house there was the drive leading to the garage, and on the other there was a lawn with a small paddling pool and a dolls' summer house. Natasha squeezed into it and sat down on the bench.

It was hot. She was dressed in shorts, which revealed her lovely long legs, with a short cut away top, and her long blond hair was nonchalantly tied in a ponytail.

"You're looking good," I said, "but you're behaving strangely. Has the heat got to your head?"

She laughed.

"No! I'll tell you straight. You can't, and you have no right, to frighten Sergio and the children. Stop it. What do you want? You've got everything. A home, children and a husband. You've got everything! What are all these nervous crises, fainting and panic attacks?"

I opened my mouth to reply.

"Don't interrupt me! I know all the memories. It hasn't been easy for us. I remember. I have nightmares too. Especially at night. I dream that I'm being followed by someone who wants to kill me if I don't sleep with him. He's beating me and in one dream I was even killed. With a knife. I barely woke up from it. I screamed as loud as I could. Do you know how awful it is when there's no-one in bed with you, no-one to offer you a shoulder to cry on? ALONE! And you? You should be ashamed of yourself! Get a grip on yourself. For the children's sake at least." She vented her fury and fell silent, looking at me anxiously.

"Natasha, darling," I cried, "he's here! He's here! I can sense him with my skin. He's somewhere here, around us!"

Her eyes widened and she asked with a frightened expression, "Darling, have you been taking your pills regularly? If you don't feel well with them, I'm sure they can be changed."

I got angry.

"Please be quiet! I'm not mad. I'm not and I will never be! Did you hear what I just said to you? Bruno's here! I saw him; I spoke to him! He threatened me! Do you understand now that you, all of you, you and Sergio, are mad for not believing me? For God's sake!" I sobbed helplessly. "Me and my children, we are all in danger! And now you are as well! Is that clear?"

I said no more and watched for her reaction. She slowly assimilated my words and at that moment understood. The blood drained from her face and she turned as white as a sheet. We sat in silence looking at each other, for so long that the children came to see us. They were silent as well.

"Mummy, what's wrong?" Roberto asked quietly. His attentive gaze moved from me to Natasha and then back again.

"Nothing's wrong, my little one. Auntie and I had a little argument. You and Julia are always arguing, aren't you? Off you go and play now."

"All right, mummy. Just don't argue any more."

"All right, I promise," Natasha forced a smile.

When they had run off, she finally spoke to me.

"Are you sure? Tell me what happened."

I told her about the meeting down to the smallest detail.

"He's just the same as he was. Absolutely. Except that his head's not shaven, he's got hair."

"And he said...he said that he would find you?" she stammered.

"Yes!" I emphasised in whisper. "Do you understand everything now?"

"I think I do!" she whispered with a note of fright. "What are we going to do? What do you think he will do?"

"I think about that all the time. I'm trying to put myself in his place."

"So what do you think?" Natasha was the same helpless girl she had been ten years ago. Clearly the leading role had been assigned to me. "He probably wants to kill us," she whispered.

"Nonsense. He wants me. But he wants me alive."

"What for?" she asked in astonishment. "To force you into trafficking again?"

"No, Natasha! You silly old fool! He wants to get me back into his bed. Don't you remember that he finally fell madly in love with me?"

Her jaw dropped and remained that way. She looked so childishly foolish and naïve that I laughed involuntarily. She looked at me with an even greater expression of terror and asked me hesitantly, "Are you all right? Are you taking your medicine?"

"Oh, Natasha. You really are a fool!" I sighed. "Do you really think that with all this going on, I'll put myself to sleep with those pills? I've thrown everything out, down to the very last pill. I've barely managed to clear my brain. I need to have a clear mind now, not numbed senses. There is a war coming. I'm not sure that it hasn't already begun."

We sat in silence for a long time, each sunken in her own thoughts.

"Ioana, don't you think we need to tell Mario? You know that he's got friends and contacts everywhere," Natasha suggested timidly.

"There's no point. He can't get Interpol to issue an international search warrant. There's no grounds."

"Perhaps he can't, but I don't believe Bruno has become a decent citizen."

"That's one thing you're right about. He's a criminal and he always will be. But we need to wait for him to make his next move. I don't even know what name he goes by now. I'm sure he's got a new identity."

The day passed imperceptibly. Natasha and I looked after the children, cooked, ate dinner and later that evening when the children were sleeping sweetly, we went out onto the small terrace. I poured some white wine and we clinked our glasses. We drank in silence, looking down towards the lights of the restaurants on the shore where they formed a beautiful bright garland around the silent lake.

"Ioana, don't you think it's a little dangerous for Sergio to leave you on your own, just now when there's such a risk of something happening?" Natasha asked as she sat cross-legged on the lounger with a blanket over her legs.

The nights here were quite cold even though it was hot during the day.

I sighed.

"First of all, he's got urgent business. He's completely overworked at the moment. There's not enough people. And secondly, he doesn't believe it. He thinks that Bruno is a figment of my mind. He thinks that the past has been buried forever and that the man I saw on the island was nothing like Bruno. How can I explain it to him?" My voice gradually rose.

"Shhhh! Calm down. You'll wake the children!"

"Natasha, I know I'm right! I really do want all this to be a figment of my imagination. But it isn't. He's planning something. I know him too well."

Natasha looked at me with an expression of dread and concern.

"I can't think of anything else, apart from...apart from running away. To France or England. You know that Mario's got money, and he will give me as much as I want. The children will want for nothing." Sweet Natasha.

"Nonsense! I'm not going to spend all my life running. It will all be resolved this time. It will be a war down to the last drop of blood."

"What are you talking about? You're not thinking of killing him, are you?"

"If he does anything to threaten my children, I will kill him in the blink of an eye!" I said decisively.

"You're not really thinking of that, are you?" Natasha looked at me in fright. I shook my head and did not reply.

Natasha stayed with us for three days. Three days filled with happiness, laughter and games until we were exhausted.

Sergio called several times every day and when he did, he heard the constant laughter of the children.

"What on earth are you up to there? It's so noisy!" His curiosity eventually got the better of him while we were speaking.

"You can't imagine! Natasha really has spoilt us this time. She's brought us a whole truck load of new toys. Even a trampoline. We set it up next to the swimming pool and the children have been jumping into the water. And all sorts of other things. She's even brought us a set of bows and arrows. They're like real ones. There's a target and you can put apples on it. When you hit it, you get an ice cream. We're having a competition at the moment."

He laughed happily.

"Just make sure no one gets hurt."

"I know what I'm doing, you don't need to tell me."

"Yes, yes," he sighed. "And how are you?"

"Fine! Are you coming home soon? Natasha wants to see you. She's leaving this afternoon."

"I don't know if I'll make it. But I'll be home tomorrow at the latest. Say hello to Natasha and tell her I'm sorry. Kisses to you, darling!"

"Kisses to you as well! Ciao!" I hung up.

***

We saw Natasha back to the car. She carefully issued me with instructions.

"And the most important thing is always to switch the alarm on. Both the outside alarm and the indoor one, all right?" Her face revealed her tension and concern.

"Come on, I know that much better than you." I smiled.

"Go inside now and I'll be off. I would stay until tomorrow, but Lucia's going to see her daughter and son-in-law in Rome. I have to be in the salon." Lucia was her manager.

"Natasha, don't worry so! I can take care of my children and myself."

She nodded and pointed towards the door with her eyes. I knew her very well and I knew that she wouldn't leave until we went inside. So we kissed quickly, the children waved goodbye and we went inside. I turned on the alarm and we exchanged glances.

"Come on kiddies, let's have something to eat!"

They ran enthusiastically towards the dining room. They helped me with the dinner and when they had eaten, they bathed and went to bed.

"It was great fun, wasn't it mummy?" Julia smiled contentedly.

"Yes, your auntie's wonderful. She loves you so much."

"We love her as well. She's so good and so beautiful. She's like an angel!" Roberto looked at me and laughed. "And she can shoot a bow and arrow like William Tell. She's a good shot."

"Who's William Tell?" Julia yawned.

"I'll tell you another time," Roberto avoided the question.

"Mummy, I want you to read me a story!" Julia wouldn't give up.

"Which one?" I went over to the bookcase.

I was looking for a book with the Grimm Brothers' fairy stories, but I was thinking of other things. I was startled by Robbie's quiet voice.

"Mummy!"

I turned around and looked at him.

"Mummy, she's already asleep. Don't look for the book. Go to bed as well."

I went over to his bed and kissed him. His eyes looked at me with the intelligent and loving expression of a grown up.

"I love you, Robbie! You are the answer to my prayer to God!" I whispered to him. "Good night!"

"I love you too, mummy! Don't worry about anything! I'll look after you!" I looked at him in surprise and my heart jumped a beat. What did he mean?

"Darling, I'm the one who has to look after you. Not the other way around. Where on earth did you get that idea? Don't think things like that, go to sleep. We'll play again tomorrow, won't we?"

"Mummy, I'll look after you!" he repeated insistently and stared at me.

"All right, all right! My big boy!" I said and kissed his forehead. "Go to sleep now, to have the strength to look after me." I smiled and he smiled back at me. "Good night, my angel!" I turned off the light, closed the door and went to my bedroom.

Halfway down the corridor I stopped and listened. There was absolute silence in the house. I hesitated and went downstairs. I checked the front door and the alarm. Everything was all right. I had set the alarm and the locks to the highest security level.

I left the lights on, half-dimmed, and tiptoed back into the bedroom. I wasn't sleepy. I was tense. I walked around the room and decided to take a bath. I filled the bath, lit candles and very quietly turned on my favourite compositions of classical music. Chopin, Mozart and Mendelssohn – the perfect atmosphere for relaxation. I lay in the bath and the scent of the herb candles complemented the fragrance of the music. Music for me possessed both fragrance and colour. At the moment I could sense jasmine and lilacs. The tension of recent days dissipated under the effect of the magical sounds of the piano. Blissfully stretched out in the tender embrace of the water, I felt relaxed and half-asleep. I spent quite a long time like that. The water began to grow cold and the flame of the candles slowly and lazily began to flicker.

I grudgingly got out of the cosy bath and found myself in my room. The moon peered in through the thin material of the curtains and cast a silver sliver of light onto the floor. I slowly approached the window. The sky glistened with the festive decorations of millions and billions of stars. It was beautiful and inexplicably exciting.

I suddenly felt an acute need for Sergio. I needed his reliable presence next to me. I needed his warm body and strong arms.

"I'll call him," I said to myself out loud. I really did miss him!

I looked for the telephone. It wasn't there. Where on earth could I have forgotten it? It must be downstairs in the living room. I fought against my unwillingness to go downstairs at that late hour, and my desire to call him. Love won out, and I smiled and opened the door.

Just at that moment, I heard something. A slight clattering sound, or something similar. I froze with my hand on the door handle. I stood there without moving while feverish thoughts spun around my head. What was it? I felt my entire body shivering, from head to foot, and I was so cold. I had to take a decision. I looked slowly around the room. There was nothing to hand which might serve as a weapon of self-defence.

Just wait! What do you think it might be? I asked myself. A burglar? Mouse? Or...Bruno? At that moment I realised that it was not a figment of my imagination.

I had to leave the room to see what was happening. Even if it cost my life. But what about the children? As the thoughts came into my head, I was already in the corridor walking towards their room. The corridor was empty. The house was peaceful and calm, and the lights were shining just as I had left them. To the left was the children's room, to the right the guest room.

My heart was pounding so loudly that I could hear it in my ears. I slowly pressed the handle and the door opened. It was dark in the room. I reached for the light switch as I stared in the direction of the children's beds.

The light softly took hold of the darkened room and I stood frozen to the spot. The beds were empty. Both of them. The shock was even greater than the shock of meeting Bruno. The blood drained from me. I looked at the empty beds and realised that the war had begun. I was paralysed by fear but I realised that I had to overcome it. Immediately.

I mustered all my strength, made every effort to stand up, and then roaring and howling like a mortally wounded female wolf, I ran outside.

***

I ran down the stairs jumping two or three at a time. When I got downstairs to the dining room, I looked around wildly. There was nothing! The door? It was closed. The windows had not been touched.

God, help me! The thought went through my mind. *They must be here, somewhere!* In the kitchen? There was no-one there! They seemed to have just vanished.

I ran back upstairs. I stopped at the top of the stairs panting, and looked around. Yes! The guest room. Yes. They must be there. They're probably hiding from me. I ran inside: it was silent and empty. I froze suddenly. The curtain was flapping. The window was wide open.

I had not opened it today.

It was all coming clear to me now. Nonsense! It wasn't clear at all! The second floor? A ladder? I looked around. There was nothing! Complete darkness. And silence.

"My children!!!" I cried out at the top of my voice. I ran back down the stairs. The telephone. "My God!" I yelled until I found it.

Sergio picked up after the third ring.

"Darling! What is it?" he asked with a note of concern.

"They're gone! He's taken them. Oh my God!" I sobbed.

"Ioana!" Sergio shouted with a rasping voice. "Calm down! Are you feeling all right?"

"I can't calm down!" I cried out wildly. "He's taken them!"

"Ioana, I'm sending the police. I'm leaving as well. Just calm down."

"I can't calm down," I sobbed inconsolably. "I will never calm down. My children!"

"Ioana, listen to me, I beseech you! Stay where you are and don't do anything! I'll hang up now and call for the police. They'll be there in a couple of minutes. As soon as I tell them, I'll call you back and I'll speak to you all the time. I'm on my way home. Just keep your phone by you. Take one of your red pills."

"Go to hell with your pills," I cried out and hung up.

I sat in the living room, shaking and looking at the phone. I couldn't calm down. It was good, however, that I could still move, shout and think...but what to think?

I tried to clarify my thoughts. I couldn't. A single thought occupied my conscious mind and would not let anything else in. Bruno had stolen my children! That was the explanation. Suddenly it all became clear. Yes. He would call me. He would tell me what he wanted. Until that moment the children would be in relative safety. This thought allowed me to take a deep breath. Gradually my terror gave way to my desire to fight. I began to come to my senses. I would destroy him, and I had a reason to do so. I would destroy him. Evil had to die!

The telephone in my lap rang, and I jumped up in fright.

"Ioana, darling, how are you?" Sergio spoke fast and anxiously. "Hello? I'm on my way back to you. I'll be with you in two hours. The police should be there at any moment." He paused. "Hello? Ioana?"

"I understood. Don't shout! I can hear you." I spoke quietly and briefly. "Just don't drive too fast and have an accident. Drive carefully."

"Ioana, are you all right?" His voice sounded even more anxious. "We'll find our children. I swear it!" My quiet voice had caused him to panic.

"Sergio, listen to me! I know that we will find our children. I'll find the person who stole them."

At that moment the door bell rang. I opened the door boldly. It was the police.

***

The next few days were filled with tension. Sergio did everything he could, even informing the police in Milan. They began their investigation. Mario, who had connections everywhere, even in Interpol, took an active part in looking for the children. But to no avail; there was nothing from anywhere. Natasha called constantly. I finally banned her from calling me more than once a day. All I could do was wait. I knew it was him. Only he could have been so precise.

The police examined the house and garden and found nothing. The alarm system had been deactivated very professionally. He had entered the house like its owner, walked up the stairs and completely calmly had carried the children out as I had been listening to Mozart in the bath. When I thought about that moment, I shook with anger.

Why had the window been open? That was a question no-one could answer. I couldn't sleep. I couldn't eat. I just sat and waited. I was waiting for a sign. I knew that he would give one. Sergio was extremely worried.

"Darling, please! Eat something! You'll get ill. I'm worried about you. The kidnappers will call. The police are certain of it. Both you and I know it too. We'll find our children. I'm certain!" He stared at me insistently and his entire being gave off a sense of torment and suffering.

I observed him in silence and just nodded my head. I didn't want to talk. I somehow thought that I had to save my strength because I would need it. A thought was taking shape in my head and I wanted to develop it and follow it through.

I got up and went into the garden. I stood in the middle of the garden near the swimming pool, where just a handful of days ago my children had been playing and laughing joyously. I looked at the blue water and I thought, *He's not going to call. We might as well wait for a letter from a dead person. Of course he's not going to call. He doesn't want a ransom, he wants ME! He will want to kidnap me.* At this my heart began to pound madly. By kidnapping the children, he seemed to be saying, *'Now I've got your children. I'm coming for you!'*

I shifted nervously. "Yes, I have to be kidnapped by Bruno immediately. That's the only way I will ever get to see my children again," I whispered to myself and looked around anxiously to see if anyone had heard me. There was no one there. Sergio was watching me nervously and sadly from the window of the living room. *I'm sorry, darling. I won't be around for much longer here,* I thought and almost ran back into the house.

"Ioana, are you all right?" He approached me and took my hands, and covered them with tender kisses.

"Yes! Don't worry, I'm all right." I even smiled faintly at him. "You know, Sergio, I want to go into town. I want to take a little walk around town to clear my head. I need it."

He looked at me in astonishment.

"Ioana?"

"What have I said?" I raised my voice. "I don't feel well. I want my children! But I'm going mad here in this house. I want to take a walk and clear my thoughts. Alone," I emphasised. So as not to give him the chance to argue, I added, "I'm taking the car. You stay at home, just in case."

I grabbed my handbag, telephone and ran outside. I had turned the ignition when Sergio caught up with me.

"Ioana, please! Take care when you're driving. Just look after yourself."

I nodded in agreement and drove off. In my impatience I was shaking like a deer that knows that it is being hunted.

The road wound down the hill and I carefully followed the bends. I drove slowly but my thoughts spun feverishly around my head.

I'll go down to the coastal path, I decided. If he's following me, it'll be easier for him to kidnap me there. I smiled at my own madness and pressed the accelerator resolutely.

It was a delightfully sunny and smiling day. Groups of tourists from all over the world had arrived in Locarno for the start of the film festival. I drove around the Piazza Grande some distance away and then turned down towards the coastal road. I parked in the car park and walked down towards the path. My telephone rang insistently and my heart leapt.

"Hello?"

"Ioana, it's me," I heard Sergio's anxious voice. "Where are you?"

"Walking along the coastal path. Why? What's wrong?"

"Nothing, I just wanted to hear your voice. When are you coming home? I'm just a little bit worried that you're by yourself and..."

"Calm down," I interrupted him impatiently. "I'm all right. As much as I can be, of course. I don't know when I'll be home. I've just got out of the car. I'll call you later. Ciao," and I hung up.

The path was quiet and the calm of the lake contrasted strangely with the tornado in my soul. I walked in all directions and looked around. There was no one there, and no trace of Bruno. Was I wrong? Perhaps I was just imagining it all? Perhaps someone was calling home just at that moment, setting out conditions for a ransom payment of a million?

"God, protect my children! Holy Mary, Mother of God, protect them! Wherever they might be at the moment!" I whispered in prayer and stared desperately at the emerald blue waters of the lake in search of a sign that my prayer had been heard.

At that moment, I felt someone come up to me.

"Would you follow me at a distance, please?" I looked at the man next to me in astonishment.

He was a well-dressed man, but a complete stranger. He spoke Italian. He walked past me and then turned around slightly to see where I was. I stared at his back as though hypnotised.

Yes. I was right. I was being kidnapped!

I walked behind him like a shadow. *Where is he taking me?* I tried to guess. *To the restaurant on the right? No, he's going to the harbour steps. I can see them now. All right, then, let's go. I'm ready.*

I walked boldly and with every step, I sensed that I would soon be meeting Bruno. The luxurious wooden launch onto which I stepped took me to a small but incredibly expensive yacht.

"Please take your shoes off," the man asked me and gave me a pair of beautiful slippers.

I obeyed without a murmur. I stumbled as I put the slippers on and he gently caught me. I looked into his face closely for a second. His eyes were familiar, or they reminded me of something, even though it was the first time I had seen them. He glanced back at me one last time, and then politely opened the door for me. I crossed the threshold and the door closed quietly behind me, leaving me in a darkened room. I felt for a light switch but couldn't find it.

"Oh my God!" I muttered. "Where's the light switch?"

"Over here. Next to me," said Bruno's voice. With its calm and slightly mocking tone, it made me tremble from head to toe.

I turned towards the voice, mustering all the strength I had. I said angrily, "Well turn the lights on, for God's sake! I'll fall over!"

"Ha ha ha!" He laughed completely sincerely and at that moment the light blazed from all corners of the ceiling.

It was a soft light which let me see him. He was seated on a soft white and gold couch, wearing a dressing gown, his hair casually combed and his feet in the same slippers I had. The walls were also white and gold. There was an enormous plasma television set taking up at least a metre and a half of one of the walls, and thick curtains hung at the windows.

"Welcome aboard, my dear friend!" Bruno lazily got up from the couch and came over to me.

I stood frozen like a statue, and only stared icily. He came so close to me that I could smell his breath, fresh and minty. I said nothing.

"Aren't you going to kiss me?" He stared mockingly into my eyes. "Or don't you love me anymore? Oh! The fickle nature of women!"

"Just stop all the theatrics!" I hissed. "Where are my children?"

He took two steps back and looked me up and down.

"That's why I fell in love with you ten years ago. Because you've got character. You're a strong woman! And pretty!" He winked at me. "Are you still as good at sex as you used to be?"

"Bastard!" I shouted. "Where are my children? I'll kill you!" I snarled at him threateningly.

He shook with laughter and every hair on my body stood on end, as though hordes of ants were crawling over me. I trembled.

"Calm down, darling! Your children are safe and sound."

I looked at him carefully and intently. He was enjoying the moment.

"Just sit down. We need to have a long talk. First of all, sit down and be calm. Relax." I sat on the couch at the far end from him. Bruno went to the bar.

"Do you want a drink? To relax?"

I refused silently.

"You're shaking, darling! You used to like a drink, and you were more talkative!" He laughed again and poured himself two fingers of gin.

With a pair of golden tongs, he dropped in slices of lemon, added ice and tonic and shook the tall crystal glass. The ice tinkled melodically against the thin crystal surface.

"I like that sound," he shared with me. "It's such a calming sound."

"Probably because your conscience, if you have one, must need calming."

He laughed loudly again and took a sip.

"You are so amusing! You're marvellous!"

I said nothing and looked at my wristwatch.

"There's no need to hurry. As I said, we need to have a long talk."

"If I'm late, Sergio will come looking for me. And then..."

"And then...he just won't find you," Bruno interrupted me mockingly.

"Don't be so certain about that." My voice was hoarse and unconvincing.

"Certain? What does certainty mean? We can never be certain about anything. At least I'm convinced about that." He spoke quietly and looked me in the eyes. "So that's it! Sergio! I want to tell you how I see things from this moment on." Bruno fell silent as he took a sip of his drink and evaluated what he saw.

I felt as if I was going to faint and I was frightened. The stress was beginning to take its toll on me.

"Can I have a glass of water?" I asked. My tongue was dry and swollen.

"Of course, darling. Just water?"

"Don't you call me 'darling'! Yes, just water!"

"Why are you so cold with me? I'm just trying to be hospitable." Bruno gave me a bottle of Evian and a glass. "Shall I pour it out for you?"

"No thanks, there's no need. I can do it myself." I drank thirstily straight from the bottle.

"Darling, it's bad manners to drink like that."

"Fuck you, Bruno. I've had enough of your tricks. I just want to hear what you want in exchange for my children's freedom."

"You!" he said, quietly and laconically.

However right I had been in my analysis of his actions, I was still shocked. I dropped the bottle on the floor. The water slowly spilled out onto the white carpet and immediately disappeared. He laughed and looked at me cruelly.

"What are you so frightened about? Did you think I was going to ask for money? I'm rich. I don't need your husband's wretched money. I need you!"

I knew it! But even so, when I heard it from his own lips it sounded terrifying, like a death sentence. I took a deep breath to relax my chest and I asked, "You want me to be with you? Really? I won't be unfaithful to Sergio. I love him."

Bruno's laughter shook the luxurious cabin.

"I'm sure you're bluffing. You can't be so stupid! I'm sure you understood me. But to be quite clear and avoid any misunderstandings, I'll say it again: I want you here, now and forever! And to make it completely clear, I will explain it to you step by step. After our meeting here on my yacht, you have two possibilities. Just accept all my demands without objection and all your problems will disappear. You will be with your children and me."

"And what if I refuse?"

"If you refuse, you can go back to your loving husband and forget about your children forever!"

My blood froze. White spots danced in front of my eyes and I rocked from side to side. When I came to, Bruno was standing over me, shaking me gently.

"Ioana. Ioana! Can you hear me?" He was patting my cheeks softly.

"Get away from me, you monster! How dare you touch me!" I slowly came to my senses.

"You fainted! I'm trying to bring you 'round and you're angry with me. You really have become so ungrateful!"

I looked at him with blood in my eyes.

"Can't you see what you're doing to me? You're a sadist. How can you threaten me with not seeing my children any more?"

"So what do you think? I've spent years looking for you. And I found you completely by chance. And you thought that I would just say, 'hello!' and carry on walking? No way! You're mine! Is that clear? Mine!"

"You think you own me? I have never been and will never be yours! Is that clear?"

We were standing face to face yelling at each other. Bruno grabbed my head. He pulled me towards him and started kissing me. I tried to twist out of his grip, but he was very strong, and I was only half-alive. He's going to rape me; the thought came into my mind. *Never!*

But he didn't. He pushed me away from him and said with a panting voice, "I can have you, you know I can, but not like this. I want you to come to me of your own free will."

He was mad! Mother of God, what was I going to do?

"Bruno, let's talk about this. Can we?"

He nodded. I sat down on the couch again.

"Bruno, I want to know where my children are."

"I can't tell you."

I bit my lips.

"Are they in good health?"

"Yes, they're fine."

"Are they crying for me?"

"Not any more."

The words had an evil ring to them.

"I will ask you again, Bruno! If you're lying to me, I swear to God, I will kill you! Are my children in good health?"

"Yes, Ioana. And to prove that I am not lying, you can hear them now."

Bruno got up and went out. My heart was beating like a cathedral bell; all my blood rushed to my head. Bruno came back in, holding a telephone.

"Take it." He gave me the telephone.

"Hello?"

"Mummy!" Roberto's voice shook me.

"My little boy! How are you?" I was suffocating with pain.

"All right."

"Robbie, can you hear me? How's Julia?"

Roberto spoke slowly and softly, as though he had been drugged.

"Julia's fine. Mummy, are you going to come?"

I almost died. My heart was bleeding, I was sure of it.

"I'll come, my child. I'll be with you very soon. You just look after yourself. And take care of Julia. Do you hear?"

"Yes, mummy. I love you!"

The telephone went silent. I fell deathly silent as well. When I came to again, I was lying in the cabin. Bruno and another man were talking to each other.

"The injection will make her feel better, but only for a short time."

"I want you to make her better for always. She can't go on fainting every half an hour."

"Well, then don't upset her any more," the doctor stressed and left.

"Bruno!" I shouted.

He was startled and turned around.

"How are you? You really frightened me! You've got very weak nerves, you never used to be like that!"

"Bruno! You have no heart!"

"Come on now! Are you all right?"

"How do you expect me to live without my children? Roberto sounded like he was drugged. What are you doing to them?"

"Look now, darling. The children are fine. I've got plenty of people looking after them. They're being treated like a prince and princess. You're the problem. Not them. Just say yes."

"What on earth are you imagining? Do you truly think that I will just leave Sergio and my children will accept you as their father? And we'll live like a family? That's just ridiculous. Sergio will leave no stone unturned until he finds us. And you will end up in prison."

Bruno laughed quietly.

"Just say yes, and Sergio won't come looking for you."

I looked at him with shock. His words concealed a threat on the life of my husband. He was mad, that was clear. I had to play him very cleverly, like I had done in the past.

"Bruno?" I forced myself to sound tender.

"Yes, darling?"

"Give me a week."

He looked at me with an intrigued expression.

"I need a week to sort things out at home."

He looked at me with raised eyebrows, inquisitively and untrustingly.

"I've lived with him for ten years, I can't just leave him like that. He's looked after me so well."

"Yes! Oh, yes! He looked after you so well that he stole you from me," Bruno muttered angrily.

"Bruno, that is my last word. One week, to end things."

"All right. But not one hour more. And remember, if you try to do anything, or if you take any other decisions, that will be the end of your children. You will never see them again."

"I want to go home now."

"Nikola will take you to your car. Remember, I want you back here in exactly seven days. On the yacht."

I left without looking at him.

We drove for a few minutes before the car stopped and Nikola turned to me.

"Madame, you will have to walk from here. Are you capable of doing that?"

I nodded and got out of the car. I walked towards the car park where I had left my car. I saw a policeman in the distance, and looked around anxiously.

"Good evening, Signora," the uniformed policemen spoke to me. "Is that your car?"

"Yes, what's happened?" I whispered.

"Are you Signora Ioana Severini?"

"Yes, I am."

"Your husband informed the police of your disappearance at six forty-five this evening. We have been looking for you."

"That's madness. Here I am."

"And you are well? You will have to come to the police station with us." The policeman stared at me resolutely.

"But why? I would prefer to go home."

"Just wait while I call your husband."

While he was talking, I took my telephone out of my handbag. The battery had run out. Two hours later, this fact would save me to some extent from the righteous anger of Sergio. The scandal was unavoidable. He accused me of all the sins of the earth, of being the most selfish person on earth, and the most heartless woman in the world. I was irresponsible, superficial and sly, amongst other things.

When he grew tired of shouting, I told him quietly that I was going to bed, without looking into his eyes.

"So you're going to sleep? You didn't tell me where you were! Where were you, for God's sake? You were gone for five hours!"

"Sergio, I was out, that's all. I was wandering around the town. Please, I'm tired."

He turned his back on me. I went quietly up to the bedroom and fell asleep before my head hit the pillow. The next morning, I saw that I had slept alone. When I went downstairs, Sergio was sitting in the living room staring sadly in front of him.

"Good morning," I muttered. "Have you had any coffee?"

He looked at me seriously and said, "Sit down."

I sat down opposite him.

"Ioana, what is happening to you? I want to know where you were! Didn't it occur to you that I might have been frightened for you? Do I mean so little to you?"

My heart shrank with pain. The poor man. He had been so good and devoted to me. And me? I was just a mother fighting for her children. Good or bad, but I was their mother. Nothing on earth could divert me from my purpose. And my purpose was clear – to save my children.

"Look, Sergio. I have to leave."

He raised his head in shock.

"Wait, don't interrupt me. This is how things are. You know my past as a prostitute in an elite hotel in Sofia. The man who forced me into trafficking was a hardened criminal who's now made an untold fortune from the flesh trade, drugs, arms and petrol smuggling. That same man once fell in love with me and wanted us to get married. That's when you saved me; you and Mario managed to get me and Natasha out of the country. You, an ordinary respectable citizen of Italy, interfered in the plans of a high-ranking mafia boss. That same mafia boss, Bruno, has been looking for me all these years, and it was like a gift of fate for him when he saw me on the island. Everything else is clear. He stole our children just to break me, and he won't stop until he gets his hands on me. The only problem is that you're in his way and he would kill you without blinking an eyelid. He'll do such a precise job that the forensic medical services will conclude that you died from a massive myocardial arrest. I know him very well."

I stopped for a moment to catch my breath. Sergio looked at me without blinking. He was hypnotised. I used his silence to continue.

"Sergio, I can't wait for the police. They don't know anything in particular, apart from his Bulgarian name. He's got another nationality now, and another identity. Before they are able to discover him, either you or our children will be dead, and perhaps all of you, apart from me. I can't wait for that to happen; I have to act now. You and the children are all I have in this world. I will save you; I know how. It's just that you have to let me go. I'm going to Italy, and I have to go tonight."

He jumped up and with his elbow he knocked over the coffee cup in front of him. The coffee spilt, the cup tumbled to the floor and smashed. The thin porcelain fragmented into hundreds of tiny pieces.

"You must be mad to think that I will let you go by yourself. Where do you want to go and why? Do you think that while you're going to look for them in all manner of suspicious places, I'll just sit at home and watch football?"

It was my turn now to look at him in silence.

"No, darling. We're going together. We'll save the children together." He lifted me up off the chair, raised me to the level of his eyes, and kissed me passionately. "My love, we've got no time to waste. We need to make a plan!"

Two hours later, one of the company's minibuses stopped in our garden in front of the garage. Sergio went out into the garden and spoke to the driver briefly. Returning to the house, he set the lights to automatic and we got into the minibus through the garage. We had two bags packed with essentials.

"OK, Mirco!" he called to the driver, and we set off.

I had thought up that plan of getting out of the house unobserved, just in case Bruno was watching me.

We travelled in silence but constantly exchanged glances and nodded conspiratorially. It wasn't a long drive to Milan and we were soon at Natasha's place. Natasha lived near the centre, on the second floor in a luxury building.

"Ioana, Sergio, how pleased I am to see you!" she said. "Come in! It's lucky I'm not at work today, but even if I was, Ioana's got a key, haven't you? I'm just waiting for Mario."

Sergio and I exchanged glances.

"That's good!" Sergio said. "I was just about to call him and ask him to come over."

Natasha's initial joy at the unexpected visit quickly faded from her eyes and she asked anxiously, "What's happened with the children? Is there any news?"

"Nothing, Natasha! For the moment," I added hurriedly. "It's good that Mario's on his way."

"Yes! Oh yes! He should be here by now. I can't sleep with the worry. It's so good that you've come." She glanced at me crossly. "I don't dare telephone."

"Well, yes! You were phoning every half an hour!"

"Quiet!" Sergio did not let us argue. "Quiet. We have to be united now, and not argue over nonsense!" He looked towards the corridor. "That must be Mario."

The lights came on and a moment later Mario appeared in the doorway.

"Ah...what a pleasant surprise!" Mario exclaimed and approached us energetically.

He was a tall, elegant man with slightly silvering hair at his temples. He hugged me and kissed me kindly. He shook hands with my husband, hugged him and patted his back. They were very good friends. And good people.

"Darling! My favourite little girl!" He caressed Natasha's head and kissed her temples. She smiled at him softly and kissed him back.

We all sat down and Mario muttered, "Oh, I'm so thirsty!"

Natasha leapt up nimbly.

"I was just about to serve something refreshing." She disappeared into the kitchen and switched on the juice maker.

Mario looked at us inquisitively and said sadly, "So there's no positive news in the search for your children?"

I sighed deeply and tears welled in my eyes.

"That's why we're here. We need to talk to you. It's time to act," Sergio said firmly.

"What do you mean? I've spoken to the Central Office of Interpol. The police have taken all possible steps. They're looking for the children in Switzerland and here in Italy, and now in Bulgaria as well. They're looking for Bruno too. the Bulgarian police have given them his full description."

At that moment, Natasha brought in a tray of drinks.

"Here you are! I bought some fresh fruit this morning. This is blackcurrant and strawberry juice, this is lemon and mint. There's ice as well. Be my guest!" She elegantly served fruit juice to each one of us in a tall glass with a lot of ice and sat down next to Mario.

She looked at us anxiously and said, "I have a suggestion. I have a client, a very rich lady. Her husband, as far as I know, is involved in a very shady business, with stolen cars. I can ask very delicately whether he might be able to help us."

Mario interrupted. "No, I won't allow that. This is no business of hers."

"Mario," I said quietly but resolutely. "You know my husband very well, and Natasha and I understand the psychology of bandits very well. We have both come to the conclusion, independently of each other, that the best way to fight them is with other bandits. The police might be doing something, but they're not fast enough. The more time passes, the more dangerous it becomes. I met the kidnapper. I met Bruno."

Everyone froze and looked at me inquisitively. Natasha held her hand to her mouth and looked at me in horror. Mario listened carefully and only his eyes betrayed how concerned he was. Sergio already knew everything, but listened tensely and despite the air conditioning, his forehead was covered in huge beads of sweat which trickled down his cheeks.

When I had completed my account, they were all looking at me in absolute silence. I picked up my glass of juice and drank it. Then I continued.

"You will tell me what you think, but before that I want you to know that my plan to save the children is connected with the Mafia. I have to find people who will help us, either in return for money or for another service."

"What for? To kill him?" Mario turned his head.

"No, no. I will go to him in a week's time and tell him that I accept his proposal. Sergio will remain here, in Milan. We will organise a group to follow me from a distance and when we go to get the children, or when his people bring the children to us, they will organise a getaway from wherever we are. And then we can get the police involved. I will testify against him and I'll get him sent to prison."

"Ioana," said Mario, "I'm afraid that sounds like fantasy. There's no way it will work."

"No, Mario! It's a simple but brilliant plan. He's hidden the children somewhere near Locarno. He's rented a yacht and thinks he's invincible. But there is a weak link in his plan. And that's where I have the advantage."

"What is that weak link?" Mario inquired.

"Me. I'm his weakness. And I can use that."

"Ioana! I'll say it again. It's dangerous."

"Sitting here waiting for someone else to save my children is dangerous. The most dangerous thing is that I have a deadline which is running out. Mario, don't you understand that this is our chance?" My voice cracked with emotion.

Mario said nothing for a long time. Natasha sat absolutely still and Sergio looked first at Mario then at me.

"Mario, I really do think that we need to find contacts with the Mafia. Ioana's plan is feasible, but I don't agree with her going to him on the yacht. For God's sake, I'll pay someone to kill him!"

I stroked his hand silently. He was trembling.

"Don't worry, darling, we'll outwit him!" I told him. "We'll get our children back."

Mario got up and paced the room. "Don't get too excited, Sergio. Let me think for a moment." He went over to the enormous French Windows and looked outside.

The daylight was already fading and we found ourselves still sitting in Natasha's darkened living room. We said nothing. Mario had gone into the next room. He was pacing up and down talking quietly on the telephone. He came back into our room and turned on the lights. An elegant candelabra with dozens of tiny lamps in the shape of white lilies tenderly and beautifully illuminated the ceiling.

"Well, friends, all we can do now is wait. I've put things in motion. This evening we'll get an answer from some boys suitable for a job like this."

Sergio raised his head.

"I hope they're reliable!" he sighed.

"We'll see about that. Shall we have dinner while we're waiting? Girls, shall we go out for something to eat or shall we eat here?"

"No, no. We'll have dinner here," Natasha and I called out in unison. We looked at each other and laughed.

"Aha, that's how I like you. Calm. We'll get this Bruno."

We left the men to talk and Natasha and I went into the kitchen to cook dinner.

"Do you know, Ioana, how happy I am that we're all here together today? No. I didn't mean it to sound like that. It's a terrible reason to be together. The children...But the house is full of people, the way I like it. But it's not the same, because the children aren't here...God! I'm so confused!" Natasha desperately flung her arms up.

I knew exactly what she meant.

"Don't be silly! I can't be cross with you. I know. My heart is broken, but I can say that I'm pleased that we're all together now. And as far as Bruno is concerned, you just watch and wait! God protect my children!" I sighed, but the pain in my breast would not go away.

I started helping Natasha with the dinner. Natasha really was a good hostess. It was a pity that she had no family. I have to admit that she was a much better cook than me; Italian cuisine was her element.

"Ioana, please pick me some basil."

"What do you mean 'pick'? Haven't you got some in a jar?"

"Ha ha," she laughed. "No, on the balcony to the left, there's a couple of plant pots with flowers. The first of them is basil."

I pulled the sliding door of the dining room and went out on the enormous balcony in the shape of a garden. There was a small fountain, and little pond covered in greenery.

"Nat, I can't find it!" I called. "Everything here is green. Where is the basil?"

She ran over like a little deer with her long legs. She gave me a playful slap and led me to a corner with plant pots.

"That, my lady, is basil. But you wouldn't know that, of course, because you don't do any housework," she said haughtily and laughed.

"I don't believe...You're a maniac. Who grows basil? Everyone buys it."

She mockingly raised her eyebrows and dextrously picked a couple of leaves. The dinner was delicious and for the first time in many days I was able to appreciate the taste of the food. I could not stop thinking about my children, but a strange internal confidence that everything would come to a satisfactory outcome made me feel calmer.

At about ten o'clock that evening Mario got a phone call.

"Yes, yes." Mario was laconic. "Let's meet right now. Wait for me in the bar, I'll be right over. I'll have a friend with me. Ciao." He hung up and looked at us. "Girls, we're going out. You'll be alone for a while. Come on, Sergio."

My husband was already at the door.

"I'm ready."

We saw them to the door and looked at each other.

"What shall we do?" I was trembling with the tension.

"I don't know, Ioana. I'm stressed as well. Let's make some blackcurrant cake. I've got some left. Cooking is good therapy!"

I looked at her inquisitively.

"That's bizarre! I have no idea how you manage to maintain such a perfect body with an appetite like yours!"

She laughed and winked at me.

"You haven't forgotten that I've got a beauty salon, have you?"

We got down to making the cake and the time passed quickly.

It was ready when the men came home. I looked at Sergio. He looked calm and wasn't sweating any more, which made me feel calm as well.

"Sit down, girls!" Mario sniffed the air. "Something smells delicious. I can tell you've cooked something marvellous."

"Mario, please! Talk to us!" I begged.

"So, the boys we talked to are, in principle, willing to help us. We'll see them tomorrow at lunchtime to sort out the details. They'll probably make some inquiries of their own, just to get a better idea."

"You're not being entirely clear. You haven't said whether they will take the job on, or are they still thinking about it?"

"Ioana, they will take a decision in the next couple of hours. They're professionals, they have to be convinced before they say yes. It's a big job."

"How big?" I asked with a lump in my throat.

"Three hundred thousand," Sergio said briefly.

Natasha and I groaned.

"That's a huge sum of money!"

"Don't worry, darling, I'll get the money! All they have to do is to confirm!"

My husband gave me a firm hug.

"You're not alone!" Mario stretched out his arm and patted my hand. "We'll help as well."

"I can get you one hundred thousand straight away," Natasha said enthusiastically.

"First we'll see how much I've got. If I haven't got enough, then I'll ask you," Mario smiled.

My eyes were filled with tears. "God, how can I thank you for giving me such friends?"

"It really does smell good. Let's try that wonder of the culinary arts!" Mario went into the kitchen.

Natasha leapt up and ran after him. "Wait, it's still hot!"

"I like hot desserts more than anything else. Like you, hot and sweet."

They wrestled with each other. Natasha squealed and laughed happily. Sergio and I hugged in silence, each trying to give encourage and succour to the other.

***

We all got up early in the morning. Mario drank his coffee and went out. Natasha saw him to the door and rushed to get ready for work.

"You stay here and take it easy!" she instructed me. "Don't worry. I'm sure that things are going to work out and the children will soon be back with us."

"All right, Natasha. Off you go now, you'll be late!"

"Yes! Oh yes! Oh, I've got an important day. I've got two special clients coming at eleven. They're close friends of Berlusconi!"

"Natasha! Look at you, you're so important now!" I joked.

"Come off it! I've had to work hard for it all!"

"I can see, I can see. You fought so hard last night that you've got bruises on your chest!" I laughed.

She blushed and rushed over to the mirror.

"Ooo! I really do! That Mario!" She cast a nervous glance over to Sergio who tactfully pretended not to have heard or seen anything.

Natasha disguised the marks of Mario's passionate kisses and ran out of the apartment in a hurry.

I went over to the window and saw her drive out of the underground car park in her new Lancia. When she came to visit us in Locarno, Roberto had recognised it the moment he saw it. My heart shrank and a strong pain stabbed me in the stomach. I immediately sat down and pressed my stomach with both hands.

"What's wrong, darling?" Sergio stared at me with an expression of fear in his eyes.

"I'm all right!" I sighed.

"You don't look all right, you're as white as...I don't know what." My husband went to the other side of the white glass table and knelt next to me. He hugged me.

"Shall I call for the doctor? Are you feeling any better? Where does it hurt?"

"Oh...I don't know what happened to me. I just suddenly thought about Robbie and my heart hurt. And my stomach. It's all right, it'll pass. Don't worry. I'm just sick with worry about the children. I'll die without them. Can you understand that?"

"I know. Just wait for another couple of hours. We'll see what they have to say. And if they refuse, I've got a plan B."

I looked at him inquisitively. "What is it?"

"It also involves the mafia. If these lads don't want to do it, I'll find some others. Giovanni knows some other people from the same organisation. They won't refuse. But let's see what these lads have to say first of all. Mario and I arranged to meet at one o'clock."

"I just hope they're serious."

"Well, they want a serious amount of money for the job, so I imagine they'll do it for us. Come and lie down; I'm worried about you." Sergio pulled me over to him on the bed and lay down next to me. He put his arms around me.

"You know how much I love you!" I cried. "And how much it hurts me to cause you all this suffering because of my past."

"Darling, don't talk such nonsense! You can't possibly hurt me. It's that bastard who thinks he can rule your life, like he used to when you were a defenceless child. But he doesn't know what's coming to him."

My husband caressed me tenderly and I relaxed. I fell asleep without realising it, and dreamt a strange dream. We were with our children on the island again, just the same as it was on that day. We walked around the palace and then went outside into the garden. In my dream I knew that I had been there before. It felt like déjà vu, but in a dream.

So we separated, and Romina and I went to the amphitheatre and the statue of the unicorn.

She told me about the island and then we slowly walked back. We have to go back to that café. That's where my children and our husbands are waiting for us. But something catches my attention! I look around carefully to see where Bruno is. Julia runs towards me carrying ice cream and falls into the lap of the man. It's Bruno. This is the moment which is important for me. I rummage around in my bag and find my gun. I take it out and, with a quick movement, I load it and raise my hand. I will shoot! Oh, no, my child is in his hands: I will shoot my child! Oh my God, help me! I know that I have to shoot him, because if I don't, the events which follow will be catastrophic. I raise my hand and aim at his head, the furthest point away from Julia. I shoot. The deafening explosion fills my conscious mind and I tense up, not knowing whether I have killed him. I wake up that very moment, sweat pouring off me and my heart pounding. Sergio stood in the doorway, looking at me anxiously.

"I was dreaming that I was shooting him. I think I killed him. I heard the gun shot," I muttered in confusion. "This time I killed Bruno on the island."

Sergio shook his head. "Ioana, darling, I'm sorry, I dropped my telephone. I have to hurry. Mario's waiting for me. It's only a couple of streets away."

"Was it your telephone I heard in my dream? I'm sure it was a pistol shot!" I said in disbelief.

"It was just a dream. Rest. I'm going now. Those mafia lads will be at the restaurant at any moment. I want to talk to Mario before they arrive."

"All right, all right! Off you go!"

He waved at me and closed the door. I stayed in bed, thinking about the dream. I wanted to remember every detail. It was important for me. I wanted to have killed Bruno. *Will that change anything?* I thought sceptically. Nevertheless, I retained some mad hope that in my dream I had killed him. While I waited for Sergio to come back from the meeting, I called Natasha.

"Can you talk?"

"Yes! What's happened?" she asked.

"I'm still waiting; I don't know anything yet. I just can't keep still from worrying."

"I'm impatient as well. What can I say? We just need to keep calm. Our men are clever. They'll think of something."

"I know. But I just can't take any more, Natasha. I just feel as though I'm going mad when I think of my children. Julia is so sensitive. And Roberto is probably suffering more because he's so clever and understands everything."

"Oh, please don't, you'll make me cry. Stop it. You said yourself that the bastard had guaranteed that they're fine and being looked after well."

"Yes. That's what he said, but I know very well what he means by 'fine.'"

"Don't think about it now. I don't want something to happen to you now, just when things are going to get sorted out." Natasha was very upset. "Just think that in a couple of days' time you'll all be together again. Please!"

And then to try and cheer me up, she added, "Oh, I nearly forgot. I had a little break and rushed out to Montenapo. I bought you a lovely dress and shoes."

"How? Without me trying them on?" I objected.

"Come on! You know we're the same size. They're marvellous. They're by Dior."

"You must be mad! They're so expensive!"

"Darling, they were on sale! Are you happy now?"

"We'll see about that! I doubt whether they'll fit me, I've put on weight."

"For God's sake! You've just melted away with all this worry. Have you looked in the mirror recently?"

"All right, all right! Bye now!" I gave in. "Hold on, when are you coming back?"

"As soon as I can! Kisses!" Natasha hung up.

I really couldn't sit still. Every couple of minutes I looked through the window and listened for the front door to open. A little after two o'clock in the afternoon, Sergio came home. I ran up to him.

"At last! Tell me what happened, before I go mad with the stress."

I looked for the answer in his face but I couldn't read anything.

"Darling, just give me a second!" He went into the bathroom and I could hear him washing. I peered in. He was pouring cold water over his head.

"Are you feeling all right? What's happened?" I asked anxiously.

"I don't know. It's all the stress, making me feel really hot. Oh, that's better, even though my head is still burning."

He dried his face with a towel and looked at me. I stood at the bathroom door looking at him. I loved him so much, with his wet hair and red, puffy eyes, and his damp shirt and wet jeans. The father of my two wonderful children.

"Sergio, I love you so much! You're the love of my life!" I murmured.

He looked at me shyly and for the first time in ages, I saw a smile on his face; a radiant and marvellous smile.

"But if you keep me in suspense for much longer, I'll bite your head off, believe me!" I said and hugged him.

A hot, steaming kiss acted upon me like a magical potion. I felt everything around us melt away and disappear. Sergio carried me in his arms to the chair. He placed me down carefully and he sat down opposite me.

"Darling. They've agreed to take the job on. They've agreed."

"That's fantastic! Tell me more details!" I exclaimed.

"And because I knew that you would want all the details – and not just because of that – I made a recording of the meeting."

My eyes nearly popped out.

"A recording? What?"

"This recording. I recorded it all on this Dictaphone. I brought it with me from home."

We really did have a Dictaphone. A small one, but it was powerful. I had bought it years ago. I liked it and had played with it for a long time.

"Are you playing at gangsters now?" I smiled.

"Well, if I'm going to be gangster, I thought I might as well do it properly," Sergio sighed.

I laughed. "Let's hear it then!"

He took the Dictaphone out of his pocket and turned it on.

Mario: I don't want to talk about money any more. I'll give you the entire amount.

Sergio: Mario, I can't let you do that. They're my children after all.

Mario: Yes, but you're my best friend. Sometime in the future, if you can, you can pay me back. They're coming.

Sound of footsteps and several voices talking over each other.

Buongiorno! Mario, Sergio! How are you?

Sound of chairs being pulled out.

Well, thank you! Would you like something to eat?

First man: No, thank you. We'll have a beer.

Sergio: I'll order some.

Mario: Here's the waitress, shall I order? Yes, a Moretti for each of us.

Waitress: So five Moretti's?

Sergio: Yes, please!

I looked at Sergio.

"So there were three of them, were there?"

"Yes, darling! Just wait. Let's listen."

Mario: So, we would like to hear what you have to say about our problem.

First man: In brief, to sum up the information you gave us last night: we've got two children kidnapped, and they don't want ransom money. The woman is the target, the children are collateral. The kidnapper is a Bulgarian. You say he comes from the former mafia organisations there. You don't know whether he's still involved. He's probably changed his identity. He lives on a luxury yacht. A conversation took place with him on board the yacht in Lago Maggiore near Locarno. The children were kidnapped eight days ago from a house in Locarno.

Sergio: Nine days now. Today is the ninth day.

First man: Yes!

Sergio: He's given us a deadline of seven days. Today is the second day.

Second man: She can't identify the yacht?

Sergio: No.

Mario: Those are all the facts that we have. What do you say? Will you take the job on?

Short silence.

Third man: We'll take it on. It's not going to be easy because we only have a couple of days. We'll take it on, but there's one thing. We will need complete cooperation on your part. Especially your wife.

Sergio, anxiously: What in particular?

They were speaking Italian, of course. But what I heard shocked me. The third voice sounded strangely familiar. It reminded me of someone.

"Sergio, who is that? Is he Italian?"

"I don't know. He's got an accent. A slight one. He might be a foreigner. Why?"

"I don't know. He just reminds me of someone. Let me just hear it all first."

Third man: I want to meet her, to get a detailed description of the man and prepare for our next steps.

Sergio, anxiously: Does that mean that you want to take part in the operation to rescue our children? Isn't that dangerous?

Third man: There's no other way!

Mario intervenes: Gentlemen. We'll help in whatever way we can. However, I want to say that we want an unconditional guarantee that the lives of Sergio's wife and children will be in no danger.

Third man, affronted: We can't give any such guarantee. Do you accept or not?

Sergio: We accept. How do you want the payment to be made?

First man: In cash. When we've completed the operation.

Mario: Don't you want anything in advance?

Third man: No, we don't need anything. I would like a meeting with the woman tomorrow at six, here.

Sergio: OK.

Sound of chairs moving.

All: Ciao!

The recording ended there. Sergio looked at me pensively.

"I don't know, Ioana. I'm a little afraid. Not just a little, I'm very afraid. What do they want to get you involved for?"

I couldn't stop thinking about the stranger. Why did he remind me so much of someone? But whom? I searched through my memories.

"Ioana, I'm talking to you!"

I was startled. "What?"

"Where are you? I was saying that there's no way I want you to get involved! Isn't that why we're paying so much, for them to do the job? I don't know why I don't just call Giovanni."

"Oh, no, Sergio. We don't have the time for that. I have to be involved in some way. I'm the only link between him and the children. Don't even think about it. I'll take part."

"I don't want to think about you going to meet him. And you'll be alone, in his hands. God, I just want to kill the bastard."

"Don't you worry yourself with stupid thoughts like that. I'm clever and cunning. And I know him very well. I just can't imagine what plans the man we're going to meet tomorrow might have."

"You'll see. Let's have something to eat. I'm hungry. And I don't feel very well."

I jumped up and went to lay the table. A man's a man and has to eat.

"Darling, there's left overs from last night. Or do you want me to make you an omelette? With salad?" I called out from the kitchen.

No answer.

"Sergio, where are you?" I ran into the living room and cried out. There was blood pouring out of my husband's nose, and he lay there looking at me helplessly.

"Sergio! Lie down, immediately!" I shouted and ran into the bathroom.

I soaked two towels and ran back to him. He was lying on the floor. I washed his face and screwed up the ends of the other one to plug his nostrils.

"Raise your right hand higher," I ordered him.

"Why?"

"Don't ask, just do it! Lay there and don't move. I'll call for an ambulance."

"I don't want one."

"I'm going to call for one, whether you like it or not. Shut up and don't talk. God, what was the number? 113?"

I called for an ambulance.

While we waited for it to arrive, I prayed to God not to take away from me everything I loved and perform a miracle to bring my family back to me and to save Sergio's life.

The doctor frowned as he examined Sergio.

"When is the last time you measured your blood pressure?"

Sergio shrugged his shoulders.

"I don't remember... Last year, perhaps, when I had a check-up."

"And what was it?"

"Normal. Why?"

"Now it's very high! Two hundred over one-fifty. I'll give you an injection but you'll have to go into the hospital."

Sergio got up.

"I can't go into hospital. I have some very important things to do."

"You will have to forget about everything else, because this is serious."

"Sergio!" I intervened. "Don't be so stubborn. Go with them, and we'll see how you are tomorrow."

"Ioana, how do you think I could stay in the hospital with everything that's going on here?"

"You're no good to me dead. The children and I want you alive."

The doctor put an end to the argument. He gave Sergio an injection and ordered the paramedics to bring a stretcher.

"Ioana! You can't go by yourself tonight at six."

"Of course I can. I'll call Mario now. But first I'm coming with you. What hospital are you taking him to, doctor?"

"To..."

"No, you're not coming with me. Stay here. I don't want you going outside too much." Sergio whispered, "I'll call you from hospital."

"All right then. You're right."

The paramedics arrived, picked my husband up and took him away. The doctor said goodbye.

"Aren't you going to come with us, Signora?"

"Yes! Oh yes! I'll set off in a moment and follow you. Goodbye and thank you."

I closed the door and ran to the window. The ambulance was just leaving.

"God, help me!" I sighed.

I looked at my watch. It was already five. I needed to get ready, but first of all I needed to phone Mario.

"Hello? Ioana, what's wrong? What?? Which hospital? What happened?"

I told him briefly.

"All right. You get ready. I'm going to the hospital and then I'll come and get you. We'll go together. The restaurant's close by, so keep calm."

"Yes, I will!" I said and sighed with relief.

If Mario was with me, everything would be all right. It really would be. He was something like a modern wizard. He sorted everything out easily. He was so organised that sometimes I really thought that he had supernatural powers.

I needed to get dressed. I had spent all day in a tee-shirt and shorts, I couldn't go out looking like that, and I had precisely fifteen minutes. I didn't need to dress up and I was so stressed out that I didn't really care what I looked like. I took a quick shower and put on the first dress that I laid my hands on. I quickly brushed my hair, put on a pair of dark glasses and I was ready.

In the meantime, Natasha came home.

"Where's Sergio? Oh my God, blood!" She was looking at the floor where I had forgotten to wash the blood away.

"Calm down, Nat! Sergio fainted with very high blood pressure and he's been taken to the hospital."

As always in situations like this, her eyes nearly popped out and she clasped her hand so tightly to her mouth that her fingers went white.

"Don't worry! He'll be all right."

"But all this blood?"

"He had a bad nose bleed."

"Oh, God, will this never end? And where do you think you're going with that dress inside out?"

I looked at her.

"Is it really? I hadn't noticed! I'm going to a meeting."

Natasha looked at me and her eyebrows leapt.

"Who are you going to meet?"

"The mafia."

"By yourself? You can't!"

"I'm going with Mario. He knows what happened to Sergio. He'll be here any moment."

"I just don't know what to do!" Natasha fussed about.

"You should rest. You've been working all day."

"I'm fine. I'll go to the hospital to keep Sergio company."

"Let's wait and see what Mario has to say first."

"There he is, he's coming." Natasha went to meet him.

"Hello!" Mario was calm and unperturbed. "What happened? How's Sergio?"

"He's on a drip. He's had a very bad attack of hypertonia. All the stress has been too much for him."

"Shall I go and see him?" Natasha asked with concern. "While you're with those people?"

"No. Let him rest for the moment. You stay here. We'll be off now. Ciao!"

The restaurant was almost full. Mario and I took our seats.

"Would you like something to drink?"

"I don't know, Mario. Sometimes I feel like that I would like to get really drunk. I'm stressed as well."

"I know. This is a huge test for your family. And for all of us."

"Mario, there aren't enough words to express how grateful I am for everything you're doing. First when you saved Nat and me from trafficking, and now all this... And the money."

He raised his hand.

"Please, don't say anything! I haven't done so much. And what I have done has been from my heart."

"I know. That is why I am so grateful to you and I shall be for the rest of my life." My eyes filled with tears.

"Come on now, don't cry, they'll be here any moment."

Just then I heard someone behind my back.

"*Buona sera.*"

I turned around instinctively and froze. There were two men standing behind me. One of them was painfully familiar. I would clearly never get away from my past.

"*Buona sera.* Hello!" Mario pointed to the vacant chairs. "Let me introduce you. This is Signora Severini."

"Pleased to meet you," I nodded and offered my hand to Krasi.

Yes, it was Krasi: another significant figure from my past.

"The pleasure is all mine," he replied, gallant as ever.

After the introductions, the two men took their seats. Krasi looked at me and performed his part expertly. But for me, this was all getting too much! Within the space of one month, I had managed to get involved with all the key figures of my past life. Evidently I was never going to be able to run away from it.

I looked at Mario. He was giving the order to the waitress.

"Ioana, what would you like?"

"An alcohol free citrus cocktail."

"And so, gentlemen, I have brought you the lady in question. I would ask you to take into account the fact that she is very worried."

"And I am willing to help you," I added.

Krasi began. He acted completely calmly, as though he had never seen me in his life. He spoke perfect Italian.

"I would first like to tell Signora Severini that I am also Bulgarian. When I heard about the case, my initial reaction was to refuse, but when I heard that you were a compatriot, I decided to assist. As far as we are concerned, you can be quite sure that we will do everything possible to get your children back."

His words were mixed with recollections of the time when we were in love with each other, and suddenly tears poured out of my eyes like a river.

The more I tried to stop them, the stronger they became. Everyone at the table maintained a respectful silence. I was so grateful to them for not trying to reassure me. Several minutes passed before Mario patted me gently on the hand.

"Come on now, my girl! Calm down now. You're a fighter, aren't you?"

I nodded. I wiped the tears from my wet face and that moment my eyes stared into Krasi's. He was quite implacable, well dressed, beautiful. Only his eyes spoke to me, those deep, expressive, blue eyes which I had loved so much. Those eyes at that moment were caressing me, smiling at me and saying, like they once used to, *'Come on, baby, stop crying, blow your nose and smile. We don't want these people to think that Sofia girls are cry babies.'*

This time I nodded at him and he understood that everything was all right and that I had accepted his message.

"Signora, I suggest that to avoid any further upset we get straight down to business."

"I'm ready."

There was another man with Krasi. He was younger with raven black hair and swarthy skin. He took out a miniature notebook and got ready to take notes.

Krasi asked countless questions about Bruno's character, distinguishing marks, habits and anything else I could think of and he hadn't asked. He asked me to describe the yacht as far as I could, the appearance of the other man who took me there and to recount the entire conversation verbatim. He asked for a photograph of the children. I transferred them from my telephone onto his. I told him everything about them. What they like, what they don't like. I told him what Robbie had said when we were talking on the phone. He asked me whether I had noticed any sounds other than the voice of my son. Millions of details.

He asked for a complete description of Bruno's circumstances and the people around him in Bulgaria. He asked for their names and external appearances, everything I could remember about the time when I was his slave, everything, until Krasi finally said, "Thank you." Two hours must have passed. I felt exhausted, but relieved when we had finished. It was strange, but I now felt certain of a positive outcome.

"Signora, I will give you this telephone. You will use it only to talk to me. I will call you when I need to. Keep it switched on at all times and fully charged."

The two men stood up and said goodbye. Mario and I exchanged glances.

"Are you tired?"

"No, quite the opposite, I feel relieved and hopeful."

"That's good news. Let's go." He pulled my chair back and helped me to get up. By way of an apology for keeping the table occupied for so long for such a small bill, he left an enormous tip for the waiter who bowed very deeply with a contented smile.

Natasha was waiting for us with dinner served on the table. She was clearly agitated but tried not to show it.

"You were gone a long time," she only dared say.

"Yes, darling. But it was very important that Ioana underwent such a detailed questioning."

She nodded.

"Let's have dinner!"

"I'm sorry but I have to leave," said Mario. "They're expecting me at home. And I have to pop into the hospital." Natasha frowned but said nothing. I was silent. That was her drama in life. She was young and beautiful as an angel, loving and devoted, but...he was married and would always remain so.

"When will you come to see me again? Tomorrow?" she asked nervously. ·

"I'll call you. Ioana, you call me from Natasha's home telephone. Keep me updated. Ciao, girls. Be careful."

He kissed Natasha passionately, stroked her head, waved goodbye to me and closed the door. Natasha and I remained alone. It felt awkward and my heart ached for her. When I looked over she was staring at the laid table with tears streaming down her cheeks.

"Nat, don't cry! I understand how difficult it is for you. And the worst thing of all is that you love him. I honestly don't know what's the right thing to do. To love him or to leave him. He's your saviour but at the same time your executioner. He saved you from the mafia, gave you everything, made you feel human again, but he's slowly killing you. He's killing your youth and your hope of having a family and children. Oh, I just don't know what to say to you..."

"Don't say anything." She sighed. "I'll end up killing myself."

"Are you mad?" I attacked her angrily. "You should be ashamed of yourself! What can I say? That bastard stole my children, threatened to kill my husband. My family's in danger and I have to fight. You're just feeling sour. Now's not the time for important decisions. Let's get all this over with and then we'll think about it. But I can say right now that I don't want you growing old as his lover. Yes, he helped you. He's helped you a lot! And he helped me as well, and is continuing to do so. But Natasha, that's enough! If he wants his family, that's where he should stay. Leave him! You'll find someone else; you're entitled to be happy! That's all I have to say."

She listened to me sadly and stared like a porcelain doll without blinking.

"Nat! Nat! Are you listening to me, you silly thing?"

"Don't shout! I can hear you," she muttered.

"Do you promise to take a decision soon?"

"I might." She sighed again.

"Let's have something to eat. You've worked so hard! And I'll call Sergio."

She got out of the sad situation and gave a painful smile.

"Let's call Sergio, really."

The duty doctor at the hospital told me that Sergio was asleep at the moment and was still on a drip.

"Come and see him tomorrow at 10.30 after the rounds. Then we'll see what the position is. But I have to tell you that he insists on leaving tomorrow which is a very foolish thing to do, because it's not just his blood pressure. His heart is out of rhythm and we've only just managed to normalise it. So there's no way he'll be leaving tomorrow or for the next four or five days."

I bit my lips. We were in a real fix. Sergio had obviously held everything inside him.

"Can he be cured, doctor?"

"We'll talk about it tomorrow. Good night!"

I hung up.

"Ioana, you're worried, I can tell! God, is there any end to this torment? What happened?"

"Nothing, silly thing, don't worry. Sergio's a true man. He'll be all right." I relayed the information quickly.

"Ioana, it's a good thing that you're so courageous and strong! I would die without you. I'm so glad I've got you!"

"Don't talk nonsense!" I said with slight irritation. "Come on, let's have dinner. It's a good job I've got you to make me eat. When all this is over, we'll live so well all of us together, and my sweet little angels will hug me again!"

We ate our dinner sadly. Natasha gobbled her food down quickly, made her apologies and went to bed. I cleaned up, put the food in the fridge and poured myself a glass of wine. I drank it almost in a single gulp and poured a second. I felt slightly dizzy. It felt good and I relaxed.

"That's quite good wine. Natasha's got taste." I looked at the label on the bottle. 'Donnafugata,' Italian wine. Sicily – how appropriate." I looked at the telephone.

There was only one number in its memory. I resolutely pressed the green button. He answered on the second ring.

"Hello," he said in Bulgarian.

I felt nervous and couldn't speak.

"Ioana?" Krasi said in a slightly tense voice. "What's up?"

I took a deep breath.

"Nothing's up. I just wanted to talk to you."

"Is there anyone around you?"

"No. I'm alone."

"Ioana, who would have believed it? I'm amazed at the vagaries of fate! Where's your husband?"

"In hospital. He's got very high blood pressure, from all the stress."

"Why aren't you with him?"

"Because I wanted to talk to you. Because I want to ask you a thousand things and to tell you that if you hadn't run away that evening, I would never have ended up in the hands of Bruno or the mafia, I wouldn't have ended up as a child prostitute, and wouldn't still be living in the nightmare which is still going on today."

"Can I come over? This is not a conversation for the telephone."

I thought. My life had completely turned head over heels when my children disappeared. Ten days ago I wouldn't have done this, but now everything was different.

"Yes," I said. "Wait for me downstairs in half an hour." I gave him the address.

I dressed quickly and tiptoed to peep in through Natasha's door. She hadn't turned off her bedside lamp, yet she was fast asleep like an angry angel. There was a packet of pills on her bedside table. I trembled, and approached the bed carefully. Oh, there was only one pill missing; she had taken a sleeping pill. I glanced at her for a moment. Asleep she was even more beautiful. In her blue satin sheets with her blond hair spread over the pillow and her graceful hands with the delicate, long fingers crossed over her breasts, she truly did resemble an angel. I caressed her with my eyes and left her room. I picked up the keys to the apartment and put both telephones in my bag, in my hurry almost forgetting to switch the alarm off before leaving. It would have woken the devil if it had gone off. It was good that Natasha would sleep heavily while I was out. I intended to tell her everything, but I didn't have the time at the moment.

Krasi was already waiting for me. I wondered what car he was in for a moment, but he saw me and flashed his lights. Dipped headlights. Then full beam. Dipped headlights. I ran over and a second later I was in his car.

He looked at me, smiled and drove off. I noticed him carefully check to see if we were being followed. He was silent.

"Where are we going?" I asked.

"To a place where we will be safe and we can talk calmly."

"And where is that place?"

Krasi smiled and answered briefly, "My house. In Como."

"You live in Como?"

"I live in many places. But I have a house in Como."

I was astonished. Destiny had taken a tight rein on my life, and this was incredible. I hadn't seen Krasi for so many, many years, and now it turned out that we were almost neighbours.

"Why are you so silent?"

"I just don't know what to say. So many years have passed since that eventful night, and here we are. You just appeared as though on command. I think you came right on time."

"We'll see about that."

I nodded my head and clasped my bag.

He tenderly took my hand in his lap and slowly raised it to his lips. He kissed my fingers and muttered, "I'll get your children back, baby! Didn't I tell you when you were a child yourself, that I would look after you? Well, God sent me to you right on time."

I didn't remove my hand but I slowly and silently sobbed. I cried for such a long time, inconsolably, that I finally ran out of tears. He said nothing and just looked ahead. When I finally stopped crying, Krasi asked quietly, "Are you feeling better now, baby?"

I nodded.

"Here we are now."

I looked around in surprise. We had stopped in front of an iron gate. Krasi activated the gate with the remote control and we entered. In the dark I could only see a garden and a house, smaller than ours in Locarno. But when we went inside, I was shocked. I hadn't expected such opulence: hidden lighting, luxury furniture and paintings which looked very expensive.

"Please come in, and make yourself at home." He turned me towards him, pulled me closer and kissed my forehead.

It was so unexpected that I looked at him in astonishment.

"Don't worry. You're completely safe from everything. Relax."

I sat in a deep, soft and comfortable armchair. Krasi smiled, then he winked slyly and asked me, "Would you like something to drink? Or are you hungry? You used to have a huge appetite."

I laughed slightly sadly.

"I did until recently. But since all this happened to my children, I've lost it somewhere."

"Everything will come back to its place, baby! Have faith in me."

I looked at him more hopefully than certainly.

"Do you really think so?"

"Yes! First tell me how much time we have."

"What do you mean? Tonight? Or until Bruno's ultimatum?"

"I'm talking about tonight, baby!" he answered. "For tonight!"

"The whole night!" I said daringly and boldly. "I even think it won't be enough."

"What for?" he asked curiously.

"For everything." I laughed.

Krasi mixed two martinis, filled a crystal bowl with olives and sat next to me.

"You're very intriguing, baby! Just like you were before, and now at such a difficult time for you. Do you want an olive?"

"Yes, three if I can."

He counted them, put them in my glass and sat on the floor next to me. He stretched out his hand and we clinked glasses.

"To you, my radiant, beautiful girl! To the imminent rescue of your marvellous little children. To your happiness! Cheers!"

I drank the glass to the bottom. I ate the olives and timidly asked for another drink.

"Oh, no! You're not going to get drunk right now! You've got enough pain, pressure and stress. Enough of everything. I understand that. But on my territory, baby, I don't allow any drunken scenes."

I looked at him as though captivated by a spell, as though I were once again that little girl whom he used to spoil and love so madly. Was it a dream? He was at my feet once again, tenderly massaging and kissing them. I took his head in both hands, raised it and stared into his eyes; those beautiful, incredible blue eyes, so deep and beautiful. Blue and beautiful like the water of Lago Maggiore. Or rather...the other way around. The water of Lago Maggiore was as beautiful as Krasi's eyes. I stared into them as though hypnotised and slowly but surely found myself sinking into them.

"I waited for you for so long that night. You weren't there. And I was slowly dying," I whispered.

Krasi stood up, took me in his arms and said,

"Here I am now..." And with that he picked me up in his arms, kicked the door open and carried me to the high bed in the bedroom.

"Princess, do you want to stop here? You're tired and vulnerable at the moment, with all these problems. We can have coffee together early in the morning and chat."

The wheel had already spun. There was no turning back now.

"No! We can drink coffee together in the morning after we spend the night together."

Krasi looked at me attentively. "I don't want to abuse the fact that you're vulnerable, but I don't want to offend you by refusing. I have to admit, baby, that our desires completely coincide."

He bent over me and our lips merged into a passionate, burning kiss. His tongue gently caressed mine, and his hands slowly, confidently and methodically removed my clothes. His kiss lasted just long enough for him to undress me, and I stood naked before his admiring eyes. Without taking his eyes off my naked body, he quickly removed his clothes and I saw a scar on his chest.

"What's that?"

"Shh." He put his hand over my lips and began gently to caress my breasts and stomach. "Baby, you're incredible! Amazing! Even more beautiful than before."

He kissed every centimetre of my body and I was excited by the touch of his lips on my skin. I was burning with passion and the desire flamed within me like a huge forest fire which I could not control. I wanted him. I had always wanted him. And he desired me no less that I wanted him. His hard flesh pulsated powerfully and with one movement he penetrated me firmly and unhesitatingly, and with every movement of his masculinity the fire within me flamed even more and more and I no longer knew where I was, who I was or where I was going.

His gentle thrusting movements filled me up, gradually becoming stronger. I felt completely taken over by his rhythm, begging him to be even more powerful. And when the fire within me was about to consume me, a huge wave of ecstasy flooded through my body, like an enormous tsunami carrying both of us on its crest. Krasi groaned with supreme pleasure and the thrusting slowly died down and only the slight trembling of my body reminded me of the wild dance of our bodies moments before. I lay in his arms and I was relaxed, content and exhausted.

***

I smiled in the darkness.

"I should cry now."

He kissed my head.

"Why? It was marvellous! I hope I wasn't disappointing?"

"Nonsense, you're incredible! Don't you know that in films married women always cry and regret showing any weakness?"

"Ha ha! You're not one of them!"

I laughed, with a slight tone of bitterness.

"No, I'm not. I'm corrupt!"

"Come on! Don't talk like that. You're wonderful!"

"Krasi, you really were the love of my life!"

"I don't know about you, baby, but I've loved you for a long time. Almost 15 years. Why didn't you come with me then? Why?"

"I don't know. I was still a child. A stupid and jealous child, and why did you run away? Did you kill that man?"

"Yes, I killed him. But it was in self defence. This scar is from him. I almost died. The knife hit a bone and didn't pierce the heart."

I felt faint.

"Don't talk like that, it's awful!"

"I thought you wanted to know? That night we had to make a huge transfer."

"What of, Krasi?"

"Some really valuable artefacts. Fourth century gold vessels and necklaces found at Perperikon. They would have made us rich and independent for once and for all. We would have lived in peace. I would have got you into school, and I..."

"And you?"

"I would have carried on trading, of course! But legally."

My heart skipped a beat.

"And what happened, Krasi?"

"What happened? Svetlin and me, you remember him?"

"Yes!"

"Well, we went to the meeting with the goods. And that bastard who promised to bring the foreigners. Some American collectors."

"And then what?"

"Well, he didn't bring them. He brought some thugs who wanted to kill us and steal the treasure. They attacked us with knives and we got into a bloody fight. Well, I didn't give in and I killed him and the thugs ran away. I told you that we should have run away. When I got home, I was injured. I was losing blood; I could have died. You got furious and went crazy but I didn't have the time to deal with you. So I left you a telephone and some money. We left Bulgaria about a month later. But you had already disappeared. I waited for you to call every day. I looked all over Plovdiv for you. And then Sofia. There was no trace of you."

"I had fallen into the hands of Bruno, and he raped me and then made me a prostitute."

"Where was this?"

"In one of the most expensive hotels in Sofia."

"The bastard. I'll kill him. But first we'll get your children back."

Krasi hugged me tightly.

"My darling little girl! I can't imagine what you've been through. Did they drug you?"

"No, no. They only drugged the girls who resisted. I gave in quickly."

I told him everything which came into my head, down to the smallest detail.

"And then when I met Sergio and Mario, I had made up my mind to run away with Nat, because my relationship with Bruno was in a dangerous phase."

He looked at me curiously.

"He was so much in love with me that he wanted to marry me. But with him, there's only one way out: you either accept or die...and I just didn't want to think about what my life would be after that. I owe everything to Sergio and Mario. They literally saved me and Natasha."

"Do you love him?" However hard he tried to control himself, I could sense his voice trembling.

"Yes. I don't want to lie that I don't love him. I love him. He's good, intelligent, devoted and caring. Everything you can imagine! He's a wonderful husband. So, yes, I love him with all my heart. But I love you as well! You are my young years, you are my madness, you are everything which I will never have again. I realised it when I saw you again. That's very sad. And I realised something else. You are my world. Perhaps, because you're Bulgarian, or perhaps because you're everything which Sergio isn't. Because you're on the other side of the barrier. And because that's where my spirit lies as well. I wanted to be with you tonight because I wanted to have a farewell. This night is ours and ours alone. I want us to live it with all the passion of our love which didn't have a future and will never have one."

He cut me off with a tender kiss and would not let me continue my sad monologue.

"Oh, my sweet Princess! I love you! I have always loved you!"

The entire night was taken up by mad, passionate and exhausting love-making. We fell asleep as dawn broke.

"Krasi, we can't fall asleep. I have to be home early in the morning," I muttered as I nearly fell asleep.

"I promise that we'll be home at eight," he replied.

"What time is it now?"

"Seven."

"Oh..." I woke up in a second and leapt out of bed. "Is it really?" My heart was pounding.

"Ha ha, I'm joking. It's only 5. Go to sleep!"

"I will kill you!" I threatened him and closed my eyes immediately.

I had just fallen asleep when he woke me.

"Come on, baby! Time to get up!"

I couldn't move.

"But I've just fallen asleep! What's wrong?"

"It's time to go. It's almost seven."

"You're lying!"

"No, I'm not! Time to get up! The coffee's going cold."

"You're awful!" I muttered and opened my eyes. Krasi stood in front of me holding a tray with cups of coffee and miniature croissants. He had a beautiful flower in his mouth. Red. Its stalk was clasped between his teeth. He was remarkable and gallant.

"Krasi, that's not fair," I said and took a cup of coffee.

"What?" he asked. He held the flower between his index finger and thumb and caressed my face with it.

"That you're so sweet with me."

He laughed happily and continued playing with the flower, stroking my body down to my breasts.

"When was I never sweet with you? Come on, pull yourself together. Eat quickly, drink your coffee and let's go, unless there's something else you want to do?"

"What, for example?" I said to irritate him, although I already knew the answer.

"This..." He took the tray away and cuddled up to me. He gently bit the nipple of one of my breasts and sucked on it with his tongue. I groaned with pleasure and burst into flame.

"Krasi, that's enough!" I didn't object very convincingly, and if I had to be honest, I even hoped that he wouldn't listen to me.

"You're so tempting! Like a real Delilah!"

I felt the growing hardness of his masculinity and the sweet pain when he penetrated me. And the world once again spun in an intoxicated dance, and we were once more on the crest of a wave, in an enormous ocean of feelings and emotions, glistening with love and passion.

***

"Don't drive so fast, I'll never forgive you if we have an accident."

"So why did you sleep so much? And then entice me into bed?" Krasi laughed. "You're a temptress!"

"But you didn't need a second invitation, did you?" I asked, slightly cuttingly.

"I'm not mad, am I? A beautiful woman in my bed and miss out on the opportunity?"

I laughed and slapped him on the back of the head.

"Rascal!"

"Delilah!"

The car flew along the road to Milan and we would soon have to part.

"Krasi, what are we going to do? We've got four days left. If I lose my children, I'll die." My voice shook.

"I know, princess. Don't worry, I'm sure he won't kill them. He's just blackmailing you. But I'll find him by tomorrow."

I looked at him anxiously.

"Who will you find by tomorrow?"

"Who? Bruno, of course. You don't imagine I was talking nonsense when I told you I would get your children back?"

"Oh, Krasi, what would I do without you?" I sobbed. "What are you, how do you do it? Are you a magician, or God?"

He said nothing.

"Tell me."

"Don't ask any more questions, baby! Remember what I used to say to you."

"People who know too much, grow old quickly," I muttered.

"That's right. Keep calm. I don't think he's as powerful as he thinks he is."

"Krasi, you're wrong. He was very high in the hierarchy."

"Of the mafia?"

"Yes."

"Don't worry, baby, we're more powerful!"

I didn't answer.

Krasi drove; the car flew and I relaxed into the comfortable seat to think about things. Natasha would already be up and about. Would she go into my room, to wake me for coffee? She still hadn't realised that I wasn't there, otherwise my phone would be burning. I took it out and checked it just in case. No one had called.

"What is it, baby? Is anyone looking for you?"

"No, I'm just looking."

"Listen to me. I'll call you this afternoon at about four, to give you instructions."

"What instructions?"

"You'll see. Is there anything else, the smallest thing, some slight detail which you might have forgotten, and which you haven't told me?"

I concentrated. I rummaged through my memory.

"Go back to the moment when you went to the yacht with that man who gave you the order to follow him."

I went back to that moment when we turned a corner and walked towards the yacht. The gangway. The polished surface of the deck. The door to the cabin. Something like a crest beneath a round dark glass.

"I don't know whether I told you about the crest."

Krasi looked at me with interest.

"What crest?"

"There was a crest on the door, just under the porthole. Gold."

"You've been like that since you were little! You see something brass, and you reckon it's gold!" He grinned.

I looked at him crossly.

"Very funny!"

"Don't be cross, baby. Anything else?"

"Anything else... He was drinking something but I didn't see what," I said with a note of anxiety in my voice.

"Don't worry, baby! I was just asking. We'll find him. Here we are, we've arrived."

"No, no. Carry on down to the end of the street. There's a very good bakery for bread and cakes. I want to buy some croissants."

We stopped in front of the bakery and I looked at him.

"Krasi, you know we can never do that again?"

"Princess," he smiled, "never say never. Ciao! I'll call you."

I leapt out of the car and pushed open the door to which a bell was attached. The aroma of freshly baked croissants was intoxicating.

"Good day, how can I help you?"

"Two croissants, please."

The shop assistant was in a good mood and smiled broadly.

"We have some freshly baked canoli...."

"No thank you! Just that." I grabbed the bag with the croissants and ran out of the shop.

The porter of the building greeted me politely.

"How are you today? What a fine day!"

I just nodded and ran up the stairs. Right in front of the door, my telephone rang. I looked. It was Natasha.

"Hello, Nat. Open the front door, I'm here."

She said nothing. The door opened immediately and she peered out with a frightened expression. She was still in her night dress. So, she was just getting up.

"Where have you been? You really frightened me. You didn't leave me a note."

There was an aroma of coffee in the corridor.

"Oh, Nat! I couldn't sleep. I went to get something for breakfast. Here I am!"

I lied to her in cold blood. I would tell her the truth one day, perhaps in many years. But I couldn't tell her now. It was very personal and very special.

"But there's plenty of food here! I thought you might have gone to see Sergio without me!"

"Oh, no. We'll go after ten. That's what the doctor said. And how are you?" I glanced at her for a moment. Her hair was tousled and she was still sleepy.

"I'm not going to take pills ever again."

"What pills, Nat?"

"Sleeping pills. I did sleep but now I feel tired and not refreshed. Just look at you, you've got a million and one problems, and you look fresh and beautiful. You're just radiant!"

Natasha kissed me kindly on the cheek. Should I tell her? No. I would be silent about it.

"Nat, pills aren't a good thing. We have to destroy the problems which are causing us the discomfort, but all we do is suppress them with pills. You understand me?"

Natasha looked at me and muttered, "If I could only be like you!"

"You can, Nat! I'll help you. But let's solve my problems first. Then we'll start on yours."

The sun was just beginning to peer in through the window. The air conditioners worked ceaselessly, otherwise it would have been impossible to breathe in the apartment. We breakfasted on the croissants which really were delicious, and Natasha went to get dressed.

I went into the bathroom to take a shower and lost myself in deep thought. Everything that was happening was so extreme that I had had no time to sort out events and arrange my thoughts, let alone analyse them. I was worried about how I would look Sergio in the eye. Whichever way I looked at it, the truth pierced me. I had been unfaithful to Sergio and what was worse, I had been unfaithful to him not just with my body, but with my heart. Yes! That was the main problem. I had done it completely consciously. What was even worse was that I had no regrets: quite the opposite. The mere thought of Krasi was like elixir for my soul. I felt twice as strong, infinitely loved and protected. I noticed that when my thoughts turned to my children, I was calmer and more confident. My panic and anxiety had disappeared, and that was all down to Krasi. I just hoped that he wouldn't disappoint me.

"No, he won't. He had never lied to me!" I said it out loud and laughed. "I just hope that all this doesn't drive me mad."

By ten we were at the hospital. I looked anxiously at the door behind which was Sergio. If he were to look into my eyes, he would probably realise the truth. Even Natasha looked at me a couple of times and eventually remarked, "I don't know why, but you look different today."

My heart leapt.

"Nonsense!"

"No, no, it's true. You seem to be all lit up."

"Natasha, don't make me laugh! What do you mean by lit up? I'm not a traffic light!"

"Ha ha! You know very well what I'm talking about. Your eyes are glowing with that very individual green sparkle. If I didn't know about your problems, I would bet that you were in love."

I didn't know how to react to this. She was much more perceptive than I had given her credit for.

"Natasha, don't make me cross..."

"Please come in, Signora Severini."

A young beautiful female doctor was standing in the doorway. I jumped up from the bench and, with trembling legs, I went into my husband's hospital room. Sergio lay still, a drip in his left arm and a monitor connected to his heart. My own heart shrank with pain and torment.

"Hello, Sergio, my darling! How are you?" I leant over and kissed his unshaven chin.

He hugged me with his free arm and pulled me passionately towards him, for a few seconds during which I realised that I was no more than a quite ordinary bitch.

"How are you, my darling girl? How are things going? Any news about the children?"

"No. I'm expecting a phone call this afternoon."

"Who from? The guys we hired?"

"Yes. Yes. Their boss is Bulgarian too," I spluttered and coughed. Tears welled up in my eyes.

"Have you caught a cold?" Sergio was worried. "You've got a bad cough!"

"No, no!" I spluttered. "He told me that he guaranteed the safe return of our children. They said they would find Bruno in the next 12 hours or so."

Sergio looked at me without blinking.

"So then, don't think about it and don't worry."

"I can't stop worrying. I'm in here lying in this bed and you're outside battling for them." His voice shook.

"Don't talk like that! I'm not doing that much. All I do is sit and wait."

"The most important thing is for you to stabilise," Natasha intervened. "Those men will do their job and everything will be all right."

Sergio nodded his head sadly.

"I want to leave. I want to be with you at this moment."

"Sergio, darling. Let's just wait for them to carry out their tests today and you can come home tomorrow. Don't be childish."

He sighed heavily and said, "All right then. But no later than tomorrow."

"I'm going to the doctors' room," I said and walked towards the door. "You stay here and chat."

I was met with unpleasant news.

"The blood tests are not good. Signor Severini doesn't know it yet, but it looks as though he will be spending longer in hospital than he might want to."

"Why?" This time I really was frightened.

"He has extremely high cholesterol, thickened blood and extremely high levels of triglycerides. And that's not all. His blood sugar levels are five times above normal. We can't let him go. His heart was out of rhythm and all that combined with high blood pressure... That's his condition at the moment. He's got complete medical insurance, I imagine?"

"Yes, yes," I confirmed anxiously.

"Then everything's fine," the doctor continued. "We'll begin therapy and complete tests, to see the source of all these problems in such a young man, but as far as I can see some of them are emotional. He's very anxious and excited, and that is not helping him at the moment."

"I'll speak to him, doctor. Thank you."

As I walked along the corridor back to the room, I thought about what I was going to do. What was I going to say to him? There were three and a half days left until the deadline. He was clearly going to stay in the hospital. There was no choice. I went boldly into the room.

Natasha turned to me with a smile.

"I just told your husband that I'm going to go out to the shop opposite and get some shaving foam and a razor. I'll give him a shave. We want to make him as handsome as possible, especially with such a young and pretty doctor."

"That's a wonderful idea," I said seriously. "Why don't you go home and get some toiletries and some other things I need. I'll stay here with him."

"Why, what's wrong?" Sergio looked at me suspiciously.

"Because, I'm sorry, you really will have to stay here for a few more days."

"Why, Ioana what's wrong? Am I going to die?"

"No, darling. You'll live a long and happy life, but you have to calm down. Most of all you mustn't worry about me and the children. In four days' time they'll be with us. But you're in bad shape and you need treatment."

I recounted my conversation with the doctor verbatim and finally asked him, "Promise me that you will do exactly as the doctors want you to do. If you want to get better quickly, you have to stop worrying. I want you home in the best of health. Don't do anything stupid. The things which have to happen in a couple of days' time, will happen. You know that those people will do everything they promised to. And they're getting paid for it."

Sergio remained silent and disgruntled.

"Sergio. Please!" I took his free hand and kissed it. "Sergio! You don't want to leave me a widow and the children fatherless? Pull yourself together!"

He hugged me tightly and nodded silently.

"I'll keep you informed but don't you worry. Just think calmly that everything will be all right. I'll come with the children to get you and then we'll for a long vacation."

He looked at me, his eyes heavy with tears; two drops rolled down his cheeks. My heart broke when I saw him lying helplessly.

"Darling, this is just a test. We will overcome it and we'll carry on with our lives. I promise you. Just believe in it."

"Ioana! I love you!"

"I love you too! Just believe that everything will be all right."

"I know it will."

Natasha stood there frozen.

"Go on, Nat. Go back home and bring his things."

Natasha moved. "Let's make a list so I don't forget anything."

"You're not going senile are you? Do we really need to write it down?" I said crossly.

"I'll tell you who's going senile! You came here, threw a bomb into the works, got me and Sergio worried and now you're giving orders left, right and centre. She's bad isn't she, Sergio?" She smiled playfully at my husband.

"She's marvellous! I really would die without her." He smiled for the first time since we had come in.

Natasha, however, was still pretending to be cross.

"She's marvellous? Nonsense! She's like the plague!"

I stuck my tongue out at her.

"Go on, Nat, clear off! I want to spend some time with my husband alone."

She gave a conspiratorial wink, blew a kiss from the door, and went out.

Sergio asked me, "Are you going to meet him at the yacht?"

"Probably, yes. But we'll see what our boys come up with. I'm waiting for a call this afternoon. They're still looking for him. But don't you worry about that."

"I can't not think about it. You know that very well. I'll just try not to worry."

"That's right! We'll leave everything in the hands of God."

"Yes. And in the hands of that Bulgarian," my husband added.

At that I felt a spasm in my throat. I coughed again. My conscience was clearly somewhere in the region of my throat.

"From a purely practical point of view, yes. By the way, Sergio, we have to be ready to pay the money. Is Mario really going to pay the whole amount?"

"Yes, that's what we agreed. Then we'll sort it out between us. You haven't called my parents, have you?"

They lived in Milan where we lived first all before going to Locarno. They were sweet and cultivated people. But they were old and we hadn't told them anything about the children being kidnapped. Now Sergio didn't want them to know what he was in the hospital.

"No, I haven't called them. Should I have done?"

"Of course not. I don't want to worry them. I don't know what's going to happen to me, but I think I might summon a notary to make a will. I've always put it off thinking that I was young, but it catches up with you. And now look what's happened. Just in case I die..."

"Sergio, don't you dare talk like that!" I called out passionately. "You're going to live. Don't even think about leaving me and the children. Stop talking nonsense! You'll see. In ten days' time you'll be as healthy as an ox!"

He looked at me lovingly and I impulsively fell at his feet and kissed them.

"Sergio, I love you! Forgive me for everything I've caused you. I love you!" I was completely sincere.

"Ioana, for God's sake! Come to your senses! What on earth have you done to me? You never meant to do it; it all happened just out of the blue. But perhaps it's all part of the strict logic of cause and effect? Whatever it is, you have no blame! Quite the opposite, in fact: you're a victim."

I was profoundly moved by the purity of his soul which only served once more to prove how tainted my own was.

It was all I could do to hold back from telling him the entire truth. He was so pure and noble, that he might just understand me and forgive me. But I held my tongue.

I left Sergio with kisses and promises that he wouldn't worry. Natasha went to work and I went back to the apartment. I needed to be alone. I desperately had to arrange my thoughts, and to take an impartial look at everything which was happening. I didn't know my own thoughts. I adored my family; my children and Sergio were the meaning of my life, and they continued to be so. However, Krasi's appearance had upset my equilibrium and I had taken a leap into a relationship which was not so pure or transparent.

If only I had been more resilient. But what did resilience mean? It meant standing up to temptations. So, I wasn't resilient. The worst thing was that I had absolutely no regrets – quite the opposite. The thought of everything that had happened last night made me feel lighter, as though the burden had fallen from my back. And it made me smile. How absurd it all was! If someone had told me that I would experience the thrill of love while my children had been taken away from me, kidnapped by a bandit with a terrifying past, and perhaps present, I would have spat at him! Alas. I was clearly a fallen woman with no scruples or sense of guilt.

God, that's enough of feeling sorry for myself. The most important thing at that moment was to free my children, whatever I had to go through. Sergio was out of the game, in the hands of the doctors. I hoped they would make him better; I didn't want to think about any complications. He was a wonderful man and didn't deserve this.

In fact, there was little chance that the complicated situation I found myself in would get any clearer in the next couple of days: quite the opposite. In all probability, they were to be the most sublime days of my life up to that moment. But I was prepared for them. Krasi had given me the confidence which I lacked up to that moment. My stomach was wracked with pain when I thought about him. God, how did that come into my head? I swear that I didn't want it to happen! I lived in my peaceful and beautiful world with my children, Sergio, and my small family joys. I had everything I needed, everything which had been taken away from me in my childhood, all of it. And then this! That mafia bastard had once again come back into my life, and kidnapped my children!

And then a second bomb! The greatest love of my young years had swum back to the surface from the depths of oblivion to save my children. It was enough to drive me mad! And on top of it all, Sergio, the pillar of my life, had physically collapsed and was now lying in the hospital over the road with a long list of symptoms, including the possibility of a heart attack.

I had to withstand all of this. At all costs! There were three days left. I didn't know what would happen after that. Krasi hadn't called yet. Should I call him? I suppressed my desire and set to work tidying Natasha's apartment.

Oh, and she was beginning to worry me as well! Looked at from a purely technical point of view, her anxieties paled in comparison with my misery, but I didn't want to underestimate them, since she had hinted a couple of times at suicide.

It was strange that when we lived in that hotel and any man could have us in exchange for a hundred dollars, and we lived a life of total uncertainty of whether we would be alive tomorrow, she never once protested. She calmly waited for her fate, but now? She had her own business which was rapidly expanding. She had a peaceful and guaranteed life, she lived in a luxury apartment and she drove an expensive car. But none of this gave her any joy.

I had to admit that Mario was ruining her future, but who was to blame for that? She should have clarified their relationship a long time ago. Given that he was so devoted to his own family, I couldn't believe that he would have objected to Natasha having her own. I knew her well. She was just weak. She carried her pain in her heart but didn't take any steps. God, I only hoped that she would not swallow a handful of pills!

I would have to turn my mind to her. But first I needed to get my children back.

What were they doing right now? I wondered. The moment I thought about my children, my heart pounded and I felt a sharp pain under my breasts to the left. I felt as though I was being pierced by a burning spear. And now I felt it again. My darlings! I hoped that Bruno was telling the truth that they were being looked after well.

God! How could you allow it? I have sins, but my children? What are they to blame for?

My soul was stabbed with pain and anger. I walked resolutely into the living room where my telephones lay. I would call Krasi. The moment I looked at the telephone, he rang. I shook with excitement.

"Hello? Ioana, what are you doing?" Krasi's voice immediately calmed the anger rising within me.

"Krasi, I was just about to call you. You beat me to it by a second."

"Are you alone?"

"Yes. Why?"

"I've got news for you, baby!"

My teeth chattered with excitement so much that I couldn't speak.

"Hello? Princess, are you there?"

"Yes."

"We've found him!"

"Krasi! So quickly?"

"Yes. Found and identified. I even have photographs."

"And the children?"

"We're working on that, baby! Don't worry, we'll find them as well."

"Where is he?"

"On his yacht."

"And now what?" I panted.

"Now we carry on. If we manage to do it in three days, everything will be OK. We'll get the children ourselves. If we don't, then you'll have to get involved as well. Even though I don't want it to come to that."

"Krasi, don't worry about me. I'll do everything I have to."

"I know, baby! How's your husband?"

I swallowed with difficulty.

"He's not well."

"I'm sorry about that. But don't worry! They'll fix him up."

"I'm praying for that," I whispered.

"Ciao, baby! And look after yourself!" he smiled into the telephone. "I'll keep you informed. Kiss you!"

"So do I." I hung up.

I was too anxious to sit down, so I paced up and down the apartment. It was a good job it was so big! Should I call Sergio? No. I didn't want to worry him. Yes, but he would be worried anyway with the uncertainty and everything else. On the other hand, they might be listening in to the telephone. The police, or Bruno. I didn't know how far his power extended. Best to keep quiet. I would go into the hospital in the morning.

My pulse must have been two hundred. I needed to calm myself down somehow. I rushed like a typhoon through the laundry room. I gathered up everything which needed washing, went into the bathroom, dropped my clothes into the bath and started washing madly. I concentrated on the washing and tried not to think about anything else. I drained the clothes and put them into the drier. But I still couldn't calm down. I switched on the vacuum cleaner and carefully cleaned the entire 150 square metres of the apartment. I wiped and dusted. Sweat dripped off me. I went into the bathroom and took an almost cold shower.

When I had dressed and got ready to cook dinner, Natasha came home.

"God, what's happened here?" she called out.

"Nothing much."

"Everything's shining! Did you do it all?" She looked at me suspiciously.

"Who else? Just imagine it!" I muttered sarcastically.

"Ha ha! I'm not used to seeing you in that light but it's wonderful! I won't have to clean for at least a month."

She planted a kiss on my cheek.

"Something smells very nice as well. What are you cooking?"

"Moussaka," I emphasised, because I knew that she particularly liked Bulgarian food.

"Now that's just too much! What do I owe all this spoiling to?" Natasha looked at me happily.

"Nat, they've found him."

She immediately turned pale and bit her lips.

"Bruno?"

"Yes. They've found him."

"And the children?"

"That's what I asked as well. No, not yet."

"Goodness, that's what you call quick!"

"Yes. Absolute professionalism. Wasn't I right, Nat, to make contact with the mafia?"

"Yes, you really were." Natasha was as excited as I was.

"That's why I cleaned the entire apartment and washed everything. I even washed the clothes. By hand."

Natasha stared in disbelief.

"What, the whole lot by hand?"

"Yes, I just couldn't settle. I was going mad."

"I understand that. Let's have a drink."

"Wine?"

"No, something a bit stronger! To relax our nerves."

We poured out some vodka with orange, clinked our glasses and took a drink. Natasha sighed.

"If only he could bring the children back tomorrow," she dreamed.

"It won't be so easy. I've got a premonition of that."

"God, I forgot. Do Sergio and Mario know? Have you called them?"

"No, I haven't told anyone. I want Sergio to sleep calmly tonight, and as for Mario...We can call him if you want to. Either from your phone or the home phone."

Natasha leapt up.

"The moussaka! It's burning!"

We both ran into the kitchen.

It hadn't burnt. We took out the baking tray and left it to cool. I dialled Mario.

"Hello, Mario, it's Ioana," I said. "Can I talk to you?"

Mario was somewhere very noisy.

"Yes! Oh yes! Talk to me. I can hear you."

"They've found him."

"OK. I'm glad about that. Sergio?"

"He's still in hospital. They're going to do a complete range of tests. I haven't told him. I thought I would tell him when I go tomorrow."

"Good idea. Have they found only him?"

"Yes. For the moment."

"I understand. Say hello to Sergio from me. Tell him not to worry about anything, especially about money."

"Thank you, Mario. From me and from him!"

"Tell Nati I'll call her later. Ciao!" He hung up.

Natasha was looking at me.

"I don't know. He was outside somewhere," I said to her silent question. "A very noisy place. He said he was happy that they've found Bruno, and that he would call you later. That's all I know."

Natasha bit her lips and drank her entire drink in a single gulp.

"Nat! Don't be angry! You know how busy he is. He got all sorts of things going on. To be honest, even after so many years, I don't know what business he's in. And even Sergio won't say anything when I ask him, or avoids the question."

"And do you think I know? He's so secretive! He's got offices all over Italy, but never says what he does. He says he's a businessman. But what, why and how? No one knows. He's built such an impenetrable barrier around himself. And he always keeps me outside it."

"God will probably punish me for being so ungrateful," I said. "I just told him five minutes ago how indebted Sergio and I were for the money he's promised to give us, but now I want to say something else. Nat, just get rid of him! If you have to, give everything back to him, but get rid of him and start afresh."

A silence ensued, broken by Natasha with a deep sigh.

"I don't know if I can. But I'll try. Not for any other reason, but I want a child. And he's categorically opposed to the idea! That really hurts me and takes the whole point away from my life. But the most difficult thing is that I love him."

"You love him, but you're by yourself the whole time." I interrupted her abruptly.

"Almost."

"So, you see? I don't want to interfere in your life but I do think it's time you took some serious steps."

"I promise."

"Oh Nat, do you think my children are all right? How do you think they're doing without me? It drives me mad thinking how helpless and defenceless they are at the moment."

"Don't torment yourself. Whatever happens, just concentrate on the thought that in a few days' time they'll be back with you."

"But Nat! How do you think they'll get over the trauma? Can you just imagine that?" I sobbed and tears flowed from my eyes. "They must be like two crushed flowers now."

Natasha hugged me.

"Don't cry, please, everything will be all right. They're resilient like you. They'll get back on their feet again. They resemble you. Just take a look at yourself. No one can break you. You're the bravest girl in the world."

Natasha lifted my head and kissed my wet cheeks.

"Wipe away your tears."

"And blow my nose?" I smiled and sniffed.

"Yes! Head up! We're warriors!"

"That's right, Nat! He won the battle, but I'll win the war!"

I went into the bathroom to wash my face and Natasha set the table for dinner. Once we had finished off the entire moussaka, which was really delicious, we both went into our separate rooms. After the heady whirlwind of events around me, all the emotions, fears, romantic adventures and everything else, I fell asleep.

I must have been completely exhausted, since at ten o'clock the next morning I could barely open my eyes.

When I saw what time it was, I leapt up as though stung by a wasp. I called Sergio from my bed.

"Hello, Sergio. Hi! How are you?"

"Darling! What's wrong with your voice?"

"Nothing, I'm fine. I'm just getting up. I couldn't wake up."

He sighed with relief.

"Tell me how you are, and don't laugh!"

"I'm all right. They're doing all sorts of tests. I'm taking my medicine. They've got me on a drip. And how do you feel?"

"I don't know, Sergio. Last night I was really missing you and the children."

"Ioana, there's only three days left."

"Yes. Just be calm. We'll find them. I think I'll come and see you in about two hours. Can I?"

"Why come? Better to rest!"

"No, no. I'll come. I've got something to tell you."

"What? What's happened?" Sergio immediately sounded anxious.

"Don't worry, darling! It's good news."

"All right then. I'll be waiting for you."

"Time to get up. Ciao!"

I found a note from Natasha in the kitchen.

I couldn't bring myself to wake you, you were sleeping so sweetly. I'm going to work. Have a nice and useful day!

"We'll see how useful it will be," I muttered and turned on the coffee machine.

It was quiet and calm in the hospital. Sergio was waiting for me in the corridor. He looked thin and his hair seemed grey. He kissed me passionately with love.

"My beautiful little girl! I miss you so much! I was sad for you and the children last night as well. And when I think of them…"

"Sergio," I interrupted him anxiously. "Please, didn't we agree that you weren't going to worry?"

"Yes, but I can't. That's beyond my will power. Tell me…?"

"Are you allowed to walk around?"

"Yes. Look, they've put a halter on my heart."

"What's that?" I asked with a real expression of fear.

"It monitors my heart twenty-four hours a day."

"Is it serious?"

"No, no, it's just a touch of arrhythmia. But my blood pressure's slowly getting back to normal, although my blood sugar's still high. They said the stress might have caused me diabetes."

"Oh my God! I muttered. "I'll kill that bastard for ruining our life."

"Darling, don't swear like a drunk woman. You're a lady."

"Nothing will stop me. I'll fucking kill him."

"Don't talk like that. I told you! Come on, I've been waiting for you to go down into the park."

It was very hot but we chose a shady and comfortable bench to sit on.

"Let me kiss you. I love you so much!"

He squeezed me passionately in his arms and pressed his lips against mine. I pushed him away softly and laughed.

"Sergio, we'll break the halter."

"I'd prefer to break the bed." He winked. "I can't wait."

"And that time will come as well! Just let this nightmare finish first."

"Yes. You're right. Come on, tell me the news."

I looked at him straight in the eyes and told him.

"They've found him!"

My husband didn't seem to be particularly impressed. After a short silence he said, "That's good! So they're really doing their job. But you're still going to see him on the yacht in three days' time anyway."

Small drops of perspiration appeared on his forehead.

"Darling, please don't," I said. "There's no point in getting angry. They might find the children before that."

Sergio shook his head sadly.

"I don't believe it, Ioana! I don't believe it. I've got the feeling that things are going to get mixed up and complicated."

"Don't be like that, Sergio!" I said passionately. "It's only because you're here, shut up in this hospital and not outside with me, that you're looking so pessimistically at things. I'm convinced that we'll get our children back in a couple of days, and that bastard will pay a very high price for what he's done to us."

Sergio looked at me pensively but didn't say another word.

I tried to distract him with kisses and teasing but he was anxious and there was not a trace left of his good mood from earlier. This made me feel really stressed and I finally told him off.

"Don't be like that, the world isn't going to end tomorrow. Have faith! There's no better feeling than a mother's intuition. I can feel that the end is in sight. You'll see that I'll come with the children to take you home."

My husband burst into tears like a child and this upset me.

"You know, Ioana, I would never have believed that life would play such a bad trick on me. In the most difficult moment for my family when I should be protecting them, I'm sitting in my slippers waiting for someone else to do it instead of me. I'm just a mediocre good-for-nothing. I'm not even a man. Just completely spineless!"

"Come on, Sergio! I'm fed up with your moaning. That's not true. You're the most wonderful man and father in the world. The details don't matter. You're wonderful and I'm very happy that I met you. Come on, don't talk any more nonsense. Just get better quickly because there are so many things we have to do before we get old."

I kissed with all my burning passion and tugged at him lightly to stand up.

"Come on, they're probably looking for you in the hospital. If I have any news, I'll run to you immediately."

"All right, darling! I love you so much, you know!"

***

The next day at about lunch time, the phone rang. It was Krasi.

"Hello, Ioana? What are you doing? Are you alone?"

"I'm alone, tell me…"

"Are you nervous?"

"No, I'm not. I'm just stressed."

"I want to see you. Tonight."

"I can't, Krasi. What would I say to Natasha?"

"Tell her the truth."

"What? That you're my ex-boyfriend? And that we're having sex while we're trying to save my children?"

"I don't understand your sarcasm. I just want to talk to you. If we can't do it tonight, I can come over now."

"Why not? I'll be by myself all day long. Come over. When you get here, call me from downstairs. I'll tell the concierge."

"OK, baby."

Fifteen minutes later I met him at the door.

"Hi, Princess!" He bent down to kiss me.

"Krasi, don't let's start again!"

"Look, I've brought you something!" He was holding a box of ice cream.

"Come on in." I stepped back and let him in.

He walked confidently towards the living room, sat down on one of the couches and crossed his long legs. He cast a friendly look over the surroundings and said, "Very nice spot here. Well done, baby!"

"It's got nothing to do with me. It's all Natasha's," I cut him off.

"Don't get me wrong, baby, I meant it's very nice because you're here."

I had sat down at a distance from him. He smiled and patted the couch.

"Come and sit next to me. There's something I want to show you."

I got up hesitantly.

"Krasi."

"Come over here, I said."

I went over and sat next to him.

"Come closer, Princess. I won't eat you."

I was angry but did as he said. I sat right next to him.

"There you are, that's better!" he said happily and kissed me on the back of my head.

He took out his telephone an expensive smart phone. He rummaged through it and put it in my trembling hands. I looked at the screen and my heart began pounding wildly. My son was looking back at me from the screen.

"Robbie!" I cried out and dropped the telephone. Krasi caught it deftly before it hit the floor.

"Calm down, baby! Catch your breath. Do you want some water?"

"My child!" Tears welled up from my eyes and I suddenly felt that I was losing consciousness, and I began to tip over. Krasi jumped up.

"Ioana, wake up!" He ran to the kitchen to get some water and wet my face and chest. "Drink this and calm down."

I drank, spluttered and coughed, and then drank some more water. I could hear my heartbeat in my ears.

"Krasi, let me see it again. Have you got any others? What about Julia? Where's Julia? Are you listening to me?"

"Just wait. Catch your breath. Calm down. Calm down!" Krasi was stroking my head as though I was a dog. His favourite dog. I drank some more water and, slowly, I began to breathe more easily.

"That's what I wanted. Did you see? It wasn't so hard. Now just relax and listen to me. I don't have any other photographs of the children. But since I've got this one, it means that we've found them."

"Let me see the photograph again!" I begged him in a wheezing but calmer voice. Krasi gave me his telephone. I looked at it. Robbie had been photographed from some distance away. He was dressed in denim shorts and a tee-shirt. I didn't recognise the clothes. He was standing in front of a big house, looking at someone. He was holding something in his hands, but what was it? A bow? Yes, he was holding a bow in his hands, just like his own. He looked serious, and perhaps a little sad.

"Krasi tell me, before I die," I begged him.

"All right. Bruno's hidden the children in Stresa. That's where the photograph's from."

"Stresa?"

"Yes. They've rented the house from someone called Lucia Genovese, a 78-year old woman. The yacht 'Esmeralda' also belongs to her. I wouldn't be surprised if a woman with that name doesn't exist.

Bruno clearly knows what he's up to. The house is guarded by his people. About ten lads. Plus two women."

I pricked up my ears. "Women?"

"They're a well organised group. And I'm absolutely sure that they're well armed. He really must be very rich to be able to pay so many people."

"Won't it be best to tell the police?" I was beginning to get scared.

"Princess, don't you trust me?"

"Krasi, don't be offended, but I'm just frightened that you're no match for them."

"Who told you that?" He stared at me.

"No one, I'm just worried."

"Baby, I've got enough people to fight against him. What I'm worried about is where the children will be when I attack the house."

"Why haven't you got a picture of Julia?"

"Because she wasn't in the garden at the time."

A wave of anxiety immediately overcame me. "God, what if she's sick or something worse?" I sobbed.

"Stop crying! The child's fine. They're both fine."

"How do you know?" I sobbed. "Why didn't you take a photograph of her?"

"Ioana, please be quiet! I came here to try and make you happy, and you've gone mad. I have to decide how I'm going to get the children out of there. It's clearly not going to be easy, I have to admit it. I'm leaving now. You take it easy; I'll try to call you later."

"Oh, please don't leave me alone at this moment," I sobbed.

"I have to go; I've got so many things to do. You'll be fine."

"What am I going to do?"

"Get some sleep, because I don't know how much sleep you're going to get after tomorrow. I can't exclude the possibility that you might have to go back to the yacht. Are you prepared to take on that challenge, or am I not going to be able to count on you?"

I leapt from the couch and looked daggers at him.

"I am prepared to die, if I have to, to save my children."

"All right, Princess. That's how I like you, not sulking and snivelling."

Krasi gave me a passionate kiss that took my breath away. By the time I had caught my breath again, he had gone.

I took his advice, took half of one of Natasha's pills and flew away into the world of dreams.

***

Natasha woke me.

"You were so fast asleep, I thought you were dead. What's up?"

"Oh, Nat," I said with a thick tongue. "Get me some water."

She ran back with a glass of water in her hand. I drank thirstily and drained the glass.

"I'm all right. I took one of your pills. God, they really are awful."

"What did you take a sleeping pill for?" She looked at me severely.

"Because I needed to sleep. Krasi was here."

Natasha looked at me curiously. "Here?"

"Yes, what's so strange about that?"

"It seems strange to me, after all this time. What is he doing here?"

"He's the one, the man that Mario hired."

"Krasi?! What did he come for?"

"To show me a photograph of Roberto."

"Robbie?" Natasha held her head in her hands. "Have they found them?"

"Yes. In Stresa, in an enormous house. I saw it. It's guarded by about ten armed bandits. Bruno's clearly their boss. There are two women as well."

"Women?"

"Yes."

"Oh my God!"

"What's so strange about it? They could be servants or something."

"Or governesses?" Natasha suggested.

"I wouldn't be surprised. That bastard said he'd looked after the children as though they were heirs to the throne. Oh, I'm aching all over. This excitement will be the death of me," I complained.

"Hold on, darling!" Natasha fussed around me. "I'll give you a massage."

"That sounds like a good idea. I'm still so thirsty. Nat, don't take any more of that rubbish. I really do feel dreadful."

"Yes, you're right, and I'm not going to take them anymore. Just let me get some massage oil, and you put a sheet down. I don't want to make a mess of the bed linen."

267

"Oh, you're such a fuss pot. All right. I'll go and get one."

Natasha gave me such an incredible massage that I felt like I had been kneaded in a bread making machine.

"Nat, I feel like you've taken me apart! I don't know how I'm going to walk now!" I muttered, going to the bathroom where Natasha had run me a bath with aromatic oils, herbs and some other fragrances.

"You'll feel like a new person after a bath. Believe me. I'm a professional!" She laughed.

"To hell with your professionalism. I don't know why they pay you. I won't give you a penny. I feel like I'm in a different world."

"Stop complaining!" Natasha couldn't stop giggling. "Jump into the bath."

"That's easy for you to say," I mumbled. "If only I could lift my legs high enough!"

Natasha was rattling dishes and making dinner, while I lay blissfully in the bath. Just like Krasi had told me, I was gathering strength for the forthcoming battle. I had no idea that it was only hours away.

***

The next morning, I felt anxious and my eyes were puffy. There were only 24 hours left to the deadline which Bruno had given me. I hadn't slept a wink from worry. The fact that Krasi hadn't called made me incredibly anxious. I had no idea what I was supposed to do.

I stood next to the huge French windows in the living room and looked aimlessly into the street. It was early morning and the people in this wealthy suburb were still fast asleep. It was quiet and peaceful in the apartment. Natasha was also asleep and I must have been the only person awake in the street. The telephone rang angrily and shrilly, startling me so much that I jumped up. It was my personal telephone, not Krasi's. I looked anxiously at the unfamiliar number and I picked it up with a trembling hand.

"Hello?"

"How are you?"

I felt dizzy, it was Bruno. I took a deep breath.

"How did you find my number?"

"That's not important. Where are you?"

"That's none of your business." I decided to be firm although my knees were trembling.

"You haven't changed your mind, have you?"

"What makes you think that? No, I haven't changed it."

"Because you're not at home."

I froze.

"You're wrong. I'm at home."

"No, I'm not wrong. I'm calling you from the nursery."

I thought that my heart would explode. I'm not exaggerating. I could see it pounding through my night dress. I mustered all my courage and silently begged God to be by my side, and I replied with a quiet and calm voice.

"Look, you filthy bastard! You leave my home immediately, and be so kind as to wait for me until tomorrow when I come aboard your stinking tub! Don't make me any madder, because I'm on the verge of doing something which will resolve your problems and my problems forever."

Bruno said nothing, but listened silently. I silently and passionately prayed to God that he would help me.

"Except that it won't be tomorrow."

"When?" I shouted.

"Today. At one o'clock. Not a minute later," and he hung up.

I felt my stomach heave, and I ran to the bathroom to throw up. I retched deeply until I could no more. I must have made a loud noise, since Natasha ran in and cried out.

"Ioana, wait. Let me help you! What's happening?"

She began to wipe my face with a wet towel, while I sobbed silently on my knees in front of the toilet. Natasha helped me get up, washed my face and hands and took me into the dining room. She put me on a chair, sat next to me and took my hands in her lap.

"Calm down, calm down. Breathe. Drink a little water." My teeth chattered against the side of the glass.

"God, help us!" Natasha called out.

She gave me some valerian and she took some too, just in case. She was very touching in her concern for me. It was just that there was nothing she could do to help me. Was there anyone who could? *God, where are you? Don't leave me, please!*

"Ioana, come to your senses! How are you?" Natasha fussed around me.

"Nat! It's over," I muttered.

"Tell me what's going on, please! I'll go mad!"

"Bruno just called. He's been to our house. He called from the nursery."

"What? The bastard. We have to call the police. What are they doing? Idiots!"

"Don't you dare. No police. He wants me to go there today. At one o'clock in the afternoon."

Natasha froze. She stared at me in terror without blinking, as though hypnotised. Unlike her, I was now slowly coming to my senses and had got over the initial shock. I needed to act. I looked at my watch. It was ten minutes to eight. I had only five hours left.

I phoned Krasi.

"Hello? What is it, baby?" He sounded slightly worried.

"Krasi, he called. Just a moment ago. He's been to our house. He saw that I wasn't there. He brought the deadline forward. He wants me to go there today. At one o'clock and not a moment later." I said it all in a single breath.

"Just wait. What did he say, that he wanted you there today?"

"Yes."

After a few moments which seemed like an eternity, he said, "All right. The bastard's got ahead of us. He's a piece of stinking carrion. He doesn't even play fair. I'll call you in a little while with a change in the plans. Everything will be fine, baby. Believe me."

Natasha was nervously searching through the kitchen cupboards.

"Nat, what are you looking for?"

She continued looking stubbornly. She finally turned around, holding something in her hand, and handed it to me.

"Take it. You might need it." It was a small flick knife. Despite all the stress I was under, I laughed.

"You're completely mad! You don't think I'm going to cut him up with knife like that? Nat, I'm going to shoot him!"

"Don't talk nonsense. I'm giving it to you just in case you need to cut something, or make a hole in something. I don't know, just take it!

"Where did you get it from?" I asked.

"I found it years ago. I've always known that it would come in handy one day."

"And you've never shown it to me?"

"No. But now the time has come."

"Where did you find it, Nat?"

"You won't believe it."

"Try me!" It was starting to get interesting.

"When we first came to Milan, you know I moved into my first flat by myself. One morning, I was coming out of the house and there was a note addressed to me on the door. It said, 'Bitch, leave my husband alone! He's mine!'"

"Nat, that's awful!"

"You think so?"

"Yes."

"What made it worse was the way the note was attached to the door."

I froze. My eyes leapt to the knife.

Natasha nodded.

"It can't be! Does Mario know?"

"No. I've never told him."

"That was a mistake. And you've hidden it from me! You deserve a good hiding – what if she had killed you? His wife must be mad."

"No, she's not mad. She's a pure-bred Sicilian."

"What?" I couldn't believe my ears.

"Yes. She's from Palermo."

"How do you know?"

"Mario told me once. And I don't know why he told me. Perhaps because he wanted me to understand that I have to know my place."

"My God, Nat. What else is going to happen to us? What is this mad world we're living in, and how much longer is it going to drive us crazy?"

Natasha sat opposite me and took my hands in hers.

"I've always said it and I'll say it again. You're my sister. You're everything I've got. I made my will a long time ago. All my assets from my business, my bank deposit, all my jewels in the safety deposit box, I've left it all to you, Ioana. If anything happens to me, you're my direct and sole inheritor. According to my rough calculations, it comes to about four hundred and fifty thousand. You know that I have a weakness for beautiful jewels. They alone are worth about seventy thousand." I was shocked. I knew that Natasha had made some money, but this was quite something.

"What are you talking about, Nat? For God's sake! I'm touched, but now's not the time to talk about it. I'm the one going to Bruno, and I don't know whether I should have made a will. I love you, my darling and my pain! Life brought us together in the most difficult of times, when we had no idea whether we would survive. And we did. We thought that it was a thing of the past, but when I look at things now, we're in a right mess. I don't know what I could leave you in my will. I haven't got anything apart from my children and Sergio. If anything happens to me, marry Sergio and look after the children. I know that you love them as much as you love me. That way I'll be at peace and I'll look down on you from heaven and smile at you. And you might even have some more. That would be good."

It was Natasha's turn to object.

"Now you've gone mad!" We fell into each other's arms and sobbed for a long time.

Each of us cried for ourselves, and then for each other. Natasha cried for her loneliness, lack of children and the fear that she might be killed. She cried for me and the frightening uncertainty which awaited me.

I cried for my children, for Sergio's illness, for my impossible love for Krasi and the unconditional battle I was about to enter into in just a couple of hours' time, and from which someone would end up dead. I cried for Natasha, for her messed up life and her kind heart. And we would have cried for each other endlessly, if the telephone hadn't rung. I calmed down quickly and answered.

"Hello?"

"Ioana." Krasi sounded very serious. "I'll be there in twenty minutes. Get ready." He hung up before I had the chance to say anything. I panicked.

"Nat! He's coming to get me."

She jumped up.

"Who? Bruno?"

"Are you mad? Not Bruno! Krasi."

She ran off to pack my bags. She shouted, "We have to call Mario."

"Not now. I haven't got the time for that. You'll have to call him later."

"What about Sergio?"

I paused. What was I going to say to him?

"I don't know. Let Mario decide. I'm not going to call him. I haven't got the strength for him at the moment."

We were ready in ten minutes.

"Take the knife, please," Natasha pleaded.

"Oh, all right then. But he'll see it."

"Don't you remember that you were once the queen of hiding things?" Natasha said.

I laughed.

"That's right, I was."

"Let's sit down," said Natasha. "That's our custom."

We sat down and looked at each other in silence. Each of us said to the other with our eyes, "I'm with you."

We stood up and said farewell.

"Nat, remember what I said to you."

"And you too."

And then, simultaneously, as though we had rehearsed it thousands of times, "Look after yourself! I love you!" We laughed, hugged and before I burst into tears again, I left.

Krasi was waiting for me outside in the street. I looked at him in astonishment.

"Where's the car?" I asked.

"There it is." He showed me a taxi. "Come on, get in."

"Where's the driver?"

"I'm the driver. Get in without any fuss."

He put the bag in the boot, opened the door for me, walked around the car and got in. He drove off at full speed, and I looked at him in confusion.

"I don't understand..."

"What is there to understand? I'll drive you to Locarno by taxi. Otherwise how are you going to explain to him who I am? What if he's got people watching us here and there? Now just listen to me and from this moment on, you have to know that I'm your shadow and you don't need to be frightened of anything. I imagine that today, this evening at the latest, you'll be leaving Locarno and he'll take you somewhere. You just hold on and you'll see your children straight away. He won't trust you, and that will be completely normal. If he decides to check up on you, he won't take you to Stresa with the children, but somewhere else. That's even the best option, as far as I'm concerned."

"And the children?" I couldn't restrain myself from interrupting him.

"Just wait. He might take you somewhere else to test your loyalty. Do what he says and repeat that you want your children. He will give instructions for the children to be brought to you and that's when we'll act."

"That's how more or less I imagine things."

"I've always respected your resourcefulness." Krasi smiled at me. "Don't worry, baby! Everything will turn out well. Now, just give me the telephone, because he'll take it off you anyway, the moment you get on the yacht."

I gave it to him grudgingly.

"I've got a knife. Do you think he'll take it off me?"

Krasi laughed.

"He'll take it, if he sees it, of course. But he'll be looking for a telephone and possibly a gun."

"I'll put it in an obvious place," I said and I put it in a small pocket in my hand bag.

"Well done, baby! And don't go into battle without me, however much he might provoke you. Is that clear?"

"Yes. And where will you be?" I asked anxiously.

"Next to you."

"How will you be next to me?" I wouldn't leave him in peace.

"Stop asking. And remember, if you play too hard to get, he'll just get irritated. Act out a little play, 'Here I am, I'm yours,' I know you can do it. That will be best for everyone. Oh, I nearly forgot." He put his hand in his pocket and took out a little envelope. There were four small sachets in it.

"What's that?"

"Baby, if you treat him well, he'll let his guard down. Then put one of these into his drink, his coffee or his food. It doesn't have any taste."

"That reminds of a past time, when you and I..."

"Ha ha! Those good old times, you haven't forgotten. These sachets will make him more talkative and calmer. But hide them well. I don't know where."

"I do," I said confidently and put them into my pants. "I'll put them in a safer place later."

Krasi laughed and winked slyly.

"Just make sure he doesn't see you putting them in his drink."

"Don't worry. I've done it so many times before, you know that."

The car was flying towards Locarno. My heart had shrunk to the size of a button. I didn't know what would happen to me, Sergio or the children. This was all just a well shuffled game of patience which needed to be played out to the end. I sighed heavily.

"Don't worry, Princess. We're just one step away from success."

"That's easy for you to say."

Krasi looked at me and said quietly, "That's what it might look like to you, but looks can be deceiving, baby."

"Why? What's wrong? You've got everything, you don't have problems like mine."

He laughed quietly.

"No. I didn't have your problems. But from the moment I saw you, your problems became mine. So they're our problems now."

He put his hand gently on my knee and squeezed it softly.

"Baby, what would I give for the children we're going to save, to be mine!"

I looked at him inquisitively.

"Believe me if you can, but I was never able to fall in love again. You took all my love away with you."

I began to perspire.

"Krasi, you're not helping me. I'm at my wit's end with fear and stress, and you're talking to me about..."

"About us, baby. I'm talking to you about us. You were, and you still are, the only woman I've ever loved. I just want to tell you that I will do the impossible, but I will save you and your children from that psychopath. That's all. Just play the game until I intervene. I mean that you are not alone with him and there's no need to be afraid."

"I'm very pleased to hear it. But have you never...you know, after that. Well. You know what I mean."

"I know," he interrupted me. "Yes, of course I've been with other women. It was just sex. Nothing more."

"Didn't you get married?"

"No."

I said nothing more and watched the countryside fly past the windows.

"That's very sad," I said eventually.

"To some extent, I'm even grateful to that bastard, because if none of this had happened, I perhaps would never have met you again. It might sound a bit selfish, but it's the truth. And when all this ends, you'll disappear again, and I'll just have my memories of you."

"It's not fair to upset me like that," I sobbed.

"Don't upset yourself. Pull yourself together." He grinned and winked. "Stop snivelling." He looked at his watch. "We'll be there on time. Are you ready?"

"Yes," I replied sadly.

We spent the rest of the journey to Locarno in silence.

The town was green, clean and beautiful. It smelt of flowers and freshness. A cold, calm fragrance wafted from the lake. I would have to get out of the car soon.

"Krasi?"

"What is it, Princess?"

"Look after the children. I don't want them hurt."

"I'll look after them as if they were my own. I already promised you."

"Krasi?"

"What?" He looked at me playfully, tenderly and with a hint of anxiety. "I'll look after you, don't worry."

"That's not what I meant."

"What?"

I looked at him with desire and gulped. But he understood me.

"I love you too, baby! See you soon!"

I got out of the taxi, took my handbag and case and walked towards the Esmeralda, amongst a lot of other boats. The yacht looked deserted. There was no one on the deck or the bridge. However, the moment I set foot on the varnished wooden gang plank, the white door with the crest opened and, with my shoes in my hand, I entered.

I went boldly into the spacious cabin and saw him. He had not drawn the curtains and I could see that the cabin actually consisted of a number of smaller interconnected ones.

Bruno was waiting for me in the middle. He was dressed in white trousers and a blue shirt, and a captain's cap on his head. If I have to be honest, it suited him. He looked calm and contented, and smiled slightly.

"I admire your punctuality. Hello!" He offered me his hand.

I looked him up and down and said, "Hello."

"Is that all I get?" he grinned.

"What do you expect? Handstands?" I sulked. And I deliberately gave him my handbag and case. "You'll be wanting to search me? I'm not carrying any contraband."

He laughed again.

"Yes. I want to search you. Raise your arms above your head and walk towards me."

"Idiot, keep your hands to yourself! Don't you dare touch me."

He laughed out loud.

"That's how I like you. It's impossible not to love you, you're so amusing. How can I possibly search you without touching you? Why don't you take your clothes off then? Slowly and carefully," he suggested. "I'll just look without touching."

"Look, I'm not finding this very amusing. I've come here voluntarily. I haven't called the police. I'm playing honestly. I'm not like you."

Bruno walked in a circle around me and stared at me insistently.

"Are you being honest with me? Where were you all week? You probably jumped town the same day I let you go."

"No. The next day," I said, arrogantly.

He laughed out loud again.

"Where did you go?" he asked.

"To Milan, of course."

"What were you doing there?"

"That's none of your business. I had things to sort out."

After a short silence he said, "All right, I accept. What happened with your husband?" I trembled. Did he know?

"Bruno, I'm standing like a nail in the middle of this pig sty. Are you going to feel me up or shall I sit down? Are you going to examine my things or are you going to trust me?"

He approached me.

"No, darling. You wouldn't kill me, because you wouldn't get your children back without me. Isn't that right?"

I looked at him without blinking.

"Just be so kind as to give me your telephone."

I put my hand in my bag demonstratively and gave it to him. He took it.

"I hope that's the only one. Because you know what a bad temper I have."

I gave him an evil stare and said nothing.

"I'll show you to your cabin."

We went down the gleaming white steps into the bedroom. It was white and lilac. The enormous round bed had a crest above it. To the right of the bedroom there was a sliding door leading to a splendid bathroom with a small Jacuzzi. I turned to Bruno.

"And where am I going to sleep?"

"Does the bed look too small?" he asked me in a mocking tone.

"What about you?"

"You don't imagine that you're going to send me away? I'm going to sleep with you, of course."

I looked at him.

"Aren't there any other rooms?"

"Yes, there are. But you'll be here with me," he said firmly and his eyes glistened threateningly. I knew that gaze.

"All right, just leave me in peace for the moment. I want to take a shower and get changed."

"All right. I'll be waiting for you upstairs."

I threw my hair back. I was covered in sweat. I looked around the other cabins. It was a marvellous yacht. There were two separate small cabins with two beds in each and an en-suite bathroom. Everything was well appointed and perfectly maintained.

Everything gleamed with cleanliness. I looked in the cupboards and found luxury monogrammed towels and sheets. Even the bathroom accessories were monogrammed. Bruno was a huge snob. I wondered who did the cleaning. I couldn't believe he did.

I went into the bathroom and took a quick refreshing shower. I wondered what to put on. I didn't know what Natasha had put in the bag. I looked at it. Ha! She had even put a bathing suit in it. Hers. I almost laughed. The poor thing. She was so careful and thought of everything. I put on a pair of shorts and a tee shirt and tied my hair in a pony tail. I put on a hat and went out onto the upper deck.

That's when I saw the other man. He was sitting with Bruno on the bridge. They heard me and stood up. The man bowed respectfully.

"Good day, Signora. How are you?" It was the same Nikola who had brought me to the yacht the first time.

I nodded and looked inquisitively at Bruno.

"You look wonderful, darling." He turned to Nikola. "Nikola, we can get underway."

He took me by the hand and led me into the dining room.

"Come on, let's leave Nikola to do his job."

I sat on a soft and comfortable corner couch. Bruno began fussing around.

"Would you like a refreshing drink, or are you hungry?"

He paced between the fridge and the couch, placing glasses, ice cubes and freshly squeezed fruit juice on the table.

At that moment I felt the vibrations of the yacht's engine starting. I turned around and saw that we were moving away from the shore. I looked for Nikola. He was standing at the wheel staring in front of him with an expression of concentration.

"Bruno, I hope that we're going to see the children?" I asked with a trembling voice.

He continued to lay the table in silence. Utensils, plates, a bottle of wine in an ice bucket appeared on the table.

"Bruno!" I shouted in anger.

He placed two covered plates on the table. He eventually sat opposite me, grunted contentedly, poured the wine into glasses and gave me one.

"Cheers!"

I took the glass, clinked it against his and sipped.

"Bruno. Please, just tell me one thing."

He raised his eyebrows inquisitively.

"I want to play honestly. I've fulfilled my part of the bargain. Now it's your turn. I asked you a moment ago whether we were going to the children. And you didn't say anything. I'm waiting for an answer."

He coughed and said, "First of all, I still don't know your decision. The fact that you're here doesn't mean that you've fulfilled all the points of the bargain. Secondly, whether we're going to the children or they'll come to us, I haven't yet decided. We'll see what's for the best."

I looked at him angrily but said nothing. He observed me carefully. I was trying to suppress my anger, and it would be best for everyone if I did. I turned around and looked behind me. We were already some way from the pretty shore of Locarno, heading south. I trembled. Were we heading for Stresa, despite his ravings?

Bruno slowly cut off the end of a cigar, lit it and puffed on it a few times with an air of satisfaction.

"All right then, I'm listening to you. Tell me."

"What do you want me to tell you?" My voice was hoarse with anxiety.

"What is your intention?" He had that carefree expression which I knew too well. His eyes were so sharp and penetrating that you can't hide even your most precious thoughts. I quickly bent over the table to look for something to occupy the silence.

"My intention is to eat. What is there under these covers?" I asked out of interest.

He laughed and lifted one of them.

"Sea bass with fennel. I recommend it. It's very delicious."

"And the other one?"

"Mediterranean salad."

"Can I have some? I'm hungry!"

He grinned.

"No need to ask. Help yourself!" He started to serve me, but I wouldn't let him.

"Let me do it. Am I a guest, or am I the host?"

He glanced at me in surprise.

"That will be your decision."

I decisively took the utensils and divided the food between his plate and mine. He watched me.

"Bruno," I said with a full mouth. "The lunch is delicious. Why aren't you eating?"

"I'll have something to eat, don't worry. I haven't poisoned it," he joked. "I just wanted to watch and admire you. You're such a wonderful woman! You really are!"

"Well, eat and don't play around," I interrupted him and continued eating.

He extinguished his cigar, took a glass of wine and said, "Here's to you and your unfading beauty!" He drained his glass.

"Don't drink too much, and stop talking nonsense! Eat. 'Unfading beauty?' Can't you see how old I've grown? And what you did to my children will be the death of me. I don't know how much I've aged in the past two weeks!"

"No you haven't! You're as beautiful as a cinema star!" He got up and came closer to me. I realised that the situation was getting dangerous.

"Bruno. Let me have my lunch. You're not very hospitable."

He leant over me and raised my head in his hand. We stared closely into each other's eyes.

"I'm hospitable, but I'm also in love."

"In love with yourself, I imagine," I said.

He laughed. He let go of me and went back to his place.

"All right. Let's eat," he said magnanimously, looking at me.

I had clearly gauged the right tone. However anxious and tense I was, I couldn't help but enjoy the delicious tiramisu which Bruno served for dessert. I ate it all down to the last crumb. I poured Bruno a glass of wine and then a glass for myself and said, "Is there any more tiramisu, Bruno? It's absolutely wonderful."

"Of course there is, I'll bring you some. I'm glad you like it."

He got up eagerly and went into the kitchenette, to the fridge in the corner. With a lightning movement, I slipped my hand inside my bra and whipped out the little sachet, pouring its contents into his glass and then concealing the two empty halves of the sachet back in my bra just in time. Bruno returned with a new plate full of sweet treats.

"Here you are, darling. Careful not to overdo it!"

"I'm fine. Let's have it."

I took the place and looked at his glass. Everything was all right.

"Bruno. Cheers! Not just the tiramisu but the whole lunch was fantastic. And as for the wine, that was just wonderful."

"Cheers!" He smiled happily, clinked glasses and slowly drank the entire glass.

I remembered that Krasi had told me that the substance had neither taste nor fragrance. I ate the second piece of tiramisu and leant back against the couch, waiting to see Bruno's reaction, but he quietly ate the rest of his lunch and didn't seem any different.

When he finished, he leant back and lit his cigar again.

"It really was good. We can talk now, if you want to," he said.

I decided to kill a bit more time.

I looked towards the kitchen and caught sight of a wonderful little coffee machine.

"Shall I make you a coffee?" I asked.

"I can make some, if you want?"

"No, no. Just sit there. I'll make some. For you? Do you want some?"

"No thank you, I've had enough," Bruno replied.

I jumped up nimbly and fussed around with the coffee machine, deliberately taking my time. I was waiting for the powder to act. I finally appeared at the table, carrying a cup of aromatic coffee.

"Bruno, isn't Nikola going to have some lunch? Or does he just drive? Are we in a hurry?" I asked trying not to show my anxiety.

I observed him carefully. There was absolutely no sign of any change in his behaviour.

"Nikola will have lunch when he wants to. He's not in the army."

I drank my coffee slowly. It was truly delicious. I have to admit Bruno really loved his luxuries.

"Bruno, this coffee is divine. You're full of surprises! You really know how to spoil yourself. What type is it?"

He laughed. "Hacienda La Esmeralda."

"You're a great fan of that name," I exclaimed sincerely.

"That's right! But yes, it's really good coffee. And quite expensive at that. The last lot I bought cost three times more than usual."

"Bruno, I want to ask you something."

"Go on."

"Why 'Esmeralda'? Even the coffee, for goodness' sake. Don't you think it's a bit much?"

He said nothing for a long time.

"It's quite simple really. You're the reason."

"Me?" I replied in astonishment.

"Yes, you!" Bruno stressed. "I don't know whether you remember, but I was madly in love with you."

"Bruno!" I reacted with anger.

"Bruno what? I was mad about you. I adored you so much that I had decided to give it all up and take you away. All of it. My entire business. My entire empire! All of it! And begin afresh. If you could have forgiven me the filth I had dragged you through! But you deceived me in the worst possible way. You accepted and then you disappeared. I spent years looking for you. Your eyes, those incredible enormous emeralds, followed me everywhere in my dreams throughout all those years. I couldn't get rid of the memory of you and your emerald eyes. The Incas of Peru had an emerald the size of an ostrich egg. They worshipped it as the goddess Esmeralda. When the conquistadors plundered the 'Temple of the Sun' they couldn't find it. The precious stone is considered the stone of unconditional love, inspiration and infinite patience. Esmeralda is an old French word for emerald. So I armed myself with infinite patience and I knew that one day I would get my Esmeralda back. However, this time I shall be very careful not to let you out of my life again."

I listened to him as though captivated by a magic spell. I could not believe that all this was happening in real time.

"You mean that I am 'Esmeralda', is that right?" I whispered.

"That's right!"

I was completely shocked. I was shocked to hear that Bruno, the monster, had gone through his own human drama. I felt overcome by an irresistible feeling of exhaustion and dizziness.

"Bruno, I don't feel very well. I want to lie down."

Looking suddenly worried, he jumped up and caught me and led me down into the bedroom. I managed to get to the bed. He helped me lie down, carefully tucking me in, and stayed with me until he was sure that I was falling asleep, before leaving. Then I really did fall asleep. When I woke up, I initially didn't know where I was. When I eventually came to my senses I leapt out of the bed, splashed my eyes with two handfuls of water and went upstairs.

It was dark. Night had fallen. Bruno was looking at something on his laptop but stood when he saw me.

"How are you? I came down twice to see how you were," he said with concern.

"I was asleep."

"And now? How are you?"

"Let's say I'm OK. Bruno, I've been asking you all day and you haven't replied. Are we going to get the children?"

He frowned.

"Just have a little more patience. Pack your bag, if you want. Or you can leave it all here."

"Why?"

"We're going ashore. I was just waiting for you to wake up."

"Where are we?" I asked anxiously.

"Less of the questions. Do you want to take something or shall we leave straight away?"

"I'll get my stuff."

"Go on then!"

I took my handbag and luggage and went upstairs. There was no trace of Bruno. I looked around in fright.

"What the hell is happening?"

"Signora, would you follow me please?" I heard Nikola's voice from below me somewhere.

He's forever frightening me, I thought. "Where's Bruno?" I said out loud.

"Follow me."

I obeyed unquestioningly and went out onto the dark deck, with no idea where I was going. Nikola helped me not to stumble, carefully guiding me by the elbow. We soon found ourselves next to a car which I had not noticed.

"Wait here," Nikola said as he unlocked it and helped me in. We were in a small car park. I couldn't see anything else. We sat in silence and waited. Shortly afterwards the back door opened and Bruno got in, panting.

"Here we are! We can leave now."

I turned to him in the darkness and said crossly, "Bruno, what are you doing? What are all these games?"

"Don't worry, darling. I just felt as though we had someone following us."

I trembled. Krasi had said quite clearly, "I'll be with you." God, I just prayed for all this to end quickly!

Nikola drove away but I noticed him staring intently in the rear view mirror.

"Bruno, where are we going?" I continued with my questions.

There was no reply.

"And the children?"

"If you ask me that question once more, you won't be seeing them any time soon," Bruno said quietly.

I fell silent and I vowed that the next chance I had I would pour two sachets of powder into his drink. At once.

As the car flew through the night, I silently prayed to God that Krasi wouldn't lose sight of me. I was beginning to feel completely lost.

I stopped asking questions because there wasn't any point. I sat as comfortably as I could, and in an attempt to show my entire contempt and disdain, I closed my eyes and fell asleep.

When I was woken by an incessant shaking, I was completely stiff. This time Nikola had disappeared. It was warm and sunny outside, and Bruno was leaning over me tugging at my arm.

"You certainly have some talent for sleeping," he said. "Come on. Get out! We've arrived."

I rubbed my eyes.

"Just wait for a moment." I stretched my stiff legs.

Bruno helped me out of the car and I studied it. It was a Masarati Grancabrio, the latest model.

"What are you looking at?" Bruno asked. "The car's number plates?"

"Idiot! I'm looking to see if it hasn't got a crest with 'Esmeralda' on it."

He grinned. "That's a good idea."

"Where are we? Or is that confidential?" I said arrogantly.

"Cannes."

"Cannes?" I smiled.

"Honestly. We're in Cannes. That's our house." He pointed to a four-storey house. "Just down there, one block away, is Croisette Boulevard and the sea."

I looked closely at the house.

"Bruno, are you a billionaire?"

"Ha! It's not mine. I just have an apartment here. It's rented. But I wouldn't say I have to count my pennies."

"That's clear," I muttered. "Let's go. I need to use the bathroom."

We took the lift, the sound of quiet music filling it, and Bruno pushed the button for the third floor. The apartment was light, quiet and very luxurious. It was no ordinary apartment. It had an internal spiral staircase.

"Bruno. It's a maisonette!"

"You're right. I like to have lots of space. So, welcome home!"

He came closer to me. I realised that the moment when Bruno would want me to give him proof that I accepted all his conditions was approaching.

"Bruno, where's the bathroom? I told you I was in a hurry."

He laughed.

"Come on." He led me down the first corridor to the right. "Here's the toilet."

It was a huge room with mirrors, potted plants, flowers in vases and even a soft couch, in case you felt tired. Bruno was mad but I had to admit he had a taste for luxury.

After completely refreshing myself with a shower which I enjoyed with all my heart, I went into the apartment dressed in a snow-white, soft bath robe. Bruno wasn't there. I looked in all the rooms on the lower storey, but I didn't see Bruno or the bag with my clothes. I went into the kitchen which resembled a space laboratory. I found the coffee machine, and a moment later I was drinking coffee which filled the entire house with its aroma. I had no idea what fate had in store for me in the next couple of hours. In my aimlessness I went over to the window and looked down. Opposite the entrance, leaning casually against a tree, I saw Krasi, looking up at me.

I pressed myself against the glass. He saw me but pretended to drop something on the ground. He picked it up and walked slowly away.

My heart was pounding wildly but I was calm. Krasi had not lost me, for the moment.

"What are you looking at, darling?" I heard behind me.

I was startled and dropped my cup of coffee. It smashed onto the floor.

"When will you get out of that stupid habit of frightening me like that?" I shouted.

"I'm sorry! I wasn't thinking."

Bruno had taken a shower as well; upstairs, clearly. He was also dressed in a bath robe. He approached me slowly. I already knew that there were two ways out of this situation. Either seduce him, or play it out for as long as I could by refusing intimacy with him.

I took a deep breath and a smile slowly developed on my lips. With one slight movement of my shoulders, the robe slowly fell to my feet, forming a small, white, fluffy cloud. I took a grandiose step forward onto the soft textile, and said, "Here I am. I'm coming to you!"

I raised my head and put my arms around him.

Bruno was slightly shocked but took me in his arms and slowly, very slowly, he carried me up the stairs. He looked at me in disbelief as though hypnotised. I knew how to deal with men. I had learnt my lesson a long time ago, when I worked as a VIP prostitute and hated all men, especially Bruno.

He slowly put me on the bed, observing me all the time. He was still dressed in his bath robe. I summoned him with my eyes. He approached the bed and I invited him with all the gestures of my body to have me. Still in disbelief, he lay down next to me. I writhed with all the cold intent I could muster and satisfied him until he was finally unable even to breathe.

Then, exhausted and happy, he fell asleep.

I hurried to go back into the bathroom. I took a long and satisfying bath.

In order to make the performance seem as real as possible, I lay down next to him and thought. To anyone else we looked like a happy, loving couple. An evil thought came into my mind that soon, very soon, there were be a complete reversal of roles. I fell asleep, disgusted but happy. The plan was working, but I was the one who had to pay. And the price was very high, but those were the rules. For the moment.

Bruno woke me with a kiss.

"Come on, darling, wake up."

"What time is it?" I asked sleepily.

"It's almost six in the evening. You were fast asleep."

"Because...didn't you..." I objected.

"Sorry...I've been awake for two hours. I didn't move for fear of waking you."

"I can't believe it, how thoughtful you are!" I muttered. "I'm hungry!"

"I had forgotten what dynamite you were!" He grinned and turned me around with my back to him.

"You've got an incredible body."

He was stroking my back and working his way down.

"Bruno, no... Not now. I really am hungry."

"All right, all right!" he sighed with a note of resignation. "I just wanted to admire you."

I got up demonstratively and deliberately walked in front of the bed. I knew that he was watching me. I slowly bent down to fix something imaginary on my slipper, in the full knowledge that the view would be amazing. He gulped.

"Ioana, do you want me to have a heart attack? What are you doing?"

"Looking for my slipper," I said casually. "Here it is!" I stood up and turned to face him. I was still naked.

"Darling, I'll die if you stand there like that for much longer."

"Then take it easy," I said. "Get up, if you don't want us to die of hunger."

I turned around and slowly left the room, smiling secretly to myself. I knew that I had him under my spell. I returned and appeared before his eyes once again. He was lying in bed completely stunned.

"Bruno, I nearly forgot. Where are my clothes? Or do you want me to go out to dinner naked?"

"I'll kill anyone who looks at you," he muttered. "Your clothes are there. In the wardrobe."

I chose a dress, a very pretty light beige Dior. Natasha had recently bought it for me. I raised my hair in a casual bun on the back of my head and I was ready.

Bruno was looking at me in a different way. He fidgeted around me and said, "Ioana!"

"Yes?"

"I've got something for you."

My thoughts immediately turned to the children. No, no. It was probably something else. I looked at him inquisitively. Bruno went upstairs and returned with a box in his hands that had a Tiffany mark on the lid. Every woman likes jewellery, and I was no exception. But what I saw exceeded all my expectations. It was an exceptionally beautiful set of earrings and a necklace. Emeralds! Surrounded by small glistening diamonds.

"This is for you!"

I looked at them in delight. My jaw might even have dropped.

"Let me put them on you." He looked at me pleadingly.

"Bruno, these are very, very expensive jewels. I can't go out to dinner with them."

"Why not?"

"Why not? Because I might lose them."

"I don't care if you do lose them. The only thing that concerns me is not to lose you."

I ignored the last words.

"All right, put them on me."

He slowly and ceremoniously put the necklace around my neck and fastened it.

"Wait, I'll put the earrings on myself." I ran over to the huge Viennese mirror, put the earrings on and let out a sigh. I was bathed in the most incredible green light and my reflection captivated me. Bruno appeared next to me.

"Bruno, they are incredible. I'm breathless. Are they really for me?"

The green light of the emeralds surrounded me like a halo and created a magical green radiance. Bruno was also profoundly impressed. He slowly turned me around to face him. We stared into each other's eyes. When he spoke, his voice trembled.

"Ioana, this is my way of showing my feelings. I already told you that these emeralds are a symbol of unconditional love and infinite patience. When I bought them for you, many years ago, I thought I would be buying them as a wedding present for the woman I love. I thought that you would wear them at our wedding. But that didn't happen. Now I believe that this time they will fulfil their destiny."

His words brought me back to reality and froze me. He would not give up on his intentions.

"Thank you! I really don't know what to say." I raised myself up on my tiptoes and kissed him.

He waved his hand.

"Let's go and have some dinner."

I began to remove the earrings.

"Don't touch them. The restaurant at the Martinez hotel has never seen such a thing. The most beautiful woman in the world with her emeralds."

I nodded and took another glance into the mirror. They truly were beautiful.

"Let's go!" Bruno tugged at me impatiently and we went out.

***

Croisette Boulevard was a five minutes' walk from Bruno's home, and it was thronged with expensive cars, motorbikes and people. We were walking along the pavement when someone knocked my elbow.

"I'm sorry!"

I turned around. Krasi smiled at me guiltily. I nodded and he passed me by.

"What does he think he's doing?" Bruno turned around and stared angrily at his back.

"It's all right. He just bumped into me by accident. You're very nervous!"

"Yes, I am, where you're concerned."

The restaurant was quiet and half-empty.

"It looks boring here," I said.

"Don't worry. It's still early but the cuisine is marvellous. You'll be happy enough."

"And that's the most important thing." I smiled at him and winked.

The waiter took our order.

"Are you always so extravagant? Champagne, caviar, oysters and truffles!"

Bruno laughed. "No, only when I want to show off."

"That's all too much. I would be quite happy with more ordinary food."

"But you're quite extraordinary. So there's no need to be over modest, please."

I said nothing and stared at the sea. I was thinking about Krasi. He really was right next to me. But for how long? And was the end in sight?

I began to perspire at the thought. I picked up my glass of water and drank all of it.

"Are you thirsty?"

"And hungry," I added.

"And secretive."

"Pardon?"

"Secretive, I said." He stared at me inquisitively.

"That's nonsense. You're imagining things."

"No, I can feel it. You're up to something, aren't you?"

"Bruno, don't spoil things. Have you forgotten what we did today? Or was that just to get your own back on me?"

"I haven't forgotten anything."

"Then shut your mouth and don't irritate me."

His eyebrows leapt to his hairline in amazement.

"Don't you think you're going a bit too far speaking to me like that?"

"No," I emphasised. "I've got nothing else to lose. What more do you want from me?"

A mocking smile flashed across his face.

"For example, tell me what you told your husband. What does he think about it all? And what do you think about it all? Or did you just come because the deadline had expired, and you still haven't decided what to do and how things will work out?"

I gulped quickly and answered.

"It's simple. I left a short note for Sergio telling him that I was leaving him. That he was not to look for me and that my lawyers would be in touch with him."

Bruno looked at me waiting for an answer.

"Then I came to you, just like you wanted. I'm prepared to do anything for the sake of my children. Even put up with your unpleasant character."

Bruno burst into laughter.

"That's all. Why complicate things? There you are, I've been honest and frank. I want my children, immediately! And this time, I'm not joking."

He became serious.

"All right."

"What does "all right" mean? Now it's your turn. Tell me when I will see my children. If you're planning to play games, think again. Either I get my children, or ..."

"Or what?" he asked out of interest.

"Or I will kill myself. And you'll have to wear the emeralds yourself."

The last argument seemed to tip the scales.

"Then I'll have to pierce my own ears," he replied smiling.

I was agitated and frightened but tried not to show it. I was getting closer to my aim, but how much time was left? I didn't know. I tried to be as natural as possible and obediently played the role I had been assigned.

After dinner Bruno proposed that we continue the evening in a club.

"Do you want to go to Bauli? It's really good!"

"No, I'm tired. Let's go home."

"I thought you wanted some excitement? You said the restaurant was boring."

"Well, now I want to go to bed and watch a film."

"What about me?"

"What do you want? If you want, go out and take a walk. If you want, come home with me. We can watch a film together. And you've got work to do."

Bruno looked at me with a question in his eyes.

"What?"

"You have to arrange the return of the children," I said quietly and decisively.

We stared into each other's eyes for a few moments. During dinner I had managed to pop a sachet of powder into his wine. I was now waiting for the results. They weren't late in coming.

"Wonderful, but I don't mind fulfilling your whims," Bruno said pensively. "All right, let's go home."

Back at the house, Nikola was sitting in the living room talking on the telephone. He stood up when he saw us.

"Good evening!"

"Good evening, Nikola," I replied.

Bruno shook his hand.

"What's up?"

Nikola looked at me, and I realised that they wanted me to leave the room. I made my excuses and went upstairs. I rattled the door handle of the bedroom but didn't go in. I knelt and, very quietly, like a cat on four paws, I crawled back to the top of the stairs. I couldn't see them but I could hear.

They were speaking Bulgarian quietly but clearly.

"The little guy called. The goods are sailing under a Portuguese flag. According to documents, it's red wine."

"In bottles?"

"Yes."

"How much?"

"One ton."

Bruno whistled.

"You have to go, brother. I don't trust them. That's a lot of money."

"When will we hand the money over?"

"We have to be sure of the goods. First we have to get them, then we'll see."

"The money's in a bank in Liechtenstein. Two and a half million. The bank has issued a bank guarantee to the Portuguese company which is the Columbians' middle man."

"OK. And from here on we have to finance the import, is that right?"

"No, the westerners will do the importing. We just have to hand over the goods to them in Varna and from then on they'll load it onto the trucks."

"Aha...All right. When are you leaving? Tomorrow morning?"

"Yes. And how are you? How's it going with the madam?"

"She's OK, she's calm for the time being."

"Take care. She seems dangerous to me."

"Yes, I know. We'll see. By the way, don't remove the guards. I have the feeling I've got a tail."

I froze. I was frightened that if Bruno was to come up the stairs at that moment, I wouldn't be able to run away. So very quietly and carefully, on all fours I crawled back into my room and quietly closed the door. I switched on the television and collapsed into an armchair. My body was sweating with all the stress and my Dior dress was stuck to me like a second skin. I was soaked. I rushed into the bathroom and quickly turned on the water. I was now safe. I could think about what I had heard. Of course he was involved in the drugs trade. It was another matter how I was going to play my cards and save my children.

I had to play them very carefully and at the same time take risks, because the moment was approaching; I had to make the most of Nikola's absence. I needed to free my children while he was in Bulgaria.

"Where are you, darling?" Bruno's head appeared around the door. "Shall I come in as well?"

"No, I'm coming out," I answered sharply and put on my bath robe.

Bruno was sitting in the armchair observing me.

"Have you finished your conversation?" I asked casually and sat in front of the dressing table.

"As you can see," he answered lazily.

"Has Nikola gone?"

"Yes. Why?"

"I'm just asking. So that I can walk around naked."

Bruno grinned.

"You can walk around wherever you like."

I deliberately undressed slowly, crossed the room and stood in front of him.

"Can I ask you something?"

"Go on!" he said magnanimously. His eyes were glued to me.

"Bruno, please, please," I bent forward. "Arrange for my children to be brought here. Please arrange it. Now. Please!"

He looked at me as though he was hypnotised.

"Please call them now. Please! Go on, I'll be waiting for you in bed. Make the call quickly and come to bed."

He got out his telephone and dialled a number.

"Hi Carla, how are things?"

My heart was in my mouth, right behind my teeth.

"Where's Massimo? Let me talk to him. Hi, Massimo. Is everything all right? Good. Organise for two people to stay in the house, and get Luisa and Carla and the two kids in a couple of cars and bring them here. Yes. How are they? OK. No, just two people to stay in the house. You'll come with them. Leave at eight tomorrow. Yes. Ciao!" He hung up. "Are you happy now?"

"Yes," I whispered. "Yes, very. Are they coming here?"

"Yes." He approached me slowly. "You're not planning any tricks, are you?"

"Don't talk nonsense!" I whispered.

"Come on now. I want you."

There was no other way. He didn't need a second invitation.

I gave everything I could that night. I didn't care who the man was next to me. There was only one important thing. I needed to stun him, to destroy all his potential capabilities of rational thought. I needed to subordinate him entirely and make him dependent on medependent on the narcotic of sex. And with only one specific person: me.

I knew I could do it. I possessed all the levers to operate his conscious mind and I operated them skilfully. All of them.

The next morning as I made the coffee, the Bruno of old, the man I had left so many years ago was standing in front of me. He was in love and as obedient as a puppy. But that did nothing to deter me in my plan. There was still the danger that he might make a phone call and delay the arrival of my children. So I put another powder in his coffee. I was in a strange mood. My adrenaline was off the scale and I couldn't feel anything, apart from the incredible excitement that the children would be with me today.

I couldn't imagine what it would be like. How would we get away? Where was Krasi and how would I tell him? A mad plan began to take shape in my mind.

"Bruno, I want real French croissants. With butter and jam. But warm. Will you go and get some? Right away?"

He hesitated.

"OK, darling. I know a boulangerie very close. I'll go and get some."

"Hurry up then. I love warm croissants."

He left without a second thought. I rushed upstairs to look for the telephone, where I knew he had left it last night. I had learnt Krasi's number by heart. I feverishly dialled. It rang for an eternity before he answered.

"Hello?"

"Krasi, it's me."

"Are you mad?"

"Yes! The children are leaving Stresa at eight this morning. They'll be in two cars and they'll have two women with them. I don't know how many men."

"Hang up and delete the call."

"OK. Ciao!" I did what he said.

I ran down the stairs and sat at the table. I was still out of breath when Bruno came back with the croissants.

"They're still hot. Here you are!"

"Thank you, darling! You're very sweet. And the butter and jam?"

"They're in the fridge. I'll get them."

I jumped up nimbly.

"No, no, sit down. It's my turn now. I'll serve breakfast."

He looked at me with a foolish and happy smile. We had breakfast and joked. I chatted incessantly about all sorts of nonsense to make him laugh and not let him think.

"Bruno, have you been to the festival here?"

"Yes."

"What's it like? Are the actresses all pretty?"

"Not in the least! They can't possibly be compared to you. They're all artificial, stupid and pumped up with silicon."

"That's a bit extreme!"

"No, that's exactly what they're like. You're beautiful and sexy. And you're real."

I gulped with some difficulty and added, "And you're good looking too!"

He stared into my eyes and said nothing for a long time. He finally replied.

"Is that what you really think?"

"Yes. Why? You know it yourself."

He shook his head.

"I know that I've caused you a lot of pain and torment. Then...and now."

We were getting into dangerous waters. I was on my guard.

I sat down, lit a cigarette and coughed, and when I was finally calm, with tears in my eyes from coughing, I smiled timidly and said,

"Bruno, a long time ago I forgave you for what you did to me in the past. And I'm on the way to forgiving you for what you've done to me now. I know that people make mistakes sometimes and do things they don't mean to. You know what they say, 'The road to Hell is paved with good intentions.' Don't tear yourself up. I know and I can feel that it's a complicated situation. Let's leave things as they are. Here I am with you, I'm giving you everything I can give you, and in exchange I want just one thing – my children. And if you've got the slightest bit of kindness in your heart, you won't deprive me of the only thing I possess. Please, Bruno!"

He sat in silence and huge tears rolled down his cheeks.

"Bruno? Don't, what's wrong? Have I upset you?" I panicked.

I didn't expect that reaction. Or was it the drug? God, I just hoped that it didn't have the opposite effect. Aggression, for example! I had heard about things like that.

"Do you want to go out for a walk?" I was seriously frightened.

"No, I've got some business to attend to. I've got to talk to a couple of people."

I was even more worried. He wasn't himself after the powder and the conversation with me. They might realise that something was wrong with him.

"Can't they wait for an hour or two? Why don't we take a walk along Croisette?"

He got up obediently.

"All right. Are you ready?"

"Let me just put a dress on, and I'll be ready."

It took me three minutes to get dressed. We went out onto the street and I glanced left and right. There wasn't a sign of Krasi. Bruno took me by the hand.

"Where do you want to go?"

"Oh, I just want to walk along Croisette."

"All right. Do you want to do any shopping? There's lots of nice shops."

"No, no. Thank you! I'm very modest. Let's go and sit on the benches." I tugged at him.

We sat down. I looked at my watch.

"What is it? You can't wait?"

"Yes," I sighed and smiled.

We said nothing and stared at the sea. The sun was roasting but there was a light sea breeze which was pleasant and refreshing.

"Look, Bruno, that yacht looks like yours."

He turned his head and followed the direction of my hand.

"No. That one's very small. Ours will be here in two days' time."

I was surprised.

"How?"

"They sail at night."

"Why? Is it stolen?"

Bruno burst into laughter.

"No. It's completely legal. Those are just the rules."

It was eleven, and my stress levels were increasing with every moment that passed. Bruno, on the other hand, was strangely calm. Was it the powder I had given him? I didn't know.

"You're looking tense," he said.

"I am," I admitted. "I'm excited at meeting my children."

"Why? It's very simple. They'll arrive and you'll hug them."

I turned to look at him.

"It's not as simple as you think. It's strange how you underestimate everything!"

"Come on, it was just a big adventure for them."

In order to gain more time, I began to tell him about my plans to learn to draw. I invented stories about my plans to take drawing lessons, and how I would become very famous and sell my paintings in galleries all over the world. I imagined all sorts of other fantasies. I even dragged him into an argument about who was the better artist, Monet or Manet. We talked for about two hours. I finally fell silent with exhaustion.

"They should be here soon," Bruno said and looked at his watch pensively.

"I hope you're right!"

"They should have called by now."

He got out his telephone and dialled a number. He waited for a moment, hung up and tried again. No answer. He pursed his lips so tightly that the skin around them turned white from lack of blood. I was out of my mind with worry. Something had happened with the two cars and the children. I was frightened and hopeful at the same time. Was it Krasi's people? Or an accident? I felt dizzy.

"Bruno, what's going on, tell me for God's sake? Has something happened to the children?"

He said nothing but flashes of lightning sparked from his eyes.

"Hello? Rocco, what's going on? Massimo's not answering his phone. Nor are the women. Who's with him? All right." He hung up abruptly and redialled. No one answered. I was now certain that something had happened. So was Bruno. He turned to me and grabbed me harshly by the arm.

"Get up!"

I stumbled.

"What's up? Let me go! You're hurting me!"

Gripping my arm firmly above the elbow, he walked quickly, making me run alongside him.

"Will you tell me what's going on?" I asked out of breath.

We walked, almost ran, towards his house. On the way he turned to me and said, "I'm sure that you've betrayed me again. But this time you're going to pay dearly for it."

"Bruno, what are you talking about?"

We had already turned the corner into the street. In contrast to the boulevard it was empty. Right outside the house a big black car suddenly appeared out of nowhere. It stopped in front of us, and before I realised what was happening, I was being dragged into it. I turned around to look for Bruno. He was lying on the pavement and blood was streaming from his head, forming a small puddle.

I looked towards the driver, but saw only a mask. Someone sat next to me and the car drove off.

"Calm down!" I heard the man next to me say. His voice was painfully familiar. With a single movement of his hand, he removed the mask and I saw Krasi.

"Are you all right, baby?" He was taking off his gloves and looking at me with an expression of concern.

"I don't know," I stuttered. "Did you kill him?"

"No," Krasi said and smiled. "You didn't see anything, did you?"

I still couldn't calm down and come to my senses. It all happened in a split second.

"I really didn't see anything. What happened? Krasi?"

"Nothing, I just came to get you."

The car flew quickly through the streets while Krasi held my hands and spoke quietly and reassuringly.

"Everything's fine. Calm down now. You're safe and you're going to a very special place, where you're being expected."

I swallowed with difficulty.

"Where?"

"Somewhere you'll be happy."

"Krasi, the only place I can be happy is with my children."

He smiled broadly, winked and said, "That's what I'm talking about!"

I fainted.

***

The boat sailed down a dark underground river and the quiet lapping of the oars mixed with the echo of evil laughter. Without wanting to, I trembled. What could I see opposite me? It looked like Blackbeard the Pirate. I rubbed my eyes. It was him!

"Mummy, look, Blackbeard!" Roberto was pointing in admiration at the impressive figure of the pirate.

"Papa, I'm frightened. I don't want to stay here anymore. I want to go to Sleeping Beauty's palace," Julia sobbed.

"Don't look, cuddle up to me. Then we'll go for a ride in the Mad Hatter's tea cups," Sergio lovingly reassured Julia, who was sobbing with fear.

"And can we go on the merry-go-round?" she snivelled.

"We'll go on them as well."

"You're so spoilt!" Robbie mocked her.

"Papa, tell him that I'm not!"

"Shhh," I told them off. "Be quiet!"

I wanted to be strict with them but I looked at my family with love and tenderness.

Exactly a year had passed since the drama which we all been dragged into against our will.

The man who had caused us all this pain was long since dead.

The police could not find the murderer. They concluded that he had been killed with two shots to the head. They had been unable to find the weapon or the assassin. Their conclusion was that it was the result of a turf war between mafia groups.

Sergio, Natasha and Mario never asked me about what had happened. And I had no intention of telling them. The most important thing was that Krasi had kept all his promises. He had done his job well, and even more. He had told the Bulgarian authorities about Bruno's cocaine shipment and it had been prevented.

Of course, he didn't tell me that he was the informant, but there was no need. Only I knew, and then in the car when I came to my senses I told him. That was enough.

Krasi didn't take the money which he had asked for.

"I will never take any money from you, baby! For me, you are and always will be...You know, I don't have to tell you."

"You're mad! What am I going to tell Sergio?" I looked at him in terror. "You have to take the money."

"Tell him that I took the money and then gave it to your children as a present from me. We're from the same country! And we have to look after each other."

He looked at me with sparkling eyes and his smile was tender and sad.

"Krasi, do you want to drive me mad?" I sobbed.

The action took place in Natasha's home, the second day after our rescue. Sergio was still in the hospital. Natasha had gone shopping and I was alone with the children. Mario brought the money early in the morning and I was to hand it over.

I looked at the metal case and cried.

Krasi got up and came over to me. He carefully raised me to my feet and said, "Baby, I want to wish you endless days of happiness. For you and your children. And if ever, at any time, and any place, you have problems, just phone me. I will always be there for you to protect your happiness."

I burst into uncontrollable tears. My love was saying farewell.

"I don't want you to go!" I raised myself on tiptoes, grasped his head and our lips merged in a burning, ardent kiss. It was infinitely long and divinely passionate. Natasha found us like that, frozen in our fervent, impossible love. She stood in the doorway and coughed.

"Excuse me! I just wanted to say that I'm home. Where are the children?" Nat asked quietly and tactfully.

"They're asleep," I replied laconically.

"Excuse me, once again." The door closed.

"Baby, she won't cause you any problems will she?"

"Don't worry, she's like a sister to me. She won't say anything."

"OK, I don't want you to have any problems."

"I won't."

The parting was painful. My heart felt as though it was being torn into pieces.

"I don't have the strength to let you go, I'll die!"

"You're not going to die, baby! I will always be with you. You remember it, don't you?" He looked at his telephone.

"I'll write it on my forehead, just in case."

"That'll be a great tattoo," Krasi grinned. He jumped up and said, "Ciao, baby!"

And then he just disappeared without giving me the chance to stop him.

I cried for a long time, until Natasha came in. She fussed around me and eventually said, "I'm not going to ask you anything, of course, but..."

At that moment she saw the suitcase full of money. She opened it carefully and then sighed in disbelief, "Ioana, now I am going to ask you and you will tell me. Who was he?"

I looked at her, sighed deeply and said, "That man, Natasha, is the love of my life. If I had had more luck in life, that man would have been my husband; I would have had children with him. I would have graduated from university in Bulgaria. I would have had a degree in Fashion Design. I would have had a whole chain of shops, and he would have been a respected businessman trading in works of art. And you, Natasha, might not be alive now, because I wouldn't have been dragged into sex trafficking to save your life. That's how my life would have turned out, if fate hadn't intervened to separate me from that man."

Natasha's eyes widened even more and I sobbed even more uncontrollably.

Natasha understood everything. She was still captivated by my story that evening when the children fell asleep and I told her everything about my love story.

"I understand you, darling, and I don't want to know any more."

Mario, who had seen everything in the secret world in which he lived, was quite surprised to find the money with me. "He must be a very noble bandit," he said.

"The noblest sort!" I affirmed and returned the money to him.

Contrary to my fears, the children soon were back to their old selves. Initially, Julia would cry if she woke up alone in the mornings.

"Mummy, we won't be taken away again, will we?"

"Never again, darling! I promise!"

Roberto revealed a bit more.

"Mummy, they were good to us, even though they were bandits."

I froze. "What do you mean?"

"I asked for a bow and arrow and I heard one of them complain that he had spent all day looking for what I wanted."

"How did they treat Julia?"

"Good, they read her stories at night."

"Who did?"

"Carla."

Bruno hadn't lied to me. They had looked after the children well.

Sometimes when I thought about him, there was a sadness in my heart. I sometimes even grieved for him. His maniacal love for me eventually killed him. It was Krasi who pulled the trigger, but I was the reason. It weighed upon my conscience and it always would.

"Darling, what are you thinking about?" Sergio was cuddling Julia and had hold of Roberto's hand, all three heading towards me. I was sitting with a cup of fragrant coffee, exhausted by three days of galloping around Disneyland.

"Mummy, we're going to the Star Wars spaceship." Robbie's face glowed with happiness.

"I want to come too," Julia grumbled.

"You can't. Papa, she just gets in the way! She's not going to come with us!"

Sergio had got better the moment he saw the children. For him and for me, they were like a magical pill.

What could I say? I love him! Not with that burning passion which I had for Krasi, no. But this was my family. This was the dream I had pursued for so many years. I was happy. Well, not entirely. There was a little red corner of my happiness missing.

"Stop arguing, please!" Sergio looked at me with a happy smile. "We'll all go!"

"Except me. I'll wait for you here. I've got a lovely cup of coffee," I smiled. "I want to call Nat to see how she is."

Sergio nodded. "OK, lazybones, the ship's crew salute you. We're taking off."

"Enjoy the flight!" I laughed.

I took my telephone and opened the picture gallery. Natasha's wedding. Goodness, how beautiful she looked! Natasha had finally decided to leave Mario. Like a true gentleman, he withdrew but said that he would always be there for her, if she needed anything. Natasha, however, would never need anything from him. Very soon after leaving Mario, she met the Frenchman who owned the building where her beauty salon was located. Jean Pierre fell in love with her after two weekends spent together. He asked her to marry him and Natasha accepted without a second thought. The marriage had a marvellous effect on her. Two months later she was pregnant. What a miracle! Especially as, unbelievably, she was expecting twins.

"Nat, you just had to copy me!" I joked.

"I had nothing to do with it! It's the work of God!" she defended herself.

Jean Pierre would not allow her even to lift a fork.

This would make everyone laugh, but Natasha defended him. "He's just so concerned about my health!"

"Yes, we're not saying anything!" we would joke, and she would go red with anger.

She was a very touching sight.

The date of her Caesarean was approaching, and Natasha was terrified. I had promised to be with her. However, for the sake of our children, Sergio had extended our stay in Paris and I was worried about being late for the birth. We were flying to Milan tomorrow.

"I'll call and tell her," I said to Sergio.

Sergio had agreed to take ten days' leave from work to allow me to help Natasha in the beginning.

"I'll take more, if you need it, darling."

"Oh, no, Sergi! I can't be away from you for any longer than that."

I was faced with a dilemma. For many months I had been pursued by an image and a voice. I slowly dialled the number. It was ringing.

"Hello?"

My heart raced. "How are you?"

"Baby, where are you?"

"In Paris."

"Is there a problem?"

"Yes."

"Baby?"

"I can't forget you."

There was the sound of happy laughter.

"Did you hear what I said?"

"Yes, Princess! Neither can I! Where?"

"Milan."

"When?"

"In three days' time. Ten in the evening. At the Duomo."

"I'll fly like a magic dove!"

"You are a magic dove!"

"If anyone has magical powers, it's you, Princess."

His voice resonated deep within me and shook me to the very foundations.

"Baby, are you there, or am I talking to myself?"

"I'm here, but my heart is with you, that's the trouble," I whispered.

"Don't worry! We'll think of something." Krasi laughed from the bottom of his heart.

"I wasn't worrying. I'm not frightened of anything, any more. As long as you're nearby."

His voice became serious. "Since I met you for the second time, my main purpose in life is to protect you and your children. And it will be for as long as I live."

I looked in front of me. My happiness stood before me enveloped in a bright, silver radiance. I looked into myself carefully. That little red corner had slotted into its place. I sighed deeply and smiled at it. It smiled back at me and slowly drew closer.

Thank you for choosing Destiny of Choice, I do hope you enjoyed reading. Your review and rating help our cause, thus, please do not hesitate to let us know what you think by leaving us a review. In return I promise to send you a free copy of my next ebook, a discounted copy with a personal note from me and a small gift. To receive the above, please use the email below to notify me of your review.

To find out why I wrote Destiny of Choice and how I help, please visit www. maryjordannovels.co.uk. As well, if you would like to be notified for other books of mine or just to keep in touch and say hi, please do not hesitate to contact me on maryjordan.novelist@gmail.com, Facebook: Mary Jordan Author, and Twitter: @MaryJordan001.

Sincere thanks & Kindest regards,
Mary Jordan

My next upcoming book is:
The longest Dance: She was the kindest, the most beautiful and the most gifted. But all this was lost in the longest dance that life served her.